Capital, Investment and Development

Sukhamoy Chakravarty

Capital, Investment and Development

**Essays in Memory of
Sukhamoy Chakravarty**

Edited by

Kaushik Basu

Mukul Majumdar

Tapan Mitra

OXFORD

UNIVERSITY PRESS

OXFORD
UNIVERSITY PRESS

YMCA Library Building, Jai Singh Road, New Delhi 110001

Oxford University Press is a department of the University of Oxford. It furthers the
University's objective of excellence in research, scholarship, and education
by publishing worldwide in

Oxford   New York
Athens   Auckland   Bangkok   Bogota   Buenos Aires   Calcutta
Cape Town   Chennai   Dar es Salaam   Delhi   Florence   Hong Kong   Istanbul
Karachi   Kuala Lumpur   Madrid   Melbourne   Mexico City   Mumbai
Nairobi   Paris   Sao Paolo   Singapore   Taipei   Tokyo   Toronto   Warsaw

with associated companies in

Berlin   Ibadan

ISBN 0 19 564758 0

Printed in India at Saurabh Print-O-Pack, Noida, UP
and published by Manzar Khan, Oxford University Press
YMCA Library Building, Jai Singh Road, New Delhi 110 001

Contents

PART I Capital and Investment

PART II Development and Welfare

PART III Markets, Capitalism, and Socialism

List of Figures

List of Tables

List of Contributors

Bardhan, Pranab, University of California, Berkeley, California, USA

Basu, Kaushik, Cornell University, Ithaca, New York, USA

Bhaduri, Amit, Centre for Economic Studies and Planning, Jawaharlal Nehru University, New Delhi.

Bose, Amitava, Indian Institute of Management, Calcutta, India

Dixit, Avinash, Princeton University, New York, USA

Khan, M. Ali, Johns Hopkins University, Baltimore, Maryland, USA

Majumdar, Mukul, Cornell University, Ithaca, New York, USA

Mitra, Tapan, Cornell University, Ithaca, New York, USA

Radner, Roy, New York University, New York, and AT&T Bell Laboratories, Murray Hill, New Jersey, USA

Raut, Lakshmi K., University of California at San Diego, La Jolla, California, USA

Samuelson, Paul A., Massachusetts Institute of Technology, Cambridge, Massachusetts, USA

Sen, Amartya, Master, Trinity College, Cambridge University, UK

Srinivasan, T.N., Yale University, New Haven, Connecticut, USA

Tinbergen, Jan, Haviklaan 31, 2566 XD The Hague, The Netherlands

Preface

Sukhamoy Chakravarty's untimely death on August 22, 1990, was mourned by his many students, colleagues, and friends. For several years he had been suffering from serious health problems. Yet, he had an extraordinarily full life: at the time of his death, he was Chairman of the Economic Advisory Council of the Prime Minister of India, Professor of Economics at the Delhi School of Economics, and Chairman of the Indian Council of Social Science Research. In his distinguished career, he combined academic research and teaching with active participation in planning and formulation of economic policy in India.

Sukhamoy Chakravarty's publications give only a glimpse of his scholarship duly appreciated by his colleagues for its breadth and depth. He was, in the words of Professor Paul A. Samuelson, "that rare specimen of an almost empty set – namely, the logical intersection of C. P. Snow's two cultures." We regret that the present collection does not capture his wide range of interests and contributions. The essays do, however, encompass three major areas in economics that fascinated him. In addition, a personal appreciation of his life and career is given in the introductory article by Amartya Sen.

We would like to thank Mrs Lalita Chakravarty for her help at various stages. We are most grateful to the contributors for their cooperation and encouragement. The project would not have materialized without the support of Romesh Vaitilingam, Sally Davies, and Rolf Janke of Blackwell Publishers, and Teresa Thresher of Cornell University.

Kaushik Basu
Mukul Majumdar
Tapan Mitra

Sukhamoy Chakravarty: An appreciation

Amartya Sen

It was in the spring of 1950 that I first met Sukhamoy – then not yet 16, but already something of a legend in the world of Calcutta intellectuals as a student of outstanding promise and talent, who talked with his elders on equal terms, and whose gently irreverent remarks on canons of local wisdom were widely quoted. I would later have the opportunity of seeing the speed and poise with which his mind worked, when we were fellow students at Presidency College, and later colleagues at the Delhi School of Economics. What came through most powerfully in our first youthful meetings, apart from Sukhamoy's astonishing intelligence, were his abounding curiosity and his cheerful but firm convictions. The two were linked. His convictions included his enthusiastic assessment of the role of cerebral activities in transforming society and human lives. To be intellectually curious was, for him, not only a delight in itself, it was also the way to change the miserable world in which we lived.

Later on, when Sukhamoy's intellectual pursuits blossomed and his contributions started coming out in published form, I remember wondering about the relation between the beliefs and opinions of his early life and what he did in his more mature years. I think we cannot appreciate adequately the direction of Sukhamoy's works – what he attempted to do and what he chose not to pursue – without an understanding of his convictions. The world he saw as wretched and nasty, but also radically changeable through the use of scrutinized deductions and through basing social action on faultless reasoning.

Later, I shall take the liberty of commenting on this aspect of Sukhamoy's intellectual beliefs, commitments and choices, but first let me perform the task assigned to me by the editors of this volume, and put on record the basic information on Sukhamoy's distinguished life and career.

Education and teaching

Sukhamoy Chakravarty was born on July 26, 1934, in an intellectually eminent family. Several of his siblings also went on to achieve distinction in various academic disciplines. He was educated in different schools in what was then undivided Bengal (the partition of India, along with independence, took place in 1947), but his legendary reputation in Bengali intellectual circles dates from the period in which he was completing his pre-University training at the well-known Ballygunge Government School in Calcutta.

Sukhamoy did his college education at Presidency College in Calcutta, completing his bachelor's degree in 1953 and his masters in 1955. He was quite a celebrity by then – known not just as a highly promising economist but also as a tremendous scholar and something of a leader of thought among the young in Calcutta.

After some work at the Indian Statistical Institute with P. C. Mahalanobis (the physicist, turned pioneering statistician, turned applied economist and planner), Sukhamoy proceeded to the Netherlands School of Economics to work with Jan Tinbergen, who would prove to be a major influence in his academic life. He completed his PhD at Rotterdam in 1958, and after working there for a further year as a Visiting Fellow, Sukhamoy went to Massachusetts Institute of Technology as an Assistant Professor for 1959–61. He worked closely with Paul Rosenstein-Rodan, but also came to know Paul Samuelson well and Robert Solow too. Then he returned to his old alma mater, Presidency College in Calcutta, as a Professor of Economics, teaching there for two years before moving back to Massachusetts Institute of Technology as a Visiting Associate Professor during 1963–4.

In 1964, Chakravarty took up a chair at the Delhi School of Economics – a post he retaihed until his untimely death on August 22, 1990. In the early 1960s, the Delhi School was going through a period of massive intellectual reinforcement, under the leadership of

K. N. Raj, and Sukhamoy was one of the chief architects of what would soon become the premier center of graduate education in economics in India.

Sukhamoy received invitations to occupy various distinguished positions in the academic world abroad, but was determined to stay on in India on a permanent basis. However, he did accept several visiting appointments, including a Visiting Professorship at Johns Hopkins University in 1968–9, the Tinbergen Professorship at Erasmus University in 1976–7, and the Jawaharlal Nehru Visiting Professorship of Economics at the University of Cambridge (and, with that, a visiting Fellowship at Sidney Sussex College) in 1984–5. The reports on his presence and impact at these international centers of education were uniformly glowing. But he explained to me on one occasion that he too got a lot from these encounters, in particular the intellectual challenge and scrutiny that he sometimes lacked in the academic atmosphere in India.

Sukhamoy Chakravarty was not only an extremely successful lecturer, he was also a particularly committed teacher. His home was full of students and young scholars all the time. Sukhamoy and his wife Lalita, also an economist who had been a fellow student at Presidency College, seemed to have infinite time for anyone seeking their company or advice. Even though from the beginning of the 1970s Sukhamoy was increasingly tied up in his non-teaching obligations (as one of the leading public policy makers in the country), he still continued to teach with unwavering devotion, and to have his door wide open for academic visitors and students.

Public appointments and planning

Sukhamoy had a central role in the economic thinking underlying planning and public policy in India. In 1971, he was invited to join the Indian Planning Commission – a position in which he served until 1977. From 1983 until his death, he was the Chairman of the Economic Advisory Council of the Prime Minister, under several different Prime Ministers (Indira Gandhi, Rajiv Gandhi, V. P. Singh). It is a remarkable tribute to Sukhamoy's intellectual standing and talents that even when one government would fall to be replaced by another hostile to it, the new Prime Minister would ask him to head the new Economic Advisory Council again.

From 1987 onwards, he was also the Chairman of the Indian Council of Social Science Research, a public institution of importance which provides funds and support for research in the social sciences. Earlier, during 1983–5, he had chaired a Committee, set up by the Reserve Bank of India, to review the monetary system of the country. During the 1970s and 1980s, Chakravarty also held several additional public positions, including chairing the Fuel Policy Committee of the Government of India, chairing the Indo-Dutch Committee for Research in the Social Sciences, co-chairing the Indo-US Subcommission on Education and Culture, and quite a few other such posts. The putative cartoon of a dozen Sukhamoy Chakravartys seated around a round table in different capacities, vigorously consulting each other, did not in fact materialize, but the diversity of his leadership roles would have made that an understandable account.

Writings and publications

Sukhamoy's first book was his PhD thesis, *The Logic of Investment Planning*, published in 1959 by North-Holland in its series of "Contributions to Economic Analysis." The work showed the influence of both P. C. Mahalanobis (it was, in fact, a dynamic generalization of Mahalanobis's four-sector model) and Jan Tinbergen (the planning exercise was formulated in terms of Tinbergen's fixed-targets framework). The monograph paid special attention to "structural" features of underdevelopment and the need to overcome them, and also took more note of gestation lags than was then common. It was well received as a contribution to development planning. More than that, the combination of substantive insights and technical virtuosity in this monograph aroused the expectation of future contributions from this new and impressive author.

In 1962, Sukhamoy published two remarkable papers on "optimum savings," which firmly established his reputation as a resourceful theorist. Both the papers were concerned with the question of how much a nation should save, and the framework of analysis – unlike his previous book – was explicitly one of optimization (rather than one of achieving fixed targets). In the first of these two papers ("The existence of an optimum savings program," *Econometrica*, vol. 30, 1962), Sukhamoy considered the problem of determining optimum paths of savings and growth over an infinite time. This is a problem of some complexity, since the favored method of social assessment, namely comparing sum totals of utilities generated, when applied to endless time, has to deal with infinite totals for many – or even most – of the alternative efficient paths, and such totals are hard to rank and compare. The "existence" of an optimum path over an infinite horizon was far from clear.

Part of Sukhamoy's exercise was to show why and how the problem was so difficult to resolve, and the alternative methods that may be used to come to grips with it. The problem had been tackled earlier by Frank Ramsey, in a deceptively lucid paper published in 1928 in which Ramsey had assumed a maximal achievable utility level, which he had called "bliss." In this specialized framework, Ramsey had seen the problem of optimization as that of minimization of the total gap between any actual path of utilities and the hypothetical path of having bliss in every period. *That* problem, as Sukhamoy discussed, was well defined and solvable in many contexts in which the original problem of maximizing the sum total of utilities would not have been. Sukhamoy's paper discussed these and other methods of dealing with this foundational exercise, and related the mathematical problems and solutions to the demands that an actual planner might wish to make.

In contrast with this clarificatory contribution on planning for an endless time, the second paper ("Optimum savings with a finite planning horizon," *International Economic Review*, vol. 3, September 1962) examined the problem over a *finite* period only, with well-specified "terminal" requirements at the end of the horizon. He investigated the solutions to this problem and their properties, the guiding rules that a planner may follow, and the sensitivity of the exercise to changes in the terminal requirements. This paper had much similarity with an article that was published at about the same time (1961) by Richard Goodwin, arriving independently at similar conclusions. The underlying issues analyzed in these two papers were further investigated in a number of contributions that followed shortly after their publications.

Sukhamoy himself did several follow-up exercises, in the form of journal articles, on themes related to these two basic papers. He went on, then, to write his classic monograph, *Capital and Development Planning*, published in 1969 by MIT Press. This book, which included a remarkably admiring – but thoroughly justified – foreword by Paul Samuelson, combined sustained technical analysis with extensive discussions of motivation and relevance, and was clearly one of the central contributions to development planning. Its combination of technical excellence and presentational lucidity – along with its plentiful insights – has rarely been matched.

A later phase of work

The 1960s brought Sukhamoy much recognition and fame as a theorist. However, by the end of that decade, as Sukhamoy put it later, "I began to feel that I required a close exposure to real life situations" (Chakravarty, 1992). His later works had a more applied bias, and were often concerned specifically with India. The fact that by 1971 Sukhamoy was firmly installed as one of the chief planners of the economy of India reinforced this shift of general interest.

Sukhamoy never repudiated his earlier work, but drew increasingly on other types of analyses and insights. The economists whose influence became more prominent in his later works included Allyn Young and Nicholas Kaldor and, most emphatically, Joseph Schumpeter, to whom Sukhamoy turned more and more in the last decade of his life (Chakravarty, 1992). His monograph *Alternative Approaches to a Theory of Economic Growth: Marx, Marshall, Schumpeter*, based on his R. C. Dutt Memorial Lectures in Calcutta and published in 1980, is partly a tribute to the cogency of the Schumpeterian perspective on economic growth, which – buttressed by some ideas of Marx – Sukhamoy compared most favorably with modern growth theory.

In his tribute to Sukhamoy, published in this volume (chapter 12), Paul Samuelson discusses and questions Sukhamoy's "lumping Schumpeter with Marx to define a paradigm alternative to mainstream growth theories." I shall not try to enter this argument, but I can see that Sukhamoy took Schumpeter to be closer to his own view of economics than perhaps would have been justified on a neutral reading. To some extent Schumpeter had become a vehicle of expression of Sukhamoy's discontent with the present state of economic theory. That discontent was very strongly felt, and on more than one occasion Sukhamoy had outlined to me his plan to do an ambitious work of reconstruction of economic theory – more institutional and a great deal more historical than what we currently have. His untimely death has robbed us of the possibility of this work.

Sukhamoy's most significant applied work – done in the later phase of his academic career – was his book *Development Planning: The Indian Experience*, published by Clarendon Press at Oxford in 1987. This was based on his hugely successful Radhakrishnan Memorial Lectures at Oxford University. It is a patient book, spelling out in some detail the rationale, as he saw it, of the respective policy strategies used in Indian planning. It certainly is the definitive "insider's view" of Indian planning experiences. The insights he had obtained from his earlier theoretical work are present in some measure in the arguments concerning the choices facing India, but the thrust of the book is commonsensical rather than technical.

In a short chapter it is not possible to discuss each of Sukhamoy's publications, but reference should also be made at least to his joint appraisal of "alternative planning models" with Richard Eckaus (1964), his largely theoretical paper on "alternative preference functions in national investment planning" (1967), his joint survey article with Jagdish Bhagwati on contributions to Indian economic analysis (1969), his joint monograph with Paul Rosenstein-Rodan on the relationship between food aid and non-food aid (1973), his critical essay in honor of Tinbergen on the theory of development planning (1973), his submission to the Club of Rome jointly with Jan Tinbergen and others on reshaping the international order (1977), his penetrating analysis of the role of Marxist economics in understanding problems of economic development (1987), and his general reappraisal of development planning in the light of his practical experience (1989). These and other publications are more fully listed later (in the "Selected Publications").

Honors and recognitions

Sukhamoy's accomplishments as an economic theorist, as a planner and policy advisor, and as an educator were matched by the national and international recognition he received. He was elected the President of the Indian Econometric Society for 1983–5 and the President of the Indian Economic Association for 1985–6. Honors within India also included his being chosen as one of the first two recipients of the Mahalanobis Memorial Gold Medal in 1974 (the other recipient was

Jagdish Bhagwati) and his being the first recipient of the VKRV Rao
Prize in the Social Sciences in 1978.

In terms of international recognition, Sukhamoy was elected a
Fellow of the Econometric Society in 1969 and was a member of its
World Council for a great many years. He was also Vice President of
the International Economic Association during 1983–6, and in 1986
Sukhamoy was elected one of the Honorary Presidents of the Asso-
ciation for life.

What Sukhamoy would have valued at least as much as all these
institutional honors and recognitions is the fondness and admiration
with which he is viewed by his students, friends, and colleagues. He
was a wonderful person to know, to talk with, to learn from – a
remarkable combination of intellectual power and thoughtful
warmth. Sukhamoy greatly valued human relations, and thanks to
his personality (and also that of his wife, Lalita) he had as much
success in this field as in his intellectual achievements. The deep
sense of loss at his death was widespread, spontaneous, and over-
whelming.

Convictions and choices

I turn now to the postponed personal questions – raised and deferred
at the beginning of this chapter. When I first met Sukhamoy in 1950
(it was March I think – the flowers were in full bloom in the village of
Santiniketan which Sukhamoy had come to visit, where I was then
being schooled), he was bathed in glowing intelligence and what
seemed like limitless intellectual curiosity. But I was also struck by
his much-reasoned conviction about the role of intellectual activities
in transforming the world.

We had reasons for feeling agonized – the Hindu–Muslim riots
had taken a terrible toll in brutal, senseless murder in the preceding
years, the Bengal famine which we had witnessed had killed millions
only a few years earlier, and we could see nothing on the horizon
that would indicate any real hope of eliminating the abject poverty
of India. Nothing short of a revolution would seem to help (a view
that has remained popular in Bengal), but it was not obvious that a
revolution would help either.

Sukhamoy clearly felt just as agonized as the rest of us, but he had
greater belief in the power of intellect and reasoning in changing the

world for better. In politics, he was, like many of us, what I can only describe as "skeptically left," but his skepticism was qualified by his enormously affirmative belief in the power of intellectual arguments and enlightened thinking. This also made him, I think, more at peace with his own inclinations, which were outstandingly intellectual and uncompromisingly scholarly. Knowing more and reasoning better would not only give each of us the delights that we had reason to value, but also, ultimately, they would help solve the problems of the nasty world in which we lived.

Like others in Bengal at that time, Sukhamoy too read his Marx carefully, and being what he was, he was more of an expert even in this field than any of us. But the Marx that shone through was the one in the Reading Room of the British Museum, the Marx that viewed with horror the "idiocy of village life." Throughout his life, Sukhamoy maintained this combination of being politically left and having great faith in the power of knowledge and reasoning. But the form of knowledge and the type of reasoning that he took to be useful changed over the decades.

In the early years Sukhamoy had great faith in the reach and relevance of mathematical reasoning. Even the initial attraction of Mahalanobis's models of quantitative planning arose partly from the fact that these were more mathematical and technically more developed than the informal reasoning then in vogue in studies of Indian economics. Sukhamoy's subsequent works on fixed-targets planning and optimizing models, which I discussed earlier, fitted well into his belief that these contributions would help solve problems of underdevelopment in general and India's poverty in particular. When I saw him at Massachusetts Institute of Technology in 1960 (after we were students together in Calcutta and before we became colleagues at the Delhi School of Economics), he expressed much satisfaction at the fact that it was possible both to work at the frontier of economic analysis and to do work that would be ultimately useful and practical.

By the end of the decade, however, Sukhamoy felt deeply shaken, as I mentioned earlier, in his belief about the practical relevance of formal models of this kind. He could have gone, at that time, in one of three possible directions. First, he could have become a "pure theorist," without worrying too much about changing the real world. This he was not willing to do – not earlier, not then, not ever. Second, he could have looked for other types of formal theories and mathematical reasoning, with the hope that they would do better for his practical purpose. He did not pursue this line, and I believe he was by then deeply skeptical of this possibility. Third, he could have moved away from active work in mathematical reasoning and looked for insights and help elsewhere. This was, in effect, what he did, though the change was not loudly announced, nor perhaps terribly sharply felt at any particular moment, since the shift was gradual.

The invitation to join the Planning Commission of India hastened this change and encouraged Sukhamoy's move to what was earlier called the "later phase" of his work. What was still common with the earlier phase was the firm belief in the power of knowledge and reasoning in bringing about a change in the practical world. But it seemed to Sukhamoy now that the knowledge that was needed had to be more institutional and historical, and the reasoning that was required must be less formal and more hospitable to imprecise but important concepts and categories.

I don't personally think that Sukhamoy had quite reached an equilibrium in this transformation. The works that he did in this phase were, of course, valuable and creative (he was not capable of anything less), but even his highly interesting speculations on Schumpeter and Marx and his quiet defense of traditional Indian planning strategies show signs of dissatisfaction and an inclination to continue searching. It is a great loss to the world of theory as well as practice that his work in the later phase remained formative and incomplete. There are insights on which others can build, and one only wishes that Sukhamoy was himself here to bring these analyses to completion. That gap cannot be filled.

References

Chakravarty, S. 1992: Economics as seen by a dissenting economist. In P. Arestis and M. C. Sawyer (eds), *Biographical Dictionary of Dissenting Economists*, Aldershot: Edward Elgar.

Goodwin, R. M. 1961: The optimal growth path for an underdeveloped economy. *Economic Journal*, 71, 756–74.

Ramsey, F. P. 1928: A mathematical theory of saving. *Economic Journal*, 38, 543–59.

PART I
Capital and Investment

1

Theories of long-run growth: old and new

Lakshmi K. Raut and T. N. Srinivasan

1 Introduction

There has been a recent revival in theorizing about long-run growth after a hiatus of over two decades since the last spurt in the 1950s and 1960s. The latter was itself inspired much earlier by the pioneering works of Frank Ramsey (1928) on optimal saving and of von Neumann (1945) on balanced growth at a maximal rate, and also to dynamic extensions of the Keynesian model by Harrod (1939) and later by Domar (1947). In the largely neoclassical growth theoretic literature of the 1960s and earlier, one could distinguish three strands.

The first strand is *positive*, or, better still, *descriptive* theory aimed at explaining the stylized facts of long-run growth in industrialized countries (particularly the United States) such as a steady secular growth of aggregate output and relative constancy of the share of savings, investment, labor, and capital income in aggregate output. These stylized facts themselves had been established by the work of empirically oriented economists such as Abramovitz (1956), Denison (1962), and Kuznets (1966), who were mainly interested in accounting for observed growth. Solow's (1956, 1957) celebrated articles and later work by Jorgenson and Griliches (1966) and others are examples of descriptive growth theory and related empirical analysis. Uzawa (1961, 1963) extended Solow's descriptive one-sector model into a two-sector model. As Stiglitz (1990) remarked, by showing that the long-run steady state growth rate could be unaffected by the rate of savings (and investment) and that, even in the short run, the rate of growth was mostly accounted for by the rate of labor-augmenting technical progress, Solow challenged then conventional wisdom.

The second strand is *normative* theory which drew its inspiration from Ramsey's (1928) classic paper on optimal saving. In contrast with the descriptive models in which the aggregate savings rate was exogenously specified (usually as a constant over time), the normative models derived time-varying savings rates from the optimization of an intertemporal social welfare function. There were mainly two variants of such normative models: one-sector models (e.g. Cass, 1965; Koopmans, 1965) and two-sector models (Srinivasan, 1962, 1964; Uzawa, 1964). The contribution of Phelps (1961) is also normative, but it focused only on the steady state level of consumption per worker rather than on the entire transitional time path to the steady state and solved for that savings rate which maximized the steady state level of consumption per worker.

The third strand of theory is primarily neither descriptive nor normative although it is related to both. Harrod's dynamic extension of the Keynesian model (with its constant marginal propensity to save) raised the issue of stability of the growth path by contrasting two growth rates: the *warranted* rate of growth that would be consistent with maintaining the savings–investment equilibrium and the *natural* growth rate as determined by the growth of the labor force and technical change. In this model, unless the economy's behavioral and technical parameters keep it on the knife edge of equality between warranted and natural growth rates, there would be either growing under-utilization of capacity if the warranted rate exceeds the natural rate or growing unemployment if the natural rate exceeds the warranted rate. Indeed this knife-edge property resulting from Harrod's assumption that capital and labor are used in fixed proportions led Solow to look for growth paths converging to a steady state by replacing Harrod's technology with a neoclassical technology of positive elasticity of substitution between labor and capital.

von Neumann's (1945) model is also part of the third strand. In this model production technology is characterized by a finite set of constant returns to scale activities with inputs being committed at the beginning and outputs emerging at the end of each discrete production period. There are no non-produced factors of production such as labor or exhaustible natural resources. In the "primal" version, von Neumann characterized the vector of activity levels that permitted the maximal rate of *balanced growth* (i.e. growth in which outputs of all commodities grew at the same rate) given that the outputs of each period were to be ploughed back as inputs in the next period. In the "dual" version, a vector of commodity prices and an interest rate were derived which had the properties that the value of the output of each activity was no higher than the value of inputs inclusive of interest and that the interest rate was the lowest possible. Under certain assumptions about the technology von Neumann showed that, first, the maximal growth rate of output of the primal was equal to the (minimal) interest rate associated with the dual, and second, the usual complementary slackness relations obtained between the vector of activity levels, prices, growth, and interest rates.

Although *prima facie* there is no normative rationale for balanced growth and the maximization of the growth rate, particularly in a set-up with no final consumption of any good, it turned out that the von Neumann path of balanced growth at the maximal rate has a "normative" property. As Dorfman et al. (1958) conjectured and Radner (1961) later rigorously proved, given an objective that is a function only of the terminal stocks of commodities, the path starting from a given initial vector of stocks that maximizes this objective would be "close" to the von Neumann path for "most" of the time, as long as the terminal date is sufficiently distant from the initial date regardless of the initial stocks and of the form of the objective function. This so-called "turnpike" feature was later seen in other growth models in which final consumption is allowed and production involves the use of non-produced factors. For example, in the Koopmans–Cass model in which the objective is to maximize the discounted sum of the stream of utility of per capita consumption over time, a unique steady state exists which is defined by the discount rate, the rate of growth of the labor force and the technology of production. *All* optimal paths, i.e. paths that maximize the objective function and start from different initial conditions, converge to this steady state regardless of the functional form of the utility function. As such all optimal paths stay "close" to the steady state path for "most" of the time.

Barring a few exceptions to be noted below, in the neoclassical growth models production technology was assumed to exhibit constant returns to scale and in many, though not all, models smooth substitution among inputs with strictly diminishing marginal rates of substitution between any two inputs along an isoquant was also posited. Analytical attention was focused on conditions ensuring the existence and uniqueness of steady state growth paths along which all inputs and outputs grew at the same rate – the steady state being the path to which all transitional paths starting from any given initial conditions and satisfying the requirements of specified descriptive rates of accumulation or of intertemporal welfare optimality converged. The steady state growth rate was the *exogenous* rate of growth of the labor force in efficiency units so that, in the absence of (exogenous) labor-augmenting technical progress, output per worker was constant along the steady state.

Turning to the exceptions, Solow (1956) himself drew attention to the possibility that a steady state need not even exist and, if one existed, it need not be unique. Indeed output per worker could grow indefinitely even in the absence of labor-augmenting technical progress if the marginal product of capital was bounded below by a sufficiently high positive number. Helpman (1992) also draws attention to this. In addition, there could be multiple steady states some of which would be unstable if the production technology exhibited nonconvexities. We return to these issues below.

There were also exceptions to the exogeneity of technical progress and the rate of growth of output along a steady state. In the one-sector, one-factor models of Harrod and Domar and the two-sector models of Feldman (1928, as described in Domar, 1957) and Mahalanobis (1955) marginal capital–output ratios were assumed to be constant so that by definition the marginal product of capital did not decline. Growth rate was *endogenous* and depended on the rate of savings (investment) in such one-sector models and on the allocation of investment between sectors producing capital and sectors producing consumer goods in the two-sector models. Kaldor and Mirrlees (1962) endogenized technical progress (and hence the rate of growth of output) by relating productivity of workers operating newly produced equipment to the rate of growth of investment per worker. And there was the celebrated model of Arrow (1962) of "learning by doing" in which factor productivity was an increasing function of cumulated output or investment. Uzawa (1965) also endogenized technical progress by postulating that the rate of growth of labor-augmenting technical progress was a concave function of the ratio of labor employed in the education sector to total employment. The education sector was assumed to use labor as the only input. Uzawa's model has influenced recent contributions to growth theory.

The recent revival of growth theory started with the influential papers of Lucas (1988) and Romer (1986). Lucas motivated his approach by arguing that neoclassical growth theory cannot account for observed differences in growth across countries and over time and its evidently counter-factual prediction that international trade should induce rapid movements toward equality in capital–labor ratios and factor prices. He argued that

> in the absence of differences in pure technology then, and under the assumption of no factor mobility, the neoclassical model predicts a strong tendency to income equality and equality in growth rates, tendencies we can observe within countries and, perhaps, within the wealthiest countries taken as a group, but which simply cannot be seen in the world at large. When factor mobility is permitted, this prediction is powerfully reinforced.
>
> (Lucas, 1988, pp. 15–16)

He then goes on to suggest that the one factor isolated by the neoclassical model, namely variation across countries in technology,

> has the potential to account for wide differences in income levels and growth rates ... when we talk about differences in "technology" across countries we are not talking about knowledge in general, but about the knowledge of particular people, or particular subcultures of people. If so, then while it is not exactly wrong to describe these differences (as) exogenous ... neither is it useful to do so. We want a formalism that leads us to think about individual decisions to acquire knowledge, and about the consequences of these decisions for productivity.

He draws on the theory of "human capital" to provide such a formalism: each individual acquires productivity-enhancing skills by devoting time to such acquisition and away from paying work. The acquisition of skills by a worker not only increases her productivity but, by increasing the average level of skills in the economy as a whole, it has a spill-over effect on the productivity of all workers by increasing the average level of skills in the economy as a whole.

Romer also looked for an alternative to the neoclassical model of long-run growth to escape from its implications that "initial conditions or current disturbances have no long-run effect on the level of output and consumption . . . in the absence of technical change, per capita output should converge to a steady-state value with no per capita growth" (Romer, 1986, pp. 1002–3). His is "an equilibrium model of endogenous technological change in which long-run growth is driven primarily by the accumulation of knowledge by forward-looking, profit-maximizing agents" (p. 1003). While the production of new knowledge is through a technology that exhibits diminishing returns, "the creation of new knowledge by one firm is assumed to have a positive external effect on the production possibilities of other firms . . . [so that] production of consumption goods as a function of stock of knowledge exhibits increasing returns; more precisely, knowledge may have an increasing marginal product" (p. 1003).

It should be noted that the spill-over effects of the average stock of human capital per worker in the Lucas model and of knowledge in the Romer model are externalities unperceived (and hence not internalized) by individual agents. However, for the economy *as a whole* they generate increasing scale economies even though the perceived production function of each agent exhibits constant returns to scale. Thus by introducing nonconvexities through the device of a Marshallian externality Lucas and Romer were able to work with intertemporal competitive (albeit a socially nonoptimal) equilibrium. Both in effect make assumptions that ensure that the marginal product of physical capital is bounded away from zero and as such it is not surprising that in both models sustained growth in income per worker is possible. Thus both avoid facing the problem[1] that research and development (R&D) that lead to technical progress are "naturally associated with imperfectly competitive markets, as Schumpeter (1942) had forcefully argued" (Stiglitz, 1990, p. 25). Later work by others (e.g. Grossman and Helpman, 1991) formulated models in which firms operating in imperfectly competitive markets undertook R&D.

The literature on growth theory has grown by leaps and bounds in the 1980s. It is not our purpose to survey this literature critically. Instead we consider a few *selected* models that address the issues of long-run sustained growth in per capita income, possible multiplicities in long-run equilibria with different growth rates and convergence or otherwise to steady states where they exist. The models are couched in three alternative frameworks within the neoclassical paradigm: descriptive growth *à la* Solow (1956), optimal growth with infinitely lived agents *à la* Ramsey–Cass–Koopmans and finally the finitely lived overlapping generations *à la* Samuelson (1958) and Diamond (1965). Section 2 briefly reviews neoclassical growth models to set the stage for a discussion in section 3 of models that generate sustained long-run growth with possible multiple growth equilibria. Section 4 takes another approach to endogenous growth by assuming that population density has an external effect on the production process so that fertility decisions of individual households determine the dynamic evolution of production possibilities endogenously. Unlike the recent growth literature, the model of section 4 is not geared to generating steady states and, in fact, its nonlinear dynamics generates a plethora of outcomes. Section 5 concludes the chapter.

2 Neoclassical growth models

2.1 Solow

The main motivation behind Solow's growth model, as mentioned earlier, was to explain the stability of the growth rates of US output during the first half of the twentieth century by means of a simple model. Solow assumes an aggregate production function

$$Y_t = A_t F(K_t, b_t L_t) \tag{1.1}$$

where Y_t is aggregate output at time t, K_t is the stock of capital, L_t is labor hours at time t, A_t ($A_0 \equiv 1$) is the disembodied technology factor (i.e. index of total factor productivity) so that output at time t associated with any combination of capital stock and labor input is A_t multiplied by that at time zero with the same combination. Analogously b_t (with $b_0 \equiv 1$) is the efficiency level of a unit of labor in period t so that a unit of labor at time t is equivalent to b_t units of labor at time zero. Thus the technical progress induced by increases in b_t is *labor augmenting*. It is easily seen that technical progress through A_t is Hicks neutral and that through b_t is Harrod neutral.

Let us denote by $\tilde{k}_t \equiv K_t/b_t L_t$ the ratio of capital to labor in efficiency units in period t, by $k_t = K_t/L_t$ the ratio of capital to labor in natural units, and by $y_t \equiv Y_t/b_t L_t$ the level of output or income per unit of labor in efficiency units. Solow made the following crucial assumptions.

Assumption 1 (Neoclassical)

F is homogeneous of degree one in its arguments and concave.

Given assumption 1, the average product of an efficiency unit of labor, i.e. $(1/b_t L_t)F(k_t, b_t L_t)$ equals $F(\bar{k}_t, 1)$.

Let $f(\bar{k}_t) = F(\bar{k}_t, 1)$. Clearly concavity of F implies concavity of f as a function of $\bar{k}_t$. In fact f is assumed to be strictly concave with $f(0) = 0$.

Assumption 2 (Inada)

$$\lim_{k \to 0} f'(\bar{k}) = \infty \qquad \text{and} \qquad \lim_{k \to \infty} f'(\bar{k}) = 0$$

In a closed economy, assuming that labor is growing exogenously as $L_t = (1 + n)^t L_0$, human capital or skill level is growing exogenously as $b_t = (1 + b)^t$, and capital depreciates at the rate δ per period, and denoting by c_t the level of consumption per efficiency unit of labor we have

$$\bar{k}_{t+1} = \frac{A_t f(\bar{k}_t) + (1 - \delta)\bar{k}_t - c_t}{(1 + n)(1 + b)} \tag{1.2}$$

Solow further assumed that the savings rate is constant, i.e. $c_t = (1 - s)y_t$. Then (1.2) becomes

$$\bar{k}_{t+1} = \frac{sA_t f(\bar{k}_t) + (1 - \delta)\bar{k}_t}{(1 + n)(1 + b)} \tag{1.3}$$

Equation (1.3) is the fundamental difference equation of the Solow model. If there is no disembodied technical progress so that $A_t = 1$ for all t, then the phase diagram of the dynamic system can be represented as in figure 1.1. It is clear from the figure that starting from any arbitrary initial capital–labor ratio $\bar{k}_0 > 0$, as $t \to \infty$ the economy will converge to the steady state $\bar{k}^* > 0$ in which all the per capita variables, including per capita income, will grow at the rate b.

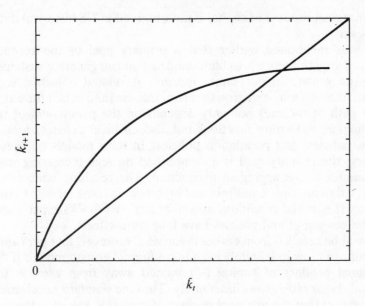

Figure 1.1 Phase diagram of Solow model.

Thus if $b = 0$ per capita income, consumption and savings do not grow along the steady state. Further, policies that permanently affect savings rate or fertility rate will have no long-run growth effects.

It is clear from figure 1.1, however, that out of the steady state (i.e. in the short run) economies will exhibit growth in per capita income even without technological change. The rate of growth will depend on the initial capital–labor ratio and the time period over which the average growth rate is calculated. It can be shown that the average growth rate *decreases* as the initial capital–labor ratio $\bar{k}_0$ (and hence initial income per head) *increases*. As the initial capital–labor ratio tends to $\bar{k}^*$, the average growth rate of per capita income converges to b, the exogenously given rate of labor-augmenting technical progress. This is indeed one of the convergence hypotheses that are tested in the recent empirical literature on growth. Policies that affect s and n clearly affect growth rates out of steady state. However, these growth effects are only temporary and the marginal product of capital will be declining over time. This predicted fall in the marginal product of capital is not observed in US historical data, however.

It was mentioned earlier that a primary goal of the recently revived growth theory is to build models that can generate sustained long-run growth in per capita income. A related objective is to ensure that the long-run growth rate of income (and in fact the entire time path of income) not only depends on the parameters of the production and utility functions but also on fiscal policies, foreign trade policies, and population policies. In most models of "new" theory, the primary goal is accomplished through increasing scale economies in the aggregate production. The resulting nonconvexities lead to multiple equilibria and hysteresis in some models so that history (i.e. initial conditions as well as any past shocks experienced by the economy) and policies have long-term effects.

It will be recalled from earlier discussion, however, that per capita output can grow indefinitely even in traditional growth models if the marginal product of capital is bounded away from zero as the capital–labor ratio grows indefinitely. Thus the standard neoclassical assumption that the marginal product of capital is a strictly decreasing function of the capital–labor ratio is not inconsistent with indefinite growth of per capita output. It has to diminish to zero as the capital–labor ratio increases indefinitely to preclude such growth. This is easily seen from equation (1.3).

Consider the simplest version of the neoclassical growth model with $b_t = 1$ and $A_t = 1$ for all t so that $\bar{k}_t = k_t$. Let $f(0) = 0$ and let the marginal product of capital, i.e. $f'(k)$, be bounded away from $(n + \delta)/s$ (i.e. $f'(k) > (n + \delta)/s$ for all k). Strict concavity of $f(k)$ together with $f(0) = 0$ implies $f(k) > kf'(k) > [k(n + \delta)]/s$ so that from (1.3) it follows that $k_{t+1} > k_t$. This in turn implies that output per worker $f(k_t)$ grows at a positive rate at all t. Moreover, given strict concavity of $f(k)$ it follows that $f'(k)$ is monotonically decreasing, and hence has a limiting value as $k \to \infty$, say γ_y, that is at least as large as $(n + \delta)/s$. As such it can be verified that the asymptotic growth rate of output and consumption will be at least as large as $[s\gamma_y - (n + \delta)]/(1 + n) \geq 0$. The savings rate s can be made endogenous using the Samuelson–Diamond overlapping generations framework or the Ramsey–Cass–Koopmans infinitely lived agent framework, thus leading to a theory of endogenous growth. Thus the neoclassical framework can endogenously generate long-run growth in per capita income. However, the assumption that the marginal product has a positive lower bound is not particularly attractive since it implies that labor is not essential for production.[2]

2.2 Ramsey–Koopmans–Cass framework

The optimal growth literature derives the savings rate endogenously by assuming that there is an infinitely lived representative agent who maximizes an additive time-separable intertemporal welfare

$$\sum_{t=0}^{\infty} \rho^t u(\bar{c}_t)$$

with respect to $\{\bar{c}_t\}_0^{\infty}$ subject to the restriction (1.2) with $A_t \equiv 1$, where $u(.)$ is a twice continuously differentiable, strictly concave, and monotonic function. It is indeed odd that per period utility $u(.)$ is a function of consumption per *efficiency unit* of labor rather than of consumption per worker. Only analytical convenience dictates this choice. Under assumption 2, it can be shown that the set of feasible $\{\bar{c}_t\}_0^{\infty}$ is compact and the above sum is a well-defined continuous[3] function of $\{\bar{c}_t\}_0^{\infty}$. Thus, the above problem has a solution. Let us denote the relationship in (1.2) with $\bar{c}_t \equiv 0$ and $A_t \equiv 1$ by the difference equation $\bar{k}_{t+1} = \psi(\bar{k}_t)$. Assuming that f satisfies the Inada condition, one can show there exists a unique positive fixed point $\bar{k}$ for ψ. Using dynamic programming techniques, one can show that the optimal capital accumulation path from any initial $\bar{k}_0 < \bar{k}$ is given by a nondecreasing policy function $\bar{k}_{t+1} = \pi(\bar{k}_t) \geq \bar{k}_t$. It can also be shown that an optimal $\{\bar{k}_t\}_0^{\infty}$ with $\bar{k}_0 \leq \bar{k}$ is a monotonic sequence bounded above, and hence $\bar{k}_t$ converges to a limit point, say $\bar{k}^* > 0$ as $t \to \infty$; $\bar{k}^*$ satisfies the following:[4]

$$f'(\bar{k}^*) = \frac{(1+n)(1+b)}{\rho} - (1-\delta) \qquad (1.4)$$

It is clear that the limit point is unique. Since it depends only on the production function and the parameters n, δ, ρ, and b, it is independent of the utility function $u(.)$. Thus, for large t we have $k_t \approx \bar{k}^* b_t$, i.e. for large t, optimal k_t, c_t, and y_t will be growing at constant rates[5] (in this case, all rates are equal to the rate of growth of b_t). This is the well-known turnpike result which states that starting from any initial capital–labor ratio the optimal path converges to the modified golden balanced growth path.

It also follows that if there is no Harrod-neutral technological change, i.e. $b = 0$, there is no growth in the capital–labor ratio and hence no growth in per capita income, and if $b > 0$, per capita income will be growing at the rate b.

It can be shown once again that, even when $b = 0$, there could still be growth in per capita income if the marginal product of capital is bounded away from zero. Moreover, the long-run growth rate in this case will depend on the rate of pure time preference ρ of the representative agent, the smaller the value ρ the larger being the rate of long-run growth. In so far as countries differ in ρ, their long-run growth rates will differ. In particular, if poverty is associated with impatience in the sense of a high value of ρ, then poor countries will have low growth rates. However, explaining intercountry differences in long-run growth entirely through differences in a parameter that represents tastes is not satisfactory since tastes need not be immutable but could be acquired.

2.3 Samuelson–Diamond overlapping generations framework

Although the overlapping generations framework was not developed by Samuelson and Diamond to examine growth issues, it turns out to be another useful approach to endogenizing savings. In addition it has all the basic features of the other two neoclassical growth frameworks discussed in sections 2.1 and 2.2. We briefly describe the framework and set up the notation for later use.

Assume that each agent lives for two periods, the first as a young person and the second as an old person. A young person of period supplies one unit of labor, earns wages w_t, consumes c_t^t and saves s_t taking the interest rate r_{t+1} between period t and $t + 1$ as given. In the next period he retires and finances his old-age consumption c_{t+1}^t with the returns from his savings while young. Formally, he maximizes his lifetime welfare $U(c_t^t, c_{t+1}^t)$ with respect to s_t subject to

$$c_t^t + s_t = w_t$$
$$c_{t+1}^t = (1 + r_{t+1})s_t$$

Denote the solution of the above problem by $H(w_t, 1 + r_{t+1})$. Assume that all markets are perfectly competitive, and producers are profit maximizers. For simplicity of exposition, we assume further that capital depreciates fully in one period and that capital has to be purchased a period ahead of its use in production. Then it follows from producer behavior that

$$\frac{w_t}{b_t} = f(\bar{k}_t) - \bar{k}_t f'(\bar{k}_t) \equiv \omega(\bar{k}_t) \text{ say} \qquad (1.5)$$

$$1 + r_{t+1} = f'(\bar{k}_{t+1}) \equiv R(\bar{k}_{t+1}) \qquad (1.6)$$

Substituting (1.5) and (1.6) in $H(,)$ and noting that $\bar{k}_{t+1} = [(1 + n)(1 + b)]^{-1} s_t$, one can write the fundamental difference equation of the Samuelson–Diamond model as

$$\bar{k}_{t+1} = \frac{H[\omega(\bar{k}_t), R(\bar{k}_{t+1})]}{(1 + n)(1 + b)} \qquad (1.7)$$

If we specialize the functional form of the utility function to be Cobb–Douglas so that $U = \alpha \log c_t^t + (1 - \alpha) \log c_{t+1}^t$, then (1.7) becomes very similar to (1.3). Even for more general utility functions, most properties of the Solow model remain valid in this framework as well.

3   Models generating sustained long-run growth and multiple equilibria

3.1   Increasing returns

At the outset a distinction should be made between generating *sustained growth* in output per head and *endogenizing* the rate of growth. For example, with the production function $Y = K^a L^b$ where $0 < a, b < 1$ and $a + b > 1$ and with the labor force growing *exogenously* at the rate n there exists a unique steady state regardless of the savings rate in which output grows at the exogenous rate $n(a + b - 1)/(1 - a) > 0$. Thus increasing scale economies together with marginal product of capital strictly diminishing to zero (i.e. $0 <$

$a < 1$) leads to *sustained* but *exogenous* growth. On the other hand, constant returns to scale with marginal product of capital bounded away from zero at a sufficiently high positive value leads to *endogenous* and *sustained* growth. Thus increasing scale economies by themselves need not generate endogenous growth.[6] While keeping this in mind, it is important to distinguish how different types of increasing returns to scale in aggregate production arise in various growth models. We consider only two types: locally increasing marginal product of capital and scale economies due to spill-over effects. For simplicity of exposition, we assume in this section that $L_t \equiv 1$, $A_t = 1$, $b_t = 1 \ \forall t \geqslant 0$. The first type arises when the marginal product of capital $f'(k)$ first increases with k and then decreases, or more generally when $f''(k) = 0$ has more than one but a finite number of solutions.

The second type arises in the models of Lucas and Romer. Building upon the work of Arrow (1962) and Sheshinski (1967), Romer (1986) considers an economy in which there are n identical firms; each has a production function of the form $Y_i = G(K_i, L_i, K)$ where K_i is the stock of knowledge capital or R&D capital employed by firm i and $K = \Sigma_{i=1}^{n} K_i$, the industry level aggregate stock of knowledge, and L_i is labor or any other inputs. K is assumed to have a positive spill-over effect on the output of each firm although the choice of K is external to the firm. Romer assumes that, for fixed K, G is homogeneous of degree one in other inputs. Supposing that all identical firms choose identical inputs, we can write $Y_i = G(K_i, L_i, nK_i)$. Define $F(K_i, L_i) \equiv G(K_i, L_i, nK_i)$. It is obvious that F exhibits increasing returns to scale in the inputs K_i and L_i. Again, besides those scale economies one needs to assume that the asymptotic marginal product of aggregate capital is positive to generate endogenous growth. Empirical support for the spill-over effect of R&D capital is found in several empirical investigations (see Bernstein and Nadiri (1989) on Canadian industry data, Jaffe (1986) on US manufacturing firm level data, and Raut (1991a) on Indian manufacturing firm level data).[7]

Following Romer, let us further assume that $L_i \equiv 1$ and denote the average product of labor by $f(k) = F(k, 1)$. Both types of increasing returns make $f(k)$ nonconcave and thus violate the neoclassical assumptions. The existence of a solution to optimal growth problems and turnpike results that were found to hold in all the neoclassical frameworks need not hold anymore. Instead, increasing returns open up the possibility for the marginal product of capital to be bounded away from zero, thus generating sustained long-run growth in these models. Moreover, the first type of increasing returns leads to multiple steady states, allowing history or the initial conditions to determine to which steady state the economy will converge. We illustrate these points with a brief discussion of a few contributions in the recent literature.

Broadly speaking given an appropriate choice of an infinite-dimensional commodity space and a topology such that the set of feasible consumption paths is compact and the social ordering is continuous, the existence of an optimal path is assured. For compactness of a feasible set some kind of bounding of the technology is necessary. Majumdar and Mitra (1983) assume that $f'(\infty) < 1 < f'(0) < \infty$ and that there exists a k_1 such that $f''(k_1) = 0$, $f''(x) > 0$ for $0 \leq x < k_1$, and $f''(x) < 0$ for $k_1 < x$. These assumptions imply that the marginal product of capital increases up to $k = k_1$ and then decreases. Somewhat more general assumptions are made by Majumdar and Nermuth (1982); they assume that $f'(\infty) < 1$ and also the following.

Assumption 3 (*Nonclassical*)

$f''(k) = 0$ has finitely many roots, and there exists $k_{\max} > 0$ such that $f(k_{\max}) = k_{\max}$, $f'(k) < 1$ for $k \geq k_{\max}$.

They show that there exists an optimal solution, and the turnpike results depend on the magnitude of the rate of time preference. Define $\hat{k} > 0$ to be a local modified golden rule if it is a local maximum of $\rho f(k) - k$ and $f(\hat{k}) > \hat{k}$. Let a steady state be any solution of $\rho f'(k) = 1$. A set of local modified golden rules could clearly be a proper subset of the set of steady states. Assume that an inflection point of $f(.)$ does not occur at a steady state, and investment is irreversible. For such an economy, if the discount factor ρ is not too large or too small, then there exist neighborhoods around each golden rule such that, depending on the neighborhood in which the initial capital–labor ratio lies, the optimal solution converges monotonically to the corresponding local golden rule. However, if ρ is too small, then all optimal programs converge to extinction, i.e. to $k = 0$ and $f(0) = 0$. If ρ is close to unity, all optimal solutions converge to the golden rule path with the largest k. It should be pointed out that the existence of multiple steady states and the dependence on the initial conditions for convergence of an optimal solution to a particular steady state are the consequences of the assumption that the production function exhibits increasing returns of the first type. In these models, there is no sustained long-run growth in any of the equilibria.

Romer (1986) posed the optimal growth problem in continuous time as follows:

$$\max_{\{c_t\} \geq 0} \int_0^\infty \exp(-\rho t)\, u(c_t)\, dt$$

subject to

$$\frac{\dot{k}_t}{k_t} = h\left[\frac{g(k_t, nk_t) - c_t}{k_t}\right] \tag{1.8}$$

where $h(.)k_t$ represents the production function of "knowledge" capital. The *rate of growth* of knowledge is a function of resources devoted to its accumulation, i.e. savings as a proportion of the existing stock of knowledge. h is assumed to be concave and *bounded above* by a constant α. The latter ensures that asymptotically there are constant returns to aggregate capital. The production function $g(k_t, nk_t)$ for output (with n being the number of firms) is assumed to be globally *convex* as a function of k so that there are increasing returns. However, for a firm which treats the total knowledge stock $K_t \equiv nk_t$ as a parameter on which it has no influence, its production function $g(k, K)$ is assumed to be concave in k. Thus economy-wide stock of knowledge is a Marshallian externality to each firm. The solution to the optimization problem that takes into account the effect of k_t on *both* arguments of g (so that the externality is internalized) is socially optimal. By contrast, one could exogenously specify the second argument K_t of $g(,)$ and solve the optimal path for its first argument k_t. Of course the solution for k_t will in general depend on the exogenously specified path for K_t. By choosing that solution for which nk_t is equal to k_t for all t, one obtains the competitive equilibrium or privately optimal path.

For the existence of optimal solutions, Romer uses the following bounding conditions.

Assumption 4 There exist positive numbers μ and θ such that $g(k, nk) < \mu + k^{\theta}$.

He then shows that, if $\alpha\theta < \rho$, then the above problem has a socially optimal solution, and under some additional assumptions there also exists a competitive equilibrium solution.

As is to be expected, the social optimal cannot be supported as a competitive equilibrium without government intervention. In the absence of appropriate intervention (such as subsidies for private acquisition of knowledge financed by lump-sum taxation of consumers) each firm would choose to acquire less than the socially optimal amount of knowledge. Under assumptions that bound the social and private marginal product of capital from below by the discount rate ρ, Romer shows that k_t and c_t grow without bound in socially and privately optimal solutions.

3.2 Endogenous Harrod-neutral technological change and human capital

One obtains long-run growth in per capita income in standard neoclassical growth models with labor-augmenting technological change. Per capita income is given by $y_t = F(k_t, b_t)$, where F is as in equation (1.1) with the further assumption that $A_t \equiv 1$ for all t. If b_t is growing exogenously at a constant rate b, as long as k_t grows at the same rate in the long run the marginal product of capital remains constant and bounded away from zero. Thus in the long run with k_t and b_t growing at the rate b, y_t will also be growing at the rate b.

The role of human capital accumulation in Uzawa (1965) and Lucas (1988) is to endogenize Harrod-neutral (i.e. labor-augmenting) technological change. Let us briefly describe this mechanism following Lucas (1988). Suppose a worker of period t is endowed with b_t of human capital or skill and one unit of labor. He has to allocate his labor endowment between accumulating skills and earning wage income. If he devotes the fraction ϕ_t of his time to the current production sector and $1 - \phi_t$ (where $0 \leqslant \phi_t \leqslant 1$) to the learning sector (such as schooling or some vocational training program), he can increase his human capital in the next period by

$$\dot{b}_t = b_t \delta(1 - \phi_t) \tag{1.9}$$

It should be noted that the marginal return to time devoted to skill accumulation is constant and does not diminish. As Lucas himself points out, this is crucial for generating sustained growth per capita consumption in the long run. Since the opportunity cost of time spent on skill acquisition is forgone income that could have been used for consumption or accumulation of physical capital, this crucial assumption should be viewed as the equivalent of assuming that the marginal product of physical capital is constant as in the Harrod–Domar model.

The budget constraint for the representative agent is given by

$$c_t + \dot{k}_t = F(k_t, \phi_t b_t) - (n + \delta)k_t \qquad (1.10)$$

From (1.10) it is clear that for given c_t and k_t, the agent faces a trade-off. He can spent more time currently (i.e. choose a larger ϕ_t) in the production sector and thus have a larger *current consumption* or *future physical capital*, or have a lower ϕ_t and thus have *larger future human capital* (i.e. higher b_t) and hence a *larger future stream of output*. It is clear that he would divide his savings between human capital and physical capital in a balanced way so that the marginal product of capital does not fall to zero. Under the further assumption that the production function is of the Cobb–Douglas form

$$F(K, L) = A(b_t)K_t^{\alpha}(b_t L_t)^{\beta} \qquad \alpha + \beta = 1 \qquad \alpha, \beta > 0$$

where the spill-over effect is given by $A(b_t) = Ab_t^{\mu}$, $0 < \mu$, it can be shown that along the balanced growth path the capital–labor ratio and hence per capita income and consumption will be growing at the rate

$$\gamma_y = \frac{1 - \beta + \mu}{1 - \beta} (1 - \phi)\delta$$

where ϕ_t is a constant equal to ϕ. Since γ_y is a function of ϕ which is endogenously determined, the growth rate of per capita income is endogenously determined. It should be noted that even if there is no spill-over effect, i.e. $\mu = 0$, γ_y is positive, and this of course is the consequence of the crucial assumption discussed above about the process of skill accumulation.

The Lucas model is essentially a two-sector growth model. Human capital and the process of its accumulation play essentially the same role as the capital goods sector in the two-sector model of Mahalanobis (1955). In this model marginal product of capital in the capital goods sector is constant – an assumption that is the equivalent of Lucas's crucial assumption about the process of human capital accumulation (Srinivasan, 1992). The rate of growth of income and consumption was endogenously determined in the Mahalanobis model by the share of investment devoted to the accumulation of capacity to produce capital goods. The share $1 - \phi_t$ of time devoted to skill acquisition plays an analogous role in the Lucas model.

Linearity of the technology of skill acquisition in the Lucas model is restrictive. It leads to a unique balanced growth solution. However, if a nonlinear (convex) technology is assumed, there could be multiple optimal balanced growth paths that are locally stable, as has been shown by Azariadis and Drazen (1990) in a Samuelson–Diamond overlapping generations model with endogenous human capital formation.

4 Agglomeration and congestion effects of population density and long-run growth

In Raut and Srinivasan (1991) we present a model that not only endogenizes growth and the process of shifts in production possibilities over time (i.e. technical change) but also generates richer dynamics than the models of recent growth theory. First, by assuming fertility to be endogenous,[8] we preclude the possibility of aggregate growth being driven solely by exogenous labor force growth in the absence of technical change. Second, by assuming that population density has an external effect (not perceived by individual agents) on the production process through either a negative congestion effect or a positive effect in stimulating innovation and technical change, we make the change in production possibilities endogenously determined by fertility decisions of individual agents. However, unlike the new growth literature, our model, which is an extension of Raut (1985, 1991b), is not necessarily geared to generating steady states. In fact, the nonlinear dynamics of the model generates a plethora of outcomes (depending on the functional forms, parameters, and initial conditions) that include not only the neoclassical steady state with exponential growth of population with constant per capita income and consumption, but also growth paths which do not converge to a steady state and are even chaotic. Per capita output grows exponentially (and super exponentially) in some of the examples.

Our model draws on the insights of Boserup (1989) and Simon (1981) who, among others, have argued that the growth of population could itself induce technical change. In the Boserup model increasing population pressure on a fixed or very slowly growing supply of arable land induces changes in methods of cultivation, not simply through substitution of labor for land by choice of techniques within a known set of techniques but, more importantly, through the invention of new techniques. Simon also attributes a positive role for increases in population density in inducing technical progress. Since having a large population is not sufficient to generate growth (Romer, 1990), it is important to examine the mechanism by which population density influences innovation. However, neither of these two authors provides a complete theory of induced innovation. We do not provide one either: we believe that the inducement to innovate will depend largely on the returns and risks to resources devoted to innovative activity, and there is no particular reason to suggest that pre-existing relative factor prices or endowments will necessarily tilt these returns towards the search for technologies that save particular factors. Instead, we simply analyze the implications of assuming that technical change is influenced by population density (strictly speaking, population size) in a world where fertility is endogenous.

More precisely, we assume that technical change in our model economy is Hicks neutral and that its rate is determined by the change in the size of the working population. Thus, instead of the aggregate production function in equation (1.1), we use the following:

$$Y_t = A(L_t)F(K_t, L_t) \tag{1.11}$$

However, for both consumers and firms in this economy $A(L_t)$ is an externality. We introduce this externality in a model of overlapping generations in which a member of each generation lives for three periods, the first of which is spent as a child in the parent's household. The second period is spent as a young person working, having and raising children, and accumulating capital. The third and last period of life is spent as an old person in retirement living off support received from one's offspring and from the sale of accumulated capital. All members of each generation are identical in their preferences defined over their consumption in their working and retired periods. Thus, in this model the only reason that an individual would want to have a child is the support the child will provide during the parent's retired life. Production (of a single commodity which can be consumed or accumulated) is organized in firms which buy capital from the retired and hire the young as workers. Markets for product, labor, and capital are assumed to be competitive.

Formally, a typical individual of the generation which is young in period t has n_t children (reproduction is by parthenogenesis!), consumes c_t^t, c_{t+1}^t in periods t and $t + 1$, and saves s_t in period t. She supplies one unit of labor for wage employment. Her income from wage labor while young in period t is w_t and that is the only income in that period. A proportion α of this wage income is given to parents as old age support. While old in period $t + 1$, she sells her accumulated saving to firms and receives from each of her offspring the proportion α of his/her wage income. She enjoys a utility $U(c_t^t, c_{t+1}^t)$ from consumption. Thus her choice problem can be stated as

$$\max_{s_t, n_t > 0} U(c_t^t, c_{t+1}^t)$$

subject to

$$c_t^t + \theta_t n_t + s_t = (1 - \alpha)w_t \qquad (1.12)$$

$$c_{t+1}^t = (1 + r_{t+1})s_t + \alpha w_{t+1}n_t \qquad (1.13)$$

where θ_t is the output cost of rearing a child while young.

Profit maximization of the producer yields (using the notation of section 2.3)

$$w_{t+1} = A(L_{t+1})[f(k_{t+1}) - k_{t+1}f'(k_{t+1})] \qquad (1.14)$$

$$1 + r_{t+1} = A(L_{t+1})f'(k_{t+1}) \qquad (1.15)$$

In equilibrium, the private rates of return from investing in children and physical capital are equal so that arbitrage opportunities are ruled out. This implies that

$$\frac{\alpha w_{t+1}}{\theta_t} = 1 + r_{t+1} \qquad (1.16)$$

Putting equations (1.14) and (1.15) in equation (1.16), we get an implicit equation linking k_{t+1}, θ_t, and α. It can be shown that under standard neoclassical assumptions on the production function, we can solve for k_{t+1} as a function $\Psi(\theta_t/\alpha)$. Since $k_{t+1} = s_t/n_t$ (given the assumption that capital depreciates fully in one generation), the budget constraints (1.12) and (1.13) become respectively $c_t^t = (1 - \alpha)w_t - S_t$ and $c_{t+1}^t = (1 + r_{t+1})S_t$, where $S_t = [\theta_t + \Psi(\theta_t/\alpha)]n_t$. S_t could be thought of as total savings.

Let us denote the solution of the above utility maximization problem as before by $S_t = H(w_t, 1 + r_{t+1})$. We can now express the solutions for n_t and s_t as

$$n_t = \frac{H(w_t, 1 + r_{t+1})}{\theta_t + \Psi(\theta_t/\alpha)}$$

and   (1.17)

$$s_t = \frac{\Psi(\theta_t/\alpha)H(w_t, 1 + r_{t+1})}{\theta_t + \Psi(\theta_t/\alpha)}$$

Equation (1.17) determines the dynamics of the system. Let us first consider the simplest case in which child rearing cost $\theta_t = \theta$ for all $t \geq 0$. It is clear that $k_{t+1} = k^*$ for all $t \geq 1$ in this case. Assuming further that the utility function is Cobb–Douglas, i.e. $U = a \log c_t^t + (1 - a) \log c_{t+1}^t$, we have $H(w_t, 1 + r_{t+1}) = (1 - a)(1 - \alpha)w_t$. Equation (1.17) now yields

$$n_t = \frac{L_{t+1}}{L_t} = \frac{(1 - \alpha)(1 - a)}{\theta + k^*} w^* A(L_t)$$

or

$$L_{t+1} = \lambda L_t A(L_t) \equiv G(L_t) \text{ say} \qquad (1.18)$$

where $\lambda = [(1 - \alpha)(1 - a)w^*]/(\theta + k^*)$. From (1.11) we note that per capita income is given by $y_t = A(L_t)f(k^*)$. Thus, the dynamics of population long-run behavior of per capita income hinge on the form of $A(L_t)$. It should be recalled that although the fertility decisions of individuals determine L_t and hence $A(L_t)$, this is an unperceived externality. A few possibilities are depicted in figure 1.2.

Suppose $G(L_t)$ is a concave function which is zero at $L_t = 0$ and satisfies the Inada condition. Then, in the long run, population will be stationary and per capita income will be constant as in the standard neoclassical growth model. This is shown in figure 1.2(a). Now suppose that $A(L_t)$ is such that $G(L_t)$ is concave and $G'(L_t)$ is bounded away from 1. In this case, we have long-run growth in L_t and hence in per capita income. This is shown in figure 1.2(b).

Suppose now that $A(L_t)$ is a logistic function with a positive asymptote, such as $A(L) = \gamma \exp[-(L - \bar{L})^2/2]$, for $L \geq 0$. It can be shown (Raut and Srinivasan, 1991; see also figure 1.2(c)) that there are multiple steady states. Let us denote the nontrivial steady states as L^* and L^{**} (see figure 1.2(c)). Let $\bar{L}$ be the maximum of $G(L_t)$. The local dynamic properties of these steady states depend on the parameter values and the position of $\bar{L}$ relative to L^{**} plays a crucial role in the local dynamics. If the maximum $\bar{L}$ is to the right of L^{**}, then L^{**} is locally stable and there exists a neighborhood around L^{**} within which the system is monotonic. On the other hand, if $\bar{L}$ is to the left of L^{**}, there can be a nongeneric set of parameter values for which the system will exhibit endogenous fluctuations that can be damped, exploding or even chaotic. However, if α is partly influenced by the government through social security schemes, since α can affect γ, the government can shift $\bar{L}$ to the right of L^{**} and thus, locally at least, a social security program can stabilize fluctuations.

We considered more general childrearing costs (Raut and Srinivasan, 1991, section 4a) involving parent's time and depending on the rate of technological change. Naturally these led to more complicated dynamical problems. We show that there could be super exponential growth in per capita income in the long run in the case of some specific functional forms for general costs of childrearing.

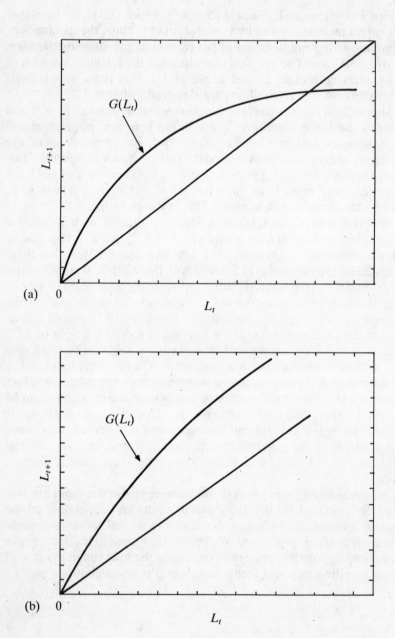

(a) 0

L_t

(b) 0

L_t

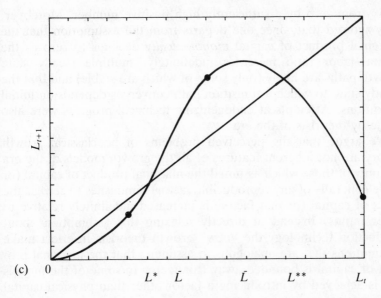

Figure 1.2 (a) Stationary population and income; (b) sustained growth in population and income; (c) complex dynamics of population and income.

5 Conclusions

The starting point of some, though not all, of the recent contributions to growth theory is a misleading characterization of the neo-classical growth theory of the 1960s and earlier as implying that a steady state growth path always exists along which output grows at a rate equal to the exogenously specified rate of growth of the labor force in efficiency units. Thus in the absence of labor-augmenting technical progress, per capita income does not grow along the steady state path. Policies that affect savings (investment) rates have only transient effects on the growth rate of per capita output although its steady state *level* is affected. Even a cursory reading of the literature is enough to convince a reader that neo-classical growth theorists were fully aware that a steady state need not exist and per capita output can grow indefinitely even in the absence of technical progress provided that the marginal product of capital is bounded away from zero by a sufficiently high positive number. Moreover, they showed that, once one departs from the assumption that the marginal product of capital *monotonically* declines to zero as the capital–labor ratio increases indefinitely, multiple steady state growth paths are likely (only some of which are stable) and that the steady state to which a transition path converges depends on initial conditions. Attempts at endogenizing technical progress were also made by theorists of the era.

We argue that the perceived problems of neoclassical growth theory are not inherent features of all the growth models of the era but only of those which assumed the marginal product of capital (or more generally of any reproducible factor) diminishes to *zero* as the input of capital (or that factor) is increased indefinitely relative to other inputs. Instead of directly relaxing this assumption about production technology the "new" growth theorists in effect make assumptions that are analogous to assuming that the marginal product of capital is bounded away from zero. In some of the models this is achieved by introducing a factor other than physical capital (e.g. human capital, stock of knowledge) which is not subject to inexorable returns. In doing so, some authors end up with an aggregate production function that exhibits increasing scale economies. Unsurprisingly in such models multiple equilibria are possible.

We present a model that takes a different approach to endogenizing technical progress and growth by assuming fertility and savings to be *endogenous* and that the size of the total population has an external effect (of a Hicks-neutral type) through either the negative influence of congestion or a positive stimulation of faster innovation. Our model generates a rich set of growth paths of per capita income and consumption, some of which do not converge to a steady state and are even chaotic.

Although the recent revival of growth theory does not constitute as much of a radical departure from its earlier roots as is sometimes thought, it contains a number of innovations, both theoretical and empirical. Further, by reviving policy interest in growth and development problems, the participants in the revival have performed a very useful service to the profession.

Notes

Dedicated to the memory of Sukhamoy Chakravarty whose premature death deprived the world of a profound scholar and India of a dedicated planner. From his earliest publication (1957) Chakravarty contributed significantly to the theoretical and empirical literature on economic growth and planning. He was one of the first (Chakravarty, 1962) among the theorists to raise deep issues of the existence of an optimal growth path. We thank John Conlisk, Isaac Ehrlick, Elhanan Helpman, Robert Lucas Jr, Mukul Majumdar, Tapan Mitra, Assaf Razin, Nouriel Roubini, Xavier Sala-i-Martin, and Robert Solow for their valuable comments on an earlier draft. We apologize to each of them for not necessarily incorporating all their suggestions in the revision and they certainly are not responsible for any errors that still remain.

1 However in Romer (1990) innovation is driven by profit-maximizing entrepreneurs.
2 One can easily prove this as follows. Suppose

$$\inf_{(K,L) > 0} \frac{\partial F}{\partial K} \equiv \gamma > 0$$

Since F is homogeneous of degree one, $F(1, L/K) = \partial F/\partial K + (L/K)\partial F/\partial L \geq \partial F/\partial K > \gamma > 0$. Now suppose $L \to 0$; then it follows that $F(1, 0) > 0$.

3 With respect to an appropriate topology in infinite-dimensional space.
4 $\bar{k}^*$ satisfying this equation is called the modified golden rule capital–labor ratio.
5 When such a relationship holds for all t, we say that the economy is on a balanced growth path.
6 We thank Robert Solow and Xavier Sala-i-Martin for pointing this out to us.
7 However, Benhabib and Jovanovic (1991) do not find any evidence for spill-over using US macro data.
8 There are a number of models in the literature in which the interaction of endogenous fertility and productive investment in human capital are analyzed in a growth context. Our purpose is not to survey this literature either. We refer the interested reader to one very interesting such model by Becker et al. (1990).

References

Abramovitz, M. 1956: Resource and output trends in the United States since 1870. *American Economic Review, Papers and Proceedings*, 46, 5–23.

Arrow, K. J. 1962: The economic implications of learning by doing. *Review of Economic Studies*, 29, 155–73.

Azariadis, C. and Drazen, A. 1990: Threshold externalities in economic development. *Quarterly Journal of Economics*, 105 (2), 501–26.

Becker, G. S., Murphy, Kevin M. and Tamura, Robert 1990: Human capital, fertility, and economic growth. *Journal of Political Economy*, 98 (5), Part 2, S12–S37.

Benhabib, J. and Jovanovic, B. 1991: Externalities and growth accounting. *American Economic Review*, 81 (1), 82–113.

Bernstein, J. and Nadiri, M. 1989: Research and development and intra-industry spillovers: an empirical implication of dynamic duality. *Review of Economic Studies*, 56, 249–68.

Boserup, E. 1989: *Population and Technical Change: A Study of Long-Term Trends*, Chicago, IL: Chicago University Press.

Chakravarty, S. 1957: The Mahalanobis model of development planning. *Arthaniti*, 1, 57–69.

—— 1962: The existence of an optimum saving program. *Econometrica*, 30 (1), 178–87.

Diamond, P. A. 1965: National debt in neoclassical growth models. *American Economic Review*, 55, 1126–50.

Domar, E. 1957: *Essays in the Theory of Economic Growth*, London: Oxford University Press.

—— 1947: Expansion and employment. *American Economic Review*, 37, 34–55.

Dorfman, R., Samuelson, P. and Solow, R. 1958: *Linear Programming and Economic Analysis*, New York: McGraw-Hill.

Cass, D. 1965: Optimum growth in an aggregative model of capital accumulation. *Review of Economic Studies*, 32, 233–40.

Denison, E. F. 1962: *Sources of Economic Growth in the United States and the Alternatives Before Us*. New York: Committee for Economic Development.

Fel'dman, G. A. 1928: K teorii tempov narodnogo dokhoda. *Planovoe Khoziaistvo*, 11, 146–70; 12, 152–78. This is discussed in Domar, E. 1957: *Essays in the Theory of Economic Growth*, London: Oxford University Press, ch. 9.

Grossman, G. and Helpman, E. 1991: *Innovation and Growth in the Global Economy*, Cambridge, MA: MIT Press.

Harrod, R. F. 1939: An essay in dynamic theory. *Economic Journal*, 49, 14–33.

Helpman, E. 1992: Endogenous macroeconomic growth theory. *European Economic Review*, 36, 237–67.

Jaffe, A. B. 1986: Technological opportunity and spillovers of R&D: evidence from firms' patents, profits, and market value. *American Economic Review*, 76 (5), 984–1001.

Jorgenson, D. W. and Griliches, Z. 1966: Sources of measured productivity change. *American Economic Review*, 56, 50–61.

Kaldor, N. and Mirrlees, J. 1962: A new model of economic growth. *Review of Economic Studies*, 29 (3), 174–92.

Koopmans, T. C. 1965: On the concept of optimal economic growth. In *The Econometric Approach to Development Planning*, Amsterdam: North-Holland (for Pontificia Acad. Sci.).

Kuznets, S. 1966: *Modern Economic Growth: Rate, Structure and Spread*, New Haven, CT: Yale University Press.

Lucas, R. E. 1988: On the mechanics of economic development. *Journal of Monetary Economics*, 22, 3–42.

Mahalanobis, P. C. 1955: The approach of operational research to planning in India. *Sankhya: The Indian Journal of Statistics*, 16, Parts 1 and 2, 3–62.

Majumdar, M. and Mitra, T. 1983: Dynamic optimization with a non-convex technology: the case of a linear objective function. *Review of Economic Studies*, 50, 143–51.

—— and Nermuth M. 1982: Dynamic optimization in non-convex models with irreversible investment: monotonicity and turnpike results. *Zeitschrift für Nationalökonomie*, 42, 339–62.

von Neumann, J. 1945: A model of general equilibrium. *Review of Economic Studies*, 13, 1–9.

Phelps, E. S. 1961: The golden rule of accumulation: a fable for growthmen. *American Economic Review*, 51, 638–43.

Radner, R. 1961: Paths of economic growth that are optimal with regard only to final states: a turnpike theorem. *Review of Economic Studies*, 28, 98–104.

Ramsey, F. P. 1928: A mathematical theory of saving. *Economic Journal*, 38 (152), 543–59.

Raut, L. 1985: Three essays on inter-temporal economic development. Unpublished doctoral dissertation, Graduate School, Yale University.

—— 1991a: R&D spillover and productivity growth: evidence from Indian private firms. Mimeo, University of California at San Diego.

—— 1991b: Capital accumulation, income distribution and endogenous fertility in an overlapping generations general equilibrium model. *Journal of Development Economics*, 34, 123–50.

—— and Srinivasan, T. N. 1991: Endogenous fertility, technical change and growth in a model of overlapping generations. Economic Growth Center Discussion Paper 628, Yale University.

Romer, P. M. 1986: Increasing returns and long-run growth. *Journal of Political Economy*, 94 (5), 1002–37.

—— 1990: Endogenous technological change. *Journal of Political Economy*, 98 (5), Part 2, S71–S102.

Samuelson, P. A. 1958: An exact consumption–loan model of interest with or without the social contrivance of money. *Journal of Political Economy*, 66, 467–82.

Schumpeter, J. 1942: *Capitalism, Socialism and Democracy*, New York: Harper.

Sheshinski, E. 1967: Optimal accumulation with learning by doing. In Karl Schell (ed.), *Essays on the Theory of Optimal Growth*, Cambridge, MA: MIT Press.

Simon, J. L. 1981: *The Ultimate Resource*, Princeton, NJ: Princeton University Press.

Solow, R. M. 1956: A contribution to the theory of economic growth. *Quarterly Journal of Economics*, 70, 65–94.

—— 1957: Technical change and the aggregate production function. *Review of Economics and Statistics*, 39, 312–20.

Srinivasan, T. N. 1962: Investment criteria and choice of techniques of production. *Yale Economic Essays*, 2, Spring, 59–115.

—— 1964: Optimal savings in a two-sector model of growth. *Econometrica*, 32 (3), 358–73.

—— 1992: Comments on Paul Romer, "Two strategies for economic development: using ideas vs. producing ideas." *Proceedings of the World Bank Conference on Development Economics*, forthcoming.

Stiglitz, J. 1990: Comments: Some retrospective views on growth theory. In P. Diamond (ed.), *Growth/Productivity/Unemployment*, Cambridge, MA: MIT Press.

Uzawa, H. 1961: On a two-sector model of economic growth, Part I. *Review of Economic Studies*, 29, 40–7.

—— 1963: On a two-sector model of economic growth, Part II. *Review of Economic Studies*, 30, 105–18.

—— 1964: Optimum growth in a two-sector model of capital accumulation. *Review of Economic Studies*, 31, 1–24.

—— 1965: Optimum technical change in an aggregative model of economic growth. *International Economic Review*, 6, 18–31.

2

Pareto optimality and productive efficiency in the overlapping generations model

Amitava Bose

The overlapping generations model is a simple but powerful device for analyzing competitive equilibrium over time. The model is especially suitable for studying questions of intertemporal welfare economics. In the paper that launched the model, Samuelson (1958) demonstrated the existence of a competitive equilibrium that fails the test of Pareto optimality. This result can be viewed as a *paradox of infinity*: whereas under "normal" conditions a competitive equilibrium does realize a Pareto optimum over finite horizons, the same conditions do not suffice in Samuelson's infinite horizon model.

Samuelson's paradox was the second of its kind. A few years earlier, Malinvaud (1953) had noted the following paradox of infinity for production programs: there exist infinite programs that are competitive in production but fail to realize an efficient allocation of resources over time. The difference between the two results stems from the fact that there are no consumers in the Malinvaud world and there is no production in the Samuelson world. Thus, while the Malinvaud result constitutes a *production paradox*, the Samuelson result yields a *distribution paradox*.

In this chapter I study a model capable of displaying both kinds of paradoxes. This is an overlapping generations model with productive capital. My principal objective is to obtain a complete characterization of programs that are Pareto optimal with respect to feasible changes in distribution as well as production. If goods are always desirable (preference monotonicity), no inefficient program can be Pareto optimal, but the converse is false. It is easy to construct a feasible program that has an efficient production sequence but a Pareto-inoptimal utility sequence – see the example in section 1.2. However, the main result states that in every such case only a finite number of changes are required to effect a Pareto improvement, i.e. efficient programs that are inoptimal are in fact *finitely* inoptimal (theorems 1 and 4). Such programs are said to fail the test of *short-run Pareto optimality*, which is discussed in section 1.3.

This chapter draws on two strands of the literature on intertemporal equilibrium. First there is the work on productive efficiency over infinite horizons. Apart from the pioneering papers of Malinvaud (1953) and Phelps (1961), there is a wealth of papers, beginning with the seminal contribution of Cass (1972), that have addressed the question of completely characterizing efficient programs under diverse technological conditions. We have particularly relied on the papers by Cass (1972), Majumdar et al. (1976), Benveniste (1976), and Mitra (1979b). The Cass paper is the fundamental one for characterization of efficiency in the "golden rule" model (defined and treated in section 2 below), but it does not apply to *non*golden rule cases.[1] In particular it does not apply to technologies that give rise to efficient programs that have "bounded consumption value" in a sense made precise in section 3.[2] For the latter models it is the Malinvaud condition, requiring the value of capital to converge to zero over time, that completely identifies efficiency. This has been noted in the papers of Majumdar et al. (1976), Benveniste (1976), and Mitra (1979b).

The other relevant strand is the literature on Pareto optimality in the overlapping generations model, taking off from Samuelson (1958). On the question of characterizing the conditions for Pareto optimality in the pure exchange model, perhaps the most complete treatment is in Balasko and Shell (1980). Adapting the technique of Cass (1972), a complete characterization had been obtained in Bose (1974b, chs 2, 3). One also likes to take note of Gale's elegant paper (1973) which characterizes stationary programs.[3] There is also some important work on the role of money in correcting inoptimalities, e.g. the important paper by Cass et al. (1979),[4] but that is a question not taken up here.

All the papers on overlapping generations mentioned above deal with the pure exchange case. Among those that incorporate production and capital accumulation in an overlapping generations framework, one of the earliest is the work of Diamond (1965). However, he did not directly address the question of characterizing Pareto optimality, though he demonstrated the existence of competitive programs that are inefficient. Wilson (1972) was able to generalize many of the results obtained by Gale (1973) for the pure exchange model to a model with production; these include a characterization for steady states. However, a complete characterization covering *all* feasible paths and any possible link with efficiency were questions that remained to be settled. Theorem 1 below was established in the first version of this paper (Bose, 1974a), and answered both these questions. This result was then extended to a multisector closed model of production in Majumdar et al. (1976).[5]

The following section is preliminary, providing notation, basic assumptions, definitions, concepts, properties associated with short-run Pareto optimality, and initial insights into the link between Pareto optimality and efficiency. In section 2 we provide a complete characterization of long-run Pareto optimality in the context of the "golden rule" model. A complete characterization of Pareto optimality for the pure exchange model is also obtained as a corollary. In section 3, the result obtained for the golden rule model is extended to an important class of *non*golden rule models. Finally, in the appendix it is shown how the separability assumption, used to make the proofs for the golden rule model more readable, can be dispensed with.

1 Preliminaries

1.1 The model

The analysis will be based on a one-good production model with overlapping generations. Production requires capital and labor. Individuals are identical except for their dates of birth, each person lives for two periods and contributes one unit of labor in each period, and there are no bequests.

A t-person, born at the beginning of period t, consumes x_t when young and y_{t+1} when old. Preferences are given by a stationary utility function u, defined on the lifetime consumption vector (x, y):

$u: \mathbb{R}^2_+ \to \mathbb{R}$. Let u_t stand for the utility level of a t-person. Then

$$u_t = u(x_t, y_{t+1}) \qquad (2.1)$$

Population grows at a constant rate $n - 1$. For each $(t - 1)$-person, the number of t-persons will be n; hence, if c_t is per capita consumption in period t, then for all $t \geq 0$

$$(1 + n)c_t = nx_t + y_t \qquad (2.2)$$

Production takes place in accordance with a neoclassical production function f, where $f: \mathbb{R}_+ \to \mathbb{R}_+$. Output not consumed gets added to the existing stock of capital and passed on to the future. Let k_t be the per capita capital stock. Then for all $t \geq 0$

$$f(k_t) = c_{t+1} + k_{t+1} \qquad (2.3)$$

To start with, only the following assumptions are made on u and f.

(A1) $u(x, y)$ is differentiable, strictly increasing and quasi-concave for $(x, y) \geq 0$.
(A2) $f(0) = 0$ and $f(k)$ is differentiable, strictly increasing and concave for $k \geq 0$.

A *program* is a nonnegative sequence $\langle u_t, x_t, y_t, k_t, c_t \rangle$ satisfying (2.1), (2.2), and (2.3) above.

For brevity we shall mostly use an abridged form such as $\langle k_t, x_t \rangle$ or $\langle k_t, c_t \rangle$ to denote a program.

1.2   Concepts of efficiency and Pareto optimality

In the above model, all programs are efficient over *finite* segments, i.e. they are invariably *short-run efficient*. Therefore we can refer to long-run efficiency (long-run inefficiency) as simply efficiency (inefficiency) without ambiguity.

A program $\langle k_t, c_t \rangle$ is *inefficient* if and only if there exists a program $\langle \bar{k}_t, \bar{c}_t \rangle$ and a positive integer τ such that $\bar{c}_\tau > c_\tau$, $\bar{c}_t \geq c_t$ for all $t \geq 1$, and $\bar{k}_0 \leq k_0$.

A program is *efficient* if and only if it is not inefficient.

While every program is short-run efficient, not every program is short-run Pareto optimal. Therefore it is necessary to specify whether one is talking about short-run Pareto optimality or about long-run Pareto optimality. To save breath, we shall use the terms short-run optimality and optimality instead of the terms short-run Pareto optimality and long-run Pareto optimality respectively.

A program $\langle k_t, x_t \rangle$ is *short-run inoptimal* if and only if there is a program $\langle \bar{k}_t, \bar{x}_t \rangle$ and a positive integer τ such that $\bar{k}_0 \leqslant k_0$, $\bar{y}_1 \geqslant y_1$, $\bar{u}_\tau > u_\tau$, $\bar{k}_{\tau+1} \geqslant k_{\tau+1}$, $\bar{x}_{\tau+1} \geqslant x_{\tau+1}$, and, if $1 \leqslant t \leqslant \tau$, then $\bar{u}_t \geqslant u_t$.

A program is *short-run optimal* if and only if it is not short-run inoptimal.

On the other hand,

A program $\langle k_t, x_t \rangle$ is *long-run inoptimal* if and only if there exists a program $\langle \bar{k}_t, \bar{x}_t \rangle$ and a positive integer τ such that $\bar{k}_0 \leqslant k_0$, $\bar{y}_1 \geqslant y_1$, $\bar{u}_\tau > u_\tau$, and $\bar{u}_t \geqslant u_t$ for all $t \geqslant 1$.

A program $\langle k_t, x_t \rangle$ is *optimal* if and only if it is not long-run inoptimal.

Note that an optimal program is short-run optimal but the converse is not true. Also, an optimal program is efficient but the converse is not true. To emphasize the distinctions, examples will now be provided of programs that are respectively (a) short-run inoptimal, (b) short-run optimal but long-run inoptimal, (c) efficient but long-run inoptimal.

Example 1

Let $f(k) = (3/4)k + 2\sqrt{k}$, $u(x, y) = xy$, and $n = 2$. Consider the program $\langle k_t, c_t, x_t \rangle$ such that $k_t = 16$ for all $t \geqslant 0$ and $x_t = 4$ for all $t \geqslant 1$. Then $c_t = 4$, $y_t = 4$, and $f(k_{t-1}) = 20$ for all $t \geqslant 1$. However, consider the alternative program $\langle \hat{k}_t, \hat{c}_t, \hat{x}_t \rangle$ such that $\hat{k}_0 = k_0$, $\hat{y}_1 = y_1$, $\hat{k}_t = k_t$, $\hat{x}_t = x_t$ for $t > 1$, and $\hat{x}_1 = x_1 - 1$. In other words, reduce the first generation's consumption by one unit each in the first period, invest the saving generated, and distribute the extra output thus obtained to the same persons in the next period. No other generation will be affected and neither will the capital stock from the (end of the) second period be disturbed. Clearly, $\hat{k}_1 = k_1 + 2/3$, and $f(\hat{k}_1) > f(k_1) + 1/2$, so that $\hat{y}_2 > y_2 + 3/2$ and $\hat{u}_1 - u_1 > x_1 y_2 - 3/2 - y_2 + (3/2)x_1 = (1/2)x_1 - (3/2) = 1/2$. Thus $\langle k_t, c_t, x_t \rangle$ is short-run inoptimal.

Example 2

Let f and u be as in example 1. Consider the program $\langle k_t, c_t, x_t \rangle$ such that $k_t = 36$ for all $t \geq 0$ and $x_t = 54/23$ for all $t \geq 1$. Then $c_t = 3$ and $y_t = 99/23$ for all $t \geq 1$. It may be checked that, since $[u_x/u_y] = 11/6 = nf'(k)$, the given program is short-run optimal. However, it is long-run inoptimal because a redistribution of consumption from the young to the old in every period makes everybody better off. Consider the alternative program $\langle \hat{k}_t, \hat{x}_t, \hat{y}_t \rangle$ such that $\hat{k}_t = k_t$ for $t \geq 0$, and $\hat{x}_t = 9/4$ and $\hat{y}_t = 9/2$ for $t \geq 1$. Clearly, $\hat{c}_t = c_t = 3$ for $t \geq 1$. But, since $\hat{y}_1 > y_1$, $\hat{k}_0 = k_0$, and, for all $t \geq 1$, $\hat{u}_t - u_t = (81/8) - (54 \times 99/23^2) > 0$, the initial program $\langle k_t, c_t, x_t \rangle$ is long-run inoptimal.[6]

Example 3

Continue with f and u as in example 1. Consider the program $\langle k_t, x_t \rangle$ with $k_{t-1} = 16$ and $x_t = 5$ for all $t \geq 1$. Then $c_t = 4$, $y_t = 2$, $u_t = 10$ for all $t \geq 1$. The alternative program $\langle \bar{k}_t, \bar{x}_t \rangle$ with $\bar{k}_t = 16$ and $\bar{x}_t = \bar{y}_t = 4$ has $\bar{y}_1 > y_1$ and, for all $t \geq 1$, $\bar{u}_t = 16$, so it clearly dominates the former. Hence the former is long-run inoptimal. But note that $k_t = 16$, being exactly the unique *golden rule* stock, generates a production program that is *efficient*.

1.3 Short-run optimality

For each horizon T, $T \geq 1$, a short-run optimal program $\langle k_t, x_t \rangle$ solves the following nonlinear programming problem:

Maximize $\bar{u}_T$ subject to
(i) $\bar{u}_t \geq u_t$, $t = 1, 2, ..., T - 1$;
(ii) $(\bar{k}_{T+1}, \bar{x}_{T+1}) \geq (k_{T+1}, x_{T+1})$;
(iii) $\bar{k}_0 = k_0$, $\bar{y}_1 = y_1$;
(iv) equations (2.1), (2.2), and (2.3) for $(\bar{k}_t, \bar{x}_t, \bar{y}_t) \geq 0$ for $1 \leq t \leq T + 1$.

It will be assumed that the given program is *strictly positive* in respect of (k_{t-1}, x_t, y_t) for all $t \geq 1$. It may be checked that the above exercise can be converted into a Lagrangean saddle-point problem, unconstrained with respect to (i) and (ii), with $k_1, ..., k_T, x_1, ..., x_T$ being the choice variables. Under (A1) and (A2) it is standard, using the Kuhn–Tucker theorem, to obtain a vector of multipliers for each T.

In fact, given the structure of the problem, the interiority of solutions and the differentiability of f and u, the same multipliers obtain for all T.

Note that, thanks to the separable structure, the short-run optimality of $\langle k_t, x_t \rangle$ is equivalent to its maximizing, for each $t \geq 1$, the expression $u(\tilde{x}_t, \tilde{y}_{t+1})$ subject to $0 \leq \tilde{k}_{t-1} \leq k_{t-1}, \tilde{y}_t \geq y_t, \tilde{k}_{t+1} \geq k_{t+1}$, $\tilde{x}_{t+1} \geq x_{t+1}$, and equations (2.1)–(2.3). This means that there exists a strictly positive sequence $\langle q_t, p_t \rangle$ of prices such that, for all $t \geq 1$,

$$0 \geq q_t(\bar{u} - u_t) - p_t n(\bar{x} - x_t) - p_{t+1}(\bar{y} - y_{t+1}) \qquad (\bar{x}, \bar{y}) \geq 0 \quad (2.4)$$

$$0 \geq p_{t+1}[f(\tilde{k}) - f(k_t)] - p_t(\tilde{k} - k_t) \qquad \tilde{k} \geq 0 \quad (2.5)$$

$$q_t \equiv np_t/u_{tx} \qquad p_0 \equiv 1 \quad (2.6)$$

where u_{tx} is the partial of u with respect to its first argument, evaluated at the point (x_t, y_{t+1}). Similarly, u_{ty} is the partial of u with respect to its second argument, evaluated at (x_t, y_{t+1}). From the above it is clear that with interior solutions

$$(u_{tx}/u_{ty}) = nf'(k_t) \qquad p_t = p_{t+1}f'(k_t) \quad (2.7)$$

It should be noted that short-run optimal programs may equivalently be called *competitive* programs. For our purposes it is not necessary to invoke the idea of a competitive equilibrium over time; this has been made explicit elsewhere, e.g. Bose and Ray (1990).

In order to be able to use marginal conditions to characterize short-run optimality, we shall henceforth confine ourselves to what we call strictly positive programs.

A program $\langle k_t, x_t, y_t \rangle$ is a *strictly positive program* if and only if $(k_{t-1}, x_t, y_t) \gg 0$ for all $t \geq 1$.

The value maximal character of short-run optimal programs over T-period horizons will be used repeatedly; its general form is summarized in lemma 1 below. The "outputs" of a T-period program are (i) the vector of utilities $(u_1, ..., u_T)$, (ii) the terminal stock of capital k_{T+1}, and (iii) the consumption of the young in the terminal year, x_{T+1}. The last two variables are, in effect, the "initial inputs" to programs beginning from $T + 1$. Short-run optimal programs maximize the value of *aggregate* output: if an alternative program yields more of some outputs – e.g. utilities – then they must yield less of some other.

Lemma 1

Assume (A1) and (A2). Let $\langle k_t, x_t \rangle$ be a strictly positive and short-run optimal program. Suppose there exists a program $\langle \bar{k}_t, \bar{x}_t \rangle$ from (k_0, y_1) $\gg 0$, such that $\lim \inf_{T \to \infty} \Sigma_{t=1}^{T} q_t(\bar{u}_t - u_t) > 0$. Then

$$\lim_{T \to \infty} \inf[(1 + n)p_{T+1}(k_{T+1} - \bar{k}_{T+1}) + np_{T+1}(x_{T+1} - \bar{x}_{T+1})] > 0$$

PROOF

From the short-run optimality of $\langle k_t, x_t \rangle$, using (2.2), (2.3), (2.4), and (2.5), we obtain for all $t \geq 1$

$$0 \geq q_t(\bar{u}_t - u_t) + np_{t+1}(\bar{x}_{t+1} - x_{t+1}) - np_t(\bar{x}_t - x_t)$$
$$+ (1 + n)p_{t+1}(\bar{k}_{t+1} - k_{t+1}) - (1 + n)p_t(\bar{k}_t - k_t) \quad (2.8)$$

Summing over t from 1 to T, cancelling common terms and noting that

$$n(\bar{x}_1 - x_1) + (1 + n)(\bar{k}_1 - k_1) = 0$$

we get

$$p_{T+1}[(1 + n)(k_{T+1} - \bar{k}_{T+1}) + n(x_{T+1} - \bar{x}_{T+1})] \geq \sum_{t=1}^{T} q_t(\bar{u}_t - u_t)$$

from which the conclusion follows.   ■

1.4   Long-run inoptimality: initial insights

Short-run optimality is necessary for full optimality. So we restrict our search for the full optimality conditions to the set of programs that are short-run optimal, i.e. characterized by (2.1)–(2.7). Moreover, efficiency is another necessary condition. Focusing on programs that are short-run optimal and, hence, price supported, one is therefore naturally led to ask: Do we have examples of prices that correctly guide the intertemporal allocation of resources, i.e. generate efficiency, but at the same time completely mislead the distribution of goods across generations, i.e. generate inoptimality?

Refer back to example 2, that of a short-run optimal but long-run inoptimal program. We were able to utility-wise dominate the given program by transferring consumption from the young to the old, *leaving the capital stocks unchanged*. The device worked precisely because $u_x/u_y < n$. But note that from short-run optimality, this means that $f'(k) < 1$, i.e. the capital allocation is clearly *inefficient*.[7] Therefore we could have generated utility dominance by giving everybody in every period a positive consumption bonus instead of bothering about redistributions! Although the example is clearly special, it turns out that the message it offers is quite general: for a large class of models, the necessary and sufficient condition for a program to be optimal is that it must be short-run optimal and efficient.

For establishing the link between long-run optimality and efficiency, I shall have to impose more structure on the technology – essentially to be able to exploit the more powerful but structure-specific characterizations of efficiency. I begin by focusing on "golden rule" technologies. Subsequently (section 3), I take up an important class of other convex technologies. While it would be desirable to devise a common technique of proof applicable to a *general* structure which includes both the above types and more, this is left as an open exercise for the present.

2 Inoptimality in the golden rule model

We add the following assumptions:

(G1) $u(x, y) = g(x) + h(y)$, with g and h twice continuously differentiable, $(g'(x), h'(y)) \gg 0 \gg (g''(x), h''(y))$ for $(x, y) \geq 0$.

(G2) $f(k)$ is twice continuously differentiable with $f'(k) > 0 > f''(k)$, for $k \geq 0$, and $f'(0) > 1 > f'(\infty)$.

These regularity conditions enable the use of the technique developed by Cass (1972) to study efficiency. However, the separability assumption is nonessential;[8] it only enhances readability at this stage. There is no problem in permitting complementarity as is shown in the appendix. We also restrict attention to interior programs, defined below:

A program is called an *interior program* if there is a real number $\underline{k}$ such that $(k_t, x_t, y_t) \geq (\underline{k}, \underline{k}, \underline{k}) \gg 0$ for all integers t.

Note from (G2) that there is $\hat{k} > 0$ such that $f(\hat{k}) = \hat{k}$, and that if $\langle k_t, x_t \rangle$ is a program then there is $\bar{K}$ such that $(k_t, x_t, y_t) \leq (\bar{K}, \bar{K}, \bar{K})$ for all integers t.

In the proof of theorem 1 below, the following inequalities, which follow from the curvature assumptions in (G1) and (G2), will play a significant role.

1 For all x and η, $\underline{k} \leq x \leq \bar{K}$, $0 < \eta \leq x - \underline{k}$, there is $m_1 > 0$, independent of x and η, such that

$$n \frac{g(x) - g(x - \eta)}{g'(x)} \geq (n\eta) + m_1(n\eta)^2 \qquad (2.9)$$

2 For all k and ε, $\underline{k} \leq k \leq \bar{K}$, $0 < \varepsilon \leq k - \underline{k}$, there is $m_2 > 0$, independent of k and ε, such that

$$(1 + n) \frac{f(k) - f(k - \varepsilon)}{f'(k)} \geq (1 + n)\varepsilon + m_2[(1 + n)\varepsilon]^2 \qquad (2.10)$$

These inequalities can be obtained by taking second-order Taylor expansions of g and f around x and k respectively and applying (G1) and (G2) appropriately. To be able to apply them we need the following property.

Lemma 2

Let f and u satisfy (A1) and (A2). Suppose $\langle k_t, x_t \rangle$ is an interior program that is long-run inoptimal. Then there is an interior program $\langle \bar{k}_t, \bar{x}_t \rangle$ such that $\bar{k}_0 = k_0$, $\bar{y}_1 = y_1$, and $\bar{u}_t - u_t \geq 0$ for all $t \geq 1$ with strict inequality for some t, $t = \tau \geq 1$.

PROOF

Given the inoptimal $\langle k_t, x_t \rangle$, let $\langle \hat{k}_t, \hat{x}_t \rangle$ be a dominating program, i.e. $\hat{k}_0 = k_0$, $\hat{y}_1 = y_1$, and $\hat{u}_t - u_t \geq 0$ for all $t \geq 1$ with strict inequality for

$t = \tau \geq 1$. Define the program $\langle \bar{k}_t, \bar{x}_t \rangle$ such that $\bar{k}_t = (k_t + \hat{k}_t)/2$, $\bar{x}_t = (x_t + \hat{x}_t)/2$ for all $t \geq 1$. The legitimacy of the construction derives from the concavity of f and the nonnegativity of variables along the given program and the dominating program. In particular, since

$$\bar{c}_t = f\left(\frac{k_{t-1} + \hat{k}_{t-1}}{2}\right) - \frac{k_t + \hat{k}_t}{2}$$

it is obvious that $(\bar{c}_t, \bar{y}_t) \geq [(c_t, y_t) + (\hat{c}_t, \hat{y}_t)]/2$. Clearly, $(\bar{k}_t, \bar{x}_t, \bar{y}_t) \geq (\underline{k}, \underline{k}, \underline{k})/2 \gg 0$ where $\underline{k}$ is a uniform lower bound for the given program $\langle k_t, x_t \rangle$. Finally, the quasi-concavity of u can be used in a straightforward manner to obtain $\bar{u}_t - u_t \geq 0$ for all t with strict inequality for $t = \tau$. ∎

We are now ready for the main result.

Theorem 1

Let f and u satisfy (A1), (A2), (G1), and (G2). An interior program $\langle k_t, x_t \rangle$ is optimal if, and only if, it is (a) short-run optimal and (b) efficient.

PROOF

Since the "only if" part is trivial, given u strictly increasing in x and y, let us go directly to the "if" part. Suppose that $\langle k_t, x_t \rangle$ is an interior program that is short-run optimal but long-run inoptimal. Let $\langle \bar{k}_t, \bar{x}_t \rangle$ be a program such that $\bar{k}_0 = k_0$, $\bar{y}_1 = y_1$, and $\bar{u}_t - u_t \geq 0$ for all $t \geq 1$ with strict inequality for some t, $t = \tau \geq 1$. By lemma 2, we may assume without loss of generality that $\langle \bar{k}_t, \bar{x}_t \rangle$ is an interior program. Now,

$$\bar{u}_t - u_t = g(\bar{x}_t) - g(x_t) + h(\bar{y}_{t+1}) - h(y_{t+1})$$
$$\leq -[g(x_t) - g(x_t - \eta_t)] + h'(y_{t+1})(\bar{y}_{t+1} - y_{t+1})$$

using the concavity of h and letting $\eta_t = x_t - \bar{x}_t$. Substituting from (2.2) and (2.3), we get

$$\bar{u}_t - u_t \leq -[g(x_t) - g(x_t - \eta_t)] + h'(y_{t+1})\{(1 + n)[f(\bar{k}_t)$$
$$- f(k_t) - (\bar{k}_{t+1} - k_{t+1})] + n\eta_{t+1}\}$$

Let $\varepsilon_t = k_t - \hat{k}_t$, multiply by $p_{t+1}/h'(y_{t+1})$, and use the short-run optimality conditions (2.6) and (2.7) to get

$$q_t(\bar{u}_t - u_t) \leq -np_t \frac{g(x_t) - g(x_t - \eta_t)}{g'(x_t)} - (1 + n)p_t \frac{f(k_t) - f(k_t - \varepsilon_t)}{f'(k_t)}$$
$$+ p_{t+1}[(1 + n)\varepsilon_{t+1} + n\eta_{t+1}]$$

By long-run inoptimality, the expression on the left of the inequality is nonnegative for all $t \geq 1$. Therefore, using (2.9) and (2.10) – which we can use since both $\langle k_t, x_t \rangle$ and $\langle \hat{k}_t, \bar{x}_t \rangle$ are interior programs – and writing $\bar{\varepsilon}_t \equiv (1 + n)\varepsilon_t$ and $\bar{\eta}_t \equiv n\eta_t$,

$$p_{t+1}(\bar{\varepsilon}_{t+1} + \bar{\eta}_{t+1}) - p_t(\bar{\varepsilon}_t + \bar{\eta}_t) \geq mp_t(\bar{\varepsilon}_t^2 + \bar{\eta}_t^2)$$
$$\geq mp_t(\bar{\varepsilon}_t + \bar{\eta}_t)^2/2$$

where $m = \min(m_1, m_2)$. Now let $\delta_t \equiv \bar{\varepsilon}_t + \bar{\eta}_t$ and $\bar{m} = m/2$. Then

$$p_{t+1}\delta_{t+1} \geq p_t\delta_t(1 + \bar{m}\delta_t)$$

Therefore, taking reciprocals and noting that $\delta_t \leq (1 + 2n)\bar{K}$,

$$\frac{1}{p_{t+1}\delta_{t+1}} \leq \frac{1}{p_t\delta_t} - \tilde{m}\frac{1}{p_t}$$

where $\tilde{m} \equiv \bar{m}/(1 + \bar{m}\bar{K})$. Summing over t from 1 to T and cancelling common terms,

$$\frac{1}{p_{T+1}\delta_{T+1}} \leq \frac{1}{p_1\delta_1} - \tilde{m}\sum_{t=1}^{T}\frac{1}{p_t}$$

Now note from the proof of lemma 1 that $p_{T+1}\delta_{T+1} \geq 0$ for $T \geq 0$. Therefore the above inequality implies that $\sum_{t=1}^{\infty}(1/p_t) < +\infty$. Since $\langle k_t, x_t \rangle$ is an interior program and f satisfies (A2) and (G2), it follows from the Cass theorem (Cass, 1972) that $\langle k_t, x_t \rangle$ is inefficient. ∎

The essential feature exploited by theorem 1 is this. With each short-run optimal program one can associate a sequence $\langle q_t, p_t \rangle$ of efficiency prices. The regularity assumptions imposed enable one to identify long-run inoptimality with the long-run behavior of $\langle 1/q_t \rangle$ where q_t is the price of the "utility good." In particular, inoptimality implies $\Sigma_{t=1}^{\infty} (1/q_t) < \infty$. Now short-run optimality ensures that the intertemporal marginal rates of substitution and transformation are equal, implying that $1/q_t = g'(x_t)/np_t \geq g'(\bar{K})/np_t$. Thus inoptimality implies that $\Sigma_{t=1}^{\infty} (1/p_t) < \infty$. But this kind of behavior in $(1/p_t)$ is bad for resource allocation and we end up with inefficiency.

2.1 Inefficiency and distribution failure

Theorem 1 relates inoptimality to inefficiency. But it is not fully explicit about distribution failures. For a complete picture of the relation between Malinvaud's *production* paradox and Samuelson's *distribution* paradox, we need a result deeper than the trivial "only if" half of theorem 1.

Take a short-run optimal program that is inefficient. Productive inefficiency implies that it is feasible to obtain some *extra* units of consumption. These can always be used to generate some *extra* units of personal utility; hence the given program must be long-run inoptimal. But this argument does not address the distribution paradox; inoptimality is here obtained as a direct consequence of the assumed *production* failure. To apply Samuelson's question to the given program what we have to ask is this: Is it possible to generate extra utility by a *pure redistribution*, i.e. without changing aggregate consumption in any period? It is revealing that the answer is yes and this is shown in theorem 2 below. What this theorem exploits is the fact that the given program is *price supported*. In such a case, inefficiency implies not merely that the sequence $\langle 1/p_t \rangle$ is summable – as Cass had noted in 1972 – but also, by virtue of short-run optimality, that the sequence $\langle 1/q_t \rangle$ is summable. The latter implication is shown to signal a distribution failure of the type highlighted by Samuelson. Thus in a production model the Malinvaud paradox implies the Samuelson paradox.[9]

Theorem 2

Let u and f satisfy (A1), (A2), (G1), and (G2). Suppose $\langle k_t, x_t \rangle$ is an interior program that is short-run optimal but inefficient. Then there exists a program $\langle \bar{k}_t, \bar{x}_t \rangle$ such that

$$\bar{y}_1 = y_1 \qquad \bar{k}_{t-1} = k_{t-1} \qquad \bar{u}_t - u_t > 0 \qquad \text{for } t \geq 1$$

PROOF

Since $\langle k_t, x_t \rangle$ is interior and inefficient, there is $M < \infty$ such that $\Sigma_{t=1}^{\infty}(1/p_t) = M$. This follows from the necessity half of the Cass theorem (Cass, 1972). For $\eta_1 > 0$, define a sequence $\langle \eta_t \rangle$ as follows:

$$p_{t+1}\eta_{t+1} = p_t\eta_t(1 + M\eta_t) \qquad t = 1, 2, \ldots$$

Then we have for $t \geqslant 1$,

$$p_t\eta_t \leqslant \frac{Mp_1\eta_1}{1 - Mp_1\eta_1}$$

Pick η_1 such that $0 < \eta_1 \leqslant 1/Mp_1$. Then, for $t \geqslant 1$, $\eta_t > 0$, and since $\eta_1 < \underline{k}/(1 + \underline{k})Mp_1$, it follows that $\eta_t \leqslant \underline{k} \leqslant x_t$. Let $\delta_t = \eta_t/2$. Then for $t \geqslant 1$ we have $0 < \delta_t \leqslant x_t$ and

$$p_t\theta_t \equiv p_{t+1}\delta_{t+1} - p_t\delta_t(1 + M\delta_t) = \frac{Mp_t\eta_t}{4} > 0$$

Let $Q = \sup[-g''(x), -h''(y)]$ for $(\underline{k}, \underline{k}) \leqslant (x, y) \leqslant (\bar{K}, \bar{K})$. Then for any γ such that $0 < \gamma \leqslant \min(1, 2nQ/M)$,

$$\gamma p_{t+1}\delta_{t+1} = \gamma p_t\delta_t(1 + M\delta_t) + \gamma p_t\theta_t$$

Dividing by p_t, using (2.6) and the bound on γ,

$$\frac{nh'(y_{t+1})}{g'(x_t)}\gamma\delta_{t+1} \geqslant \gamma\delta_t\left(1 + \frac{Q}{2n}\gamma\delta_t\right) + \gamma\theta_t$$

Letting $\alpha_t \equiv \gamma\delta_t$, we have

$$h'(y_{t+1})\alpha_{t+1} \geqslant \frac{g'(x_t)\alpha_t}{n}\left[1 + \frac{Q(\alpha_t/n)}{2}\right] + \frac{\gamma\theta_t g'(x_t)}{n}$$

Define a sequence $\langle \bar{k}_t, \bar{x}_t, \bar{y}_t \rangle$ such that for all $t \geqslant 1$

$$\bar{k}_{t-1} = k_{t-1} \qquad \bar{y}_t = y_t + \alpha_t \qquad \bar{x}_t = x_t + \beta_t$$

where $\beta_t = -\alpha_t/n$. We shall now show that, for an appropriate choice of γ within the specified interval, the above sequence is a program that is utility dominant over $\langle k_t, x_t, y_t\rangle$.

Now, by definition of Q,

$$h(\bar{y}_{t+1}) - h(y_{t+1}) \geq \alpha_{t+1}h'(y_{t+1}) - \frac{Q\alpha_{t+1}^2}{2}$$

Therefore,

$$h(\bar{y}_{t+1}) - h(y_{t+1}) \geq -g'(x_t)\beta_t + \frac{Q\beta_t^2}{2} - \frac{Q\alpha_{t+1}^2}{2} + \frac{\gamma\theta_tg'(x_t)}{n}$$

Again,

$$-g'(x_t)\beta_t + \frac{Q\beta_t^2}{2} \geq g(x_t) - g(\bar{x}_t)$$

and so

$$\bar{u}_t - u_t \geq \frac{\gamma\delta_tg'(x_t)}{n} - \frac{Q\alpha_{t+1}^2}{2} \tag{2.11}$$

We now pick γ small enough so that the right-hand side of (2.11) is positive for each $t \geq 1$. Now, substituting from definitions, $\gamma\theta_t = \gamma\eta_t^2M/2$. Therefore,

$$\frac{\gamma\theta_tg'(x_t)}{n} - \frac{Q\alpha_{t+1}^2}{2} = \frac{\gamma M\eta_t^2g'(x_t) - nQ\alpha_{t+1}^2}{2n}$$

Let $\gamma M\eta_t^2g'(x_t) - nQ\alpha_{t+1}^2 \equiv A$, say. Since, from definitions, $\alpha_{t+1}^2 = (\gamma\eta_{t+1})^2/4$, we have

$$A \geq \gamma(\hat{M}\eta_t^2 - \hat{Q}\eta_{t+1}^2)$$

where $\hat{M} \equiv Mg'(\bar{K})$ and $\hat{Q} \equiv \gamma nQ/4$. By construction of $\langle\eta_t\rangle$,

$$\eta_{T+1} = \frac{\eta_1(1/p_{T+1})}{1 - Mp_1\eta_1\Sigma_1^T[1/p_t(1 + M\eta_t)]}$$

Thus there is $v > 0$ such that $(\eta_t/\eta_{t+1})^2 \geqslant v$.[10] Hence

$$A \geqslant \gamma(v\hat{M} + \hat{Q})\eta_t^2$$

and we can choose γ – and thereby $\hat{Q}$ – such that the right-hand side is strictly positive. Thus let

$$\gamma = \min\left(1, \frac{2nM}{Q}, \frac{4v\hat{M}}{nQ}\right) > 0$$

Then, from (2.11), we would have, for all $t \geqslant 1$, $\bar{u}_t - u_t > 0$. To see that $\langle \bar{k}_t, \bar{x}_t, \bar{y}_t \rangle$ is a program, note that, for all $t \geqslant 1$, $\alpha_t > 0$ so that $\bar{y}_t = y_t + \alpha_t > y_t \geqslant 0$. Also $\alpha_t = \gamma\delta_t \leqslant \delta_t \leqslant x_t \leqslant nx_t$, so that $\bar{x}_t = x_t - \alpha_t/n \geqslant 0$. Moreover, $\bar{k}_t = k_t$ for all t.

Thus we have constructed a dominating program.[11]   ∎

2.2   *The pure exchange case*

We briefly take up the Samuelsonian *pure exchange* model to demonstrate that a complete characterization of Pareto optimality for such a model can be obtained as a corollary to theorems 1 and 2.

A *pure exchange program* is a nonnegative sequence $\langle u_t, x_t, y_t \rangle$ such that

$$u_t = u(x_t, y_{t+1})$$

and

$$nx_t + y_t = C$$

where C is a positive number that is given exogenously.

A pure exchange program $\langle u_t, x_t, y_t \rangle$ is *inoptimal* if and only if there exists another pure exchange program $\langle \bar{u}_t, \bar{x}_t, \bar{y}_t \rangle$ and a positive integer τ such that $\bar{y}_1 \geqslant y_1$, $\bar{u}_\tau > u_\tau$, and, for all $t \geqslant 1$, $\bar{u}_t \geqslant u_t$. Otherwise it is *optimal*.

Note that in our one commodity model all pure exchange programs are short-run optimal; inoptimality here must always mean long-run inoptimality. For the characterization we confine ourselves to *interior pure exchange programs*, those for which the sequences $\langle x_t, y_t \rangle$ are bounded above and below by strictly positive numbers.

Theorem 3

Let u satisfy (G1). An interior pure exchange program $\langle u_t, x_t, y_t \rangle$ is inoptimal if and only if

$$\sum_1^\infty \prod_{s=1}^t \frac{g'(x_s)}{h'(y_{s+1})} < +\infty$$

PROOF

For the "only if" part we follow the proof of theorem 1 ("if"), putting $k_t = \hat{k}_t$ and $(1 + n)[f(k_t) - k_{t+1}] = C$ for all t.

The "if" part is immediate from theorem 2; just assume $(1 + n) \times [f(k_t) - k_{t+1}] = C$. ∎

This kind of characterization for the pure exchange model was obtained earlier by Bose (1974b), Balasko and Shell (1980), and Benveniste (1986).

To return to the production model, to what extent can theorem 1 be extended to convex technologies that are not of the golden rule type? I consider this question now.

3 Inoptimality in models with bounded consumption value

In the theory of efficient intertemporal allocation of resources, it is useful for many purposes to distinguish between those models in which the value of consumption is summable (i.e. $\Sigma_1^\infty p_t c_t < \infty$) and those models in which (there is always a program such that) it is not. The best example of the latter is the golden rule model of section 2; e.g. the golden rule program has $p_t = 1$ and $c_t = c^*$, a constant. In the golden rule model, the well-known sufficient condition for efficiency due to Malinvaud fails to be necessary. The Malinvaud condition is a transversality condition, namely $\lim_{t \to \infty} p_t k_t = 0$. One has to rely instead on the Cass criterion: $\Sigma_1^\infty 1/p_t = +\infty$. On the other hand the so-called *closed* models of production – labor is not essential for positive output – belong to the former class of technol ogies, and for these, efficient programs both maximize the presen value of consumption and are completely identified by the Malin vaud condition.[12] Mitra (1979b) has provided a complete character ization of convex technologies for which efficient programs have "bounded consumption value," i.e. the associated sequence $\langle p_t c_t \rangle$ is summable. Such technologies satisfy, in addition to (A1), the follow ing condition:

(B) f satisfies one of the following conditions: (i) $\sup_{k \geqslant 0} f'(k) < 1$ (ii) $\inf_{k \geqslant 0} f'(k) > 1$; (iii) there is $k^* > 0$ such that $f'(k) = 1$ for $0 \leqslant k \leqslant k^*$.

We can now establish the following extension of theorem 1.

Theorem 4

Let u and f satisfy (A1), (A2), and (B). A strictly positive program $\langle k_t, x_t \rangle$ is optimal if, and only if, it is (a) short-run optimal and (b) efficient.

PROOF

Only the sufficiency half is nontrivial. To establish sufficiency, sup pose that $\langle k_t, x_t \rangle$ is short-run optimal and efficient but long-run inoptimal; we shall arrive at a contradiction. Let $\langle \bar{k}_t, \bar{x}_t \rangle$ be a program from (k_0, y_1) that dominates $\langle k_t, x_t \rangle$. Appealing to lemma 1 and noting that $(\bar{k}_t, \bar{x}_t) \geqslant 0$, we have

$$p_t[(1 + n)k_t + nx_t] \geqslant \lambda > 0$$

for $t \geqslant \tau \geqslant 1$ for some integer τ and real number λ. But from (2.2) $nx_t \leqslant (1 + n)c_t$; hence $p_t f(k_{t-1}) \geqslant \lambda/(1 + n) > 0$. Now since $\langle k_t, x_t \rangle$ is efficient we must have

$$\lim_{t \to \infty} p_t k_t = \lim_{t \to \infty} p_t c_t = \lim_{t \to \infty} p_t f(k_{t-1}) = 0$$

which is a contradiction. Therefore, $\langle k_t, x_t \rangle$ is inefficient.

A similar theorem has been established by Majumdar et al. (1976) for a multisector closed model of production with output substitutability, using essentially the same technique. Reduced to a one-sector version, their model would be a special case of the one treated here.

Theorems 1 and 3 do not of course exhaust all possibilities for technologies satisfying (A2). There are two "boundary" cases left uncovered by (G2) and (B): (i) $\sup_{k \geq 0} f'(k) > 1$ and $\inf_{k \geq 0} f'(k) = 1$; and (ii) $\sup_{k \geq 0} f'(k) = 1$ and $\inf_{k \geq 0} f'(k) < 1$ for all $k > 0$.

Appendix

In the golden rule model, the utility function was assumed to be separable. This assumption is not essential for the results; the weaker assumption (H1), which allows for complementarity, is quite sufficient. We show this here by sketching how theorem 1 can be generalized.

(H1) $u(x, y)$ is twice continuously differentiable, $(u_x, u_y) \gg 0$, for $(x, y) > 0$ and the Hessian matrix $[u_{ij}]$ of the second-order partial derivatives of u is negative definite when evaluated at a positive vector (x, y).

Theorem 1*

Let f and u satisfy (A1), (A2), (H1), and (G2). An interior program $\langle k_t, x_t \rangle$ is optimal if, and only if, it is (a) short-run optimal and (b) efficient.

PROOF

The "only if" part is trivial, by (A1), so we focus on the "if" part. Suppose that $\langle k_t, x_t \rangle$ is an interior program that is short-run optimal and long-run optimal. We show that $\langle k_t, x_t \rangle$ is inefficient.

Let $\langle \bar{k}_t, \bar{x}_t \rangle$ be a dominating program, i.e. $\bar{k}_0 = k_0$, $\bar{y}_1 = y_1$, $\bar{u}_t \geq u_t$ for all $t \geq 1$, with strict inequality for some t. Now

$$\bar{u}_t - u_t = -(x_t - \bar{x}_t)u_{tx} - (y_{t+1} - \bar{y}_{t+1})u_{ty} - (1/2)z_t'J_t z_t$$

where z_t denotes the column vector $(x_t - \bar{x}_t, y_{t+1} - \bar{y}_{t+1})$ and $J_t = [-u_{ij}]$ is the negative of the Hessian evaluated at some vector $(\hat{x}_t,$

$\hat{y}_{t+1}$) intermediate between (x_t, y_{t+1}) and $(\bar{x}_t, \bar{y}_{t+1})$. By lemma 2, we may assume that $\langle \hat{x}_t, \hat{y}_{t+1} \rangle$ is strictly positive and bounded away from the origin.

Let $\eta_t \equiv x_t - \hat{x}_t$ and $\theta_t \equiv y_t - \bar{y}_t$. Multiply both sides of the earlier equation by q_t and use equations (2.6) and (2.7) to obtain

$$q_t(\bar{u}_t - u_t) = -np_t\eta_t - p_{t+1}\theta_{t+1} - (q_t/2)z_t'J_tz_t$$

We now claim that there is a scalar $m > 0$ such that $z_t'J_tz_t \geq m\eta_t^2$.

If this is not true then for each $m > 0$ there is a sub-sequence $\langle t_s \rangle$ such that $z_{t_s}'J_{t_s}z_{t_s} < m\eta_{t_s}^2$. Then $\eta_{t_s}^2 > 0$ and letting $w_{t_s} = z_{t_s}/\eta_{t_s}$ we obtain $w_{t_s}J_{t_s}w_{t_s} < m$. Thus there is a sub-sequence $\langle w_r \rangle$ such that

$$\bar{w}'\bar{J}\bar{w} = \lim_{r \to \infty} w_r'J_rw_r = 0$$

However, $w_r = (1, \theta_{r+1}/\eta_r)$ for each r, and so $\bar{w} \neq 0$. But then, by (H1), $\bar{w}'\bar{J}\bar{w} > 0$, a contradiction. This establishes the claim.

Note that $q_t = np_t/u_{tx} \geq np_t/a$ where a is a finite upper bound on $\langle u_{tx} \rangle$; a exists by virtue of the interiority of $\langle k_t, x_t \rangle$. Thus we obtain $q_tz_t'J_tz_t \geq 2m_3p_t(n\eta_t)^2$, where $m_3 = m/2na$. Therefore,

$$q_t(\bar{u}_t - u_t) \leq -p_t(n\eta_t) - m_3p_t(n\eta_t)^2 - p_{t+1}\theta_{t+1}$$

Let $\varepsilon_t \equiv k_t - \bar{k}_t$. From (2.2), (2.3), and (2.10), we have

$$p_{t+1}\theta_{t+1} = (1 + n)p_t\frac{f(k_t) - f(k_t - \varepsilon_t)}{f'(k_t)} - (1 + n)p_{t+1}\varepsilon_{t+1} - np_{t+1}\eta_{t+1}$$

$$\geq (1 + n)p_t\varepsilon_t + m_2p_t[(1 + n)\varepsilon_t]^2 - (1 + n)p_{t+1}\varepsilon_{t+1}$$
$$- np_{t+1}\eta_{t+1}$$

Let $\delta_t \equiv (1 + n)\varepsilon_t + n\eta_t$. Then

$$q_t(\bar{u}_t - u_t) \leq p_{t+1}\delta_{t+1} - p_t\delta_t - m_3p_t(n\eta_t)^2 - m_2p_t[(1 + n)\varepsilon_t]^2$$
$$\leq p_{t+1}\delta_{t+1} - p_t\delta_t - \mu p_t\delta_t^2$$

for $\mu = \min(m_2, m_3)/2$. From dominance, $\bar{u}_t \geq u_t$, and so

$$p_{t+1}\delta_{t+1} \geq p_t\delta_t(1 + \mu\delta_t)$$

From this point the proof is identical to the last nine lines of the proof of theorem 1, with μ replacing m. ∎

Notes

The first version of this paper was written during 1973–4 when I was a student in Rochester, and forms part of my unpublished PhD thesis. The generosity of the people who helped me with my work is still fresh in my mind. I am very grateful to William Brock, Swapan Dasgupta, James Friedman, Mukul Majumdar, Lionel McKenzie, Charles Wilson, and, especially, Tapan Mitra. The present version is dedicated to the memory of my late teacher, Sukhamoy Chakravarty. My association with him goes back to my student days at the Delhi School of Economics. That was in the late 1960s and in those days Chakravarty's effervescent enthusiasm for optimal accumulation problems and paradoxes of infinity was plainly visible.

1 For a valuable extension of the Cass technique to a significantly wider realm, see Mitra (1979a). The unifying criterion developed in that paper not only includes the Cass criterion as a special case but also covers the conditions of Benveniste and Gale (1975) and Benveniste (1976) as special cases. More general technologies are treated in Cass and Yaari (1971) for the one-good case and Majumdar (1974) for the many-good case.

2 A linear production function is a special case of such technologies.

3 See also Clark (1979). A useful piece by Benveniste (1986) offers a characterization in a general abstract model that can be interpreted either as a model for analyzing productive efficiency or as a model for analyzing Pareto optimality in a pure exchange model. An earlier paper by Starrett (1972), though focused on steady states, is also suggestive of this possibility. In Clark (1981) every overlapping generations model is shown to be isomorphic to some *non*overlapping generations model.

4 See Bose and Ray (1990) for an analysis in a model with production, and for additional references.

5 For doubts about its validity under *even more* general conditions, see example 3.3 of McFadden et al. (1980).

6 Note that $\langle \hat{k}_t, \hat{c}_t, \hat{x}_t \rangle$ fails to dominate $\langle k_t, c_t, x_t \rangle$ in a finite number of periods since the latter is short-run optimal.

7 This is one of the earliest results in intertemporal efficiency, due to Phelps; see Phelps (1961).

8 The technique used in Mitra (1976) or Benveniste (1986) can be easily adapted. In the appendix we follow Mitra (1976).

9 The converse is a trivial corollary of the "if" part of theorem 1: in the proof, simply put $k_t = \bar{k}_t$ for all t.

10 In particular, we may choose $v = (1 - p_1\eta_1 M^2)^2$.

11 Indeed from the continuity of f and u and of (2.1)–(2.3), since for utility dominance one only requires $\bar{u}_t - u_t > 0$ for some and not all t, it is obvious that from $t = 2$ onward we might actually *reduce* aggregate consumption and maintain $\bar{u}_t - u_t = 0$. Thus while $\langle \bar{k}_t, \bar{x}_t \rangle$ dominates $\langle k_t, x_t \rangle$ in terms of *utility*, the latter is the dominant path in terms of *consumption*.

12 See the analysis of Majumdar et al. (1976). See also Benveniste (1976) and Mitra (1979b).

References

Balasko, Y. and Shell, K. 1980: The overlapping-generations model, I: The case of pure exchange without money. *Journal of Economic Theory*, 23, 281–306.

Benveniste, L. M. 1976: Two notes on the Malinvaud condition for efficiency of infinite horizon programs. *Journal of Economic Theory*, 12, 338–46.

—— 1986: Pricing optimal distributions to overlapping generations: a corollary to efficiency pricing. *Review of Economic Studies*, 53 (2), 301–6.

—— and Gale, D. 1975: An extension of Cass' characterization of infinite efficient production programs. *Journal of Economic Theory*, 12, 338–46.

Bose, A. 1974a: Pareto optimality and efficient capital accumulation. Discussion Paper 74-4, Department of Economics, University of Rochester.

—— 1974b: Pareto optimum consumption loans with and without production. Unpublished PhD thesis, University of Rochester.

—— and Ray, D. 1990: Monetary equilibrium in an overlapping generations model with productive capital: existence and optimality results. Indian Institute of Management Calcutta Working Paper 131(90). *Economic Theory*, forthcoming.

Cass, D. 1972: On capital overaccumulation in the aggregative neoclassical model of economic growth: a complete characterization. *Journal of Economic Theory*, 4, 200–23.

—— and Yaari, M. E. 1971: Present values playing the role of efficiency prices in the one good growth model. *Review of Economic Studies*, 38, 331–9.

——, Okuno, M. and Zilcha, I. 1979: The role of money in supporting the Pareto optimality of competitive equilibrium in consumption-loan type models. *Journal of Economic Theory*, 20, 41–80.

Clark, S. 1979: Pareto optimality in the pure distribution economy with an infinite number of consumers and commodities. *Journal of Economic Theory*, 21 (2), 336–47.

—— 1981: A combinatorial analysis of the overlapping generations model. *Review of Economic Studies*, 48, 139–45.

Diamond, P. 1965: National debt in a neoclassical growth model. *American Economic Review*, 55, 126–50.

Gale, D. 1973: Pure exchange equilibrium of dynamic economic models. *Journal of Economic Theory*, 6, 12–36.

Majumdar, M. 1974: Efficient programs in infinite dimensional spaces: a complete characterization. *Journal of Economic Theory*, 7, 355–69.

——, Mitra, T., and McFadden, D. 1976: On efficiency and Pareto optimality of competitive programs in closed multisector models. *Journal of Economic Theory*, 13, 26–46.

Malinvaud, E. 1953: Capital accumulation and efficient allocation of resources. *Econometrica*, 21, 233–68.

McFadden, D., Mitra, T. and Majumdar, M. 1980: Pareto optimality and competitive equilibrium in infinite horizon economies. *Journal of Mathematical Economics*, 7 (1), 1–26.

Mitra, T. 1976: On efficient capital accumulation in a multi-sector neoclassical model. *Review of Economic Studies*, 43, 423–9.

—— 1979a: Identifying inefficiency in smooth aggregative models of economic growth. *Journal of Mathematical Economics*, 6, 85–111.

—— 1979b: On the value maximizing property of infinite horizon efficient programs. *International Economic Review*, 20 (3), 635–42.

Phelps, E. S. 1961: Second essay on the golden rule of accumulation. *American Economic Review*, 51, 638–43.

Samuelson, P. 1958: An exact consumption–loan model of interest with or without the social contrivance of money. *Journal of Political Economy*, 66, 467–82.

Starrett, D. 1972: On golden rules, the biological theory of interest and competitive inefficiency. *Journal of Political Economy*, 80 (2), 276–91.

Wilson, C. 1972: An analysis of a one-sector dynamic general equilibrium model with capital. Unpublished, Department of Economics, University of Rochester.

3

Irreversible investment and competition under uncertainty

Avinash Dixit

1 Introduction

Sukhamoy Chakravarty was a staunch advocate of planned development, particularly in the Indian context. But his support was no
mere act of faith; it represented his conclusions after a careful study
of the planning process, with due regard to its many difficulties. In a
recent book (Chakravarty, 1987) he offered a very detailed and
perceptive critique of the "inadequacies of design and implementation" in planning, and concluded that the solution lay "not in giving
up planning but in giving it new content."

Here I want to argue that an important component of such new
content should be the recognition of pervasive and continuing uncertainty. Even the best planners seem to regard each twist and turn of
the economic environment as an isolated unforeseeable event that
upset their best laid plans. Thus Chakravarty treats the Indian
drought of the mid-1960s and the oil price rises of the mid- and late
1970s as unpleasant surprises, and the green revolution and the
boom in the export of goods and labor services to the Gulf countries
as pleasant ones. Of course the specific details of these events could
not have been foreseen, but planning should surely have taken into
account the fact that the future is full of shocks, favorable and
unfavorable.

Such uncertainty matters most in just those decision situations that
are the most crucial in development planning, namely irreversible

investments. It affects such choices by putting a premium on flexibility, and attaching an option value to the possibility of waiting for better information.

The conceptual foundations of development planning were laid in the 1950s and 1960s, when a different set of issues was at the forefront of economists' attention. The emphasis was on aspects of interconnectedness of the economy that decentralized decisions might overlook – hence the attention given to input–output theory, shadow prices that correct for externalities etc. The impact of uncertainty on irreversible decisions first began to be understood in a different context, namely environmental economics. The work of Arrow and Fisher (1974), Henry (1974), and others clarified the concept of option value for the preservation of irreplaceable natural resources. Bernanke (1983) introduced the idea for investment decisions. In recent years, exploiting the analogy with financial options, a number of writers including Pindyck (1988) and Dixit (1989) have shown how the problem can be solved in a framework that permits its quantitative importance to be assessed.

In this chapter I shall illustrate some of these ideas by developing the theory of investment in an activity that is utterly familiar, namely one that can be expanded at constant returns to scale. The only new feature is the combination of irreversibility and ongoing uncertainty. I shall consider two modes of its organization – central planning, and decentralized choice by risk-neutral price-taking firms. In this special context, the two yield identical results. But each serves to introduce new economic concepts in the simplest possible context. Also, as usual, knowing when planned and market outcomes coincide serves as a starting point for analysis of more pertinent cases when they do not. I shall indicate some such extensions in the concluding section.

Relative to recent research, there is little new here. Readers familiar with Lucas and Prescott (1974) should recognize the correspondence between a social surplus maximization problem and a competitive equilibrium with rational expectations. Lippman and Rumelt (1985), Dumas (1988), Edleson and Osband (1989), and Leahy (1990) have studied the dynamic equilibrium of the competitive industry under slightly different assumptions. Leahy, in particular, has established the parallel between a competitive firm's and a monopolist's investment problems. What I have done is to tie these ideas together in what I hope is an illuminating way.

2 The planner's problem

The model is deliberately simplified for ease of exposition; the special assumptions can be relaxed at the cost only of technical complexity.[1] To emphasize the feature of irreversibility of investment, I shall suppose that sunk capital is the only factor of production. To produce each unit of output we need one unit of installed capital. Each unit of capital costs K to install, and has no other use.

The uncertainty occurs on the demand side. The flow of utility when the rate of output is Q is given by $XU(Q)$. The stochastic shift variable X follows a Brownian motion process:

$$\frac{\mathrm{d}X}{X} = \mu \, \mathrm{d}t + \sigma \, \mathrm{d}w \tag{3.1}$$

where $\mathrm{d}w$ is the increment of a standard Wiener process having mean zero and variance $\mathrm{d}t$.

Some readers might prefer to interpret this as a model of an intermediate good when the utility is the downstream users' surplus and the uncertainty can arise from technological change or shocks to other factor prices downstream.

The planner's objective is to maximize the expected present value of utility net of capital installation cost, and the discount rate is $\rho > 0$. The mathematics of such control problems is quite hard; see Harrison (1985). Here I shall give a brief heuristic or intuitive treatment suitable for the problem at hand.

Let $W(Q, X)$ denote the Bellman value function (the maximized objective) when the initial state has the demand shock at X and an amount Q of capacity installed. It is clearly suboptimal to install new capacity if the marginal benefit from doing so is less than the marginal cost, i.e. $W_Q(Q, X) < K$. Call the region of (Q, X) space where this inequality holds the inactive region. It is intuitively clear that higher values of X are more conducive to investment. Therefore the inactive region has a positively sloped upper boundary, say $X = H(Q)$, along which $W_Q(Q, X) = K$. Figure 3.1 depicts this.

Above the boundary, immediate investment is optimal. The amount q of new capacity installed is found by maximizing $W(Q + q, X) - qK$. The first-order condition for this is $W_Q(Q + q, X) = K$. Thus q must be chosen to put the point $(Q + q, X)$ on the boundary, and so $X = H(Q + q)$ or $Q + q = H^{-1}(X)$. Then

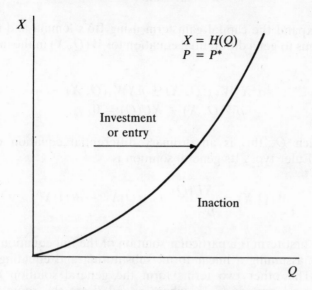

Figure 3.1 Irreversible investment.

$$W(Q, X) = \max W(Q + q, X) - qK$$
$$= W[H^{-1}(X), X] - [H^{-1}(X) - Q]K \qquad (3.2)$$

Below the boundary, Q is constant and the state moves over time because of the stochastic shifts in X. Decomposing W into the flow of utility over the next small time interval dt and the continuation value, we have

$$W(Q, X) = XU(Q)\, dt + E[W(Q, X + dX)\, \exp(-\rho\, dt)]$$

Multiply by $\exp(\rho\, dt) = 1 + \rho\, dt$ to order dt, and rearrange terms to get

$$\rho W(Q, X)\, dt = XU(Q)\, dt + E[W(Q, X + dX) - W(Q, X)]$$
$$(3.3)$$

To interpret this, regard the installed capital as an asset that has the social shadow value W. Then (3.3) says that the normal return over the time interval dt should equal the sum of the flow utility (dividend) and the appreciation (capital gain). This is a kind of social or shadow "arbitrage" relation.

Now expand the capital gain term using Itô's lemma and cancel the dt terms to get a differential equation for $W(Q, X)$ in the inactive region:

$$\tfrac{1}{2}\sigma^2 X^2 W_{XX}(Q, X) + \mu X W_X(Q, X) -$$
$$\rho W(Q, X) + XU(Q) = 0 \tag{3.4}$$

For each Q, this is an ordinary differential equation of the Cauchy–Euler type. Its general solution is

$$W(Q,X) = \frac{XU(Q)}{\rho - \mu} + A(Q)X^\alpha + B(Q)X^\beta \tag{3.5}$$

Here the first term is a particular solution of the full equation (3.4), found by assuming a linear form, substituting and equating coefficients. The other two terms form the general solution of the homogeneous part of (3.4), where α and β are the roots of the quadratic equation

$$\phi(\xi) \equiv \rho - \mu\xi - \tfrac{1}{2}\sigma^2\xi(\xi - 1) = 0 \tag{3.6}$$

The two functions $A(Q)$ and $B(Q)$ remain to be determined.

The particular solution has a useful interpretation. It is simply the expected present value of utility if no more investment is ever undertaken. The reason is that with Q held constant the utility grows with X at an expected rate μ, and is discounted back at rate ρ. For this present value to be finite, we need $\rho > \mu$. Then it is easy to see that the roots of (3.6) satisfy $\alpha < 0$ and $\beta > 1$.

Now consider what happens to the general solution (3.5) as X goes to zero. Starting from a very low value, X is unlikely to rise to the boundary $H(Q)$ in any foreseeable future, so further investment is a remote and heavily discounted event. Therefore the first term of (3.5) should be a close approximation to the full value $W(Q, X)$. But since $\alpha < 0$, the term in X^α would become dominant as $X \to 0$. To avoid that, we must have $A(Q) = 0$. This consideration enables us to write the solution as

$$W(Q, X) = \frac{XU(Q)}{\rho - \mu} + B(Q)X^\beta \tag{3.7}$$

Once again, the first term is the expected present value of utility if Q is held constant for ever. Therefore the second term must be the additional value of the ability to change Q optimally, i.e. the value of all future *options to invest*.

It remains to determine $B(Q)$. For this we must use considerations at the other end of the range of X, namely the boundary $X = H(Q)$. But the function H was merely stipulated from intuitive considerations; we must determine it as a part of the solution.

For this, first note that, along the boundary, $W_Q = K$. In terms of (3.7), this becomes

$$\frac{XU'(Q)}{\rho - \mu} + B'(Q)X^\beta = K \tag{3.8}$$

Next note from (3.2) that, just to the other side of the boundary, W_Q continues to equal K and therefore $W_{QX} = 0$. It can be shown that W is twice continuously differentiable, and so we can take the value of W_{QX} just on the other side of the boundary. Differentiating (3.7), we get

$$\frac{U'(Q)}{\rho - \mu} + \beta B'(Q)X^{\beta-1} = 0 \tag{3.9}$$

Now for any Q, (3.8) and (3.9) can be solved as a pair of equations with $B'(Q)$ and X regarded as unknowns. Eliminating $B'(Q)$, we have

$$XU'(Q) = \frac{\beta}{\beta - 1}(\rho - \mu)K \tag{3.10}$$

This holds along the boundary and therefore allows us to obtain the function H in explicit form:

$$H(Q) = \frac{\beta}{\beta - 1}\frac{(\rho - \mu)K}{U'(Q)} \tag{3.11}$$

But the implicit form (3.10) is economically the more interesting and informative. At any instant, $XU'(Q)$ is the marginal utility, or the social demand price. Then (3.10) says that new investment is triggered when this price rises to the critical level given by the right-hand side.

Moreover, the expression for this investment-triggering price has an important economic implication. When Q units are currently installed, the next marginal unit of capacity generates the marginal utility or social demand price equal to $XU'(Q)$. Since the trend rate of growth of X is μ and the discount rate is ρ, the expected present value of this marginal benefit is $XU'(Q)/(\rho - \mu)$. A textbook Marshallian calculation would tell the planner to invest when this exceeds the cost K. But a factor $\beta/(\beta - 1) > 1$ intervenes in the actual expression (3.10); a still higher price is needed before it is optimal to invest.

The reason can be found in the concept of the option value. From (3.8) and (3.9) we get

$$B'(Q) = -\frac{X^{-\beta}K}{\beta - 1} < 0 \qquad (3.12)$$

Since $B(Q)$ is the value of all future investment options when Q is the initial capacity, $-B'(Q)$ is the opportunity cost of giving up the marginal option, i.e. actually installing the $(Q + dQ)$th unit. Now in the expression for W_Q on the left-hand side of (3.8), the first term is the expected present value of the marginal utility of that unit capacity after it is actually installed. Investing as soon as the first term exceeds K would yield positive net expected value, but it would not be optimal, because that would mean forfeiting the valuable option to wait and decide later after some more information about the path of X has been observed. As (3.8) shows, only when $XU'(Q)/(\rho - \mu)$ reaches the sum of the actual installation cost K and the opportunity cost of the marginal option $-B'(Q)X^\beta$ is it optimal to go ahead, exercise the option, and install the marginal $(Q + dQ)$th unit. The factor $\beta/(\beta - 1)$ in (3.11) is the result after the solution is completed and the option value is expressed in terms of the underlying parameters.

When (3.8) is interpreted in this way, (3.9) becomes the "smooth pasting condition" for the optimal exercise of a call option in finance (see Merton, 1973, fn 60, or Malliaris and Brock, 1983, p. 124).

3 Competitive equilibrium

In this section I consider an alternative mode of organization of this industry, namely risk-neutral price-taking firms with rational expectations. With these assumptions the size of a firm is immaterial, and so without loss of generality we can define a firm as the owner of one unit of capital. There is a potential infinity of such firms, and at any instant Q denotes the actual or active ones.

Consider a currently inactive firm contemplating investment. It accepts as exogenous the stochastic process of the industry price, but entertains rational expectations about this process. When no new investment takes place, the short-run market clearing price is simply proportional to the shock

$$P = XU'(Q) \qquad (3.13)$$

When X follows the process (3.1), P follows a similar process.

$$\frac{dP}{P} = \mu \, dt + \sigma \, dw \qquad (3.14)$$

But if X, and therefore P, gets too large, new firms will enter to stop P from rising any further. In other words, the P process will have an upper reflecting barrier. I shall assume such a barrier at $\bar{P}$ and determine the value of $\bar{P}$ as a part of the solution for the industry equilibrium.

The flow of operating profits for an active firm is simply P since it produces a unit flow of output at zero variable cost. Let $V_1(P)$ denote the expected present value of these profits when the current price is P. An argument exactly like (3.4) establishes the arbitrage equation

$$\rho V_1(P) \, dt = P \, dt + E[V_1(P + dP) - V_1(P)] \qquad (3.15)$$

Then we have the differential equation

$$\tfrac{1}{2}\sigma^2 P^2 V_1''(P) + \mu P V_1'(P) - \rho V_1(P) + P = 0 \qquad (3.16)$$

and the general solution

$$V_1(P) = \frac{P}{\rho - \mu} + A_1 P^\alpha + B_1 P^\beta$$

As before, considering the limit as P goes to zero eliminates the middle term, leaving

$$V_1(P) = \frac{P}{\rho - \mu} + B_1 P^\beta \tag{3.17}$$

Now the first term is the expected present value of profits if the P process follows (3.14) and grows at rate μ without any barriers. But an active firm has no more decisions left to make, and so the second term is not an option value. Instead, it is the deduction from the expected present value to allow for the cutoff of the upside profit potential at the barrier $\bar{P}$. This is indeed what we find. To determine B_1, we have the smooth pasting condition at a reflecting barrier (see Malliaris and Brock, 1983, p. 200)

$$V_1'(\bar{P}) = 0 \tag{3.18}$$

This gives

$$B_1 = \frac{-\bar{P}^{1-\beta}}{\beta(\rho - \mu)} \tag{3.19}$$

Since $\beta > 1$, the numerical value of the right-hand side is a decreasing function of $\bar{P}$: as the barrier of the price process is lowered, the larger is the reduction in $V_1(P)$.

An idle firm is merely an option to become active. Let $V_0(P)$ denote the value of such an asset. Following familiar steps, we find

$$V_0(P) = B_0 P^\beta \tag{3.20}$$

and it remains to determine B_0 together with the optimal price P^* at which the firm will exercise its option.

As before, the conditions are (i) that the value upon becoming active must equal the cost of investment plus the opportunity cost of the forgone option

$$V_1(P^*) = K + V_0(P^*) \tag{3.21}$$

and (ii) the smooth pasting condition

$$V_1'(P^*) = V_0'(P^*) \tag{3.22}$$

Substituting from (3.17) and (3.20), these become

$$\frac{P^*}{\rho - \mu} + (B_1 - B_0)P^{*\beta} = K \tag{3.23}$$

and

$$\frac{1}{\rho - \mu} + \beta(B_1 - B_0)P^{*\beta-1} = 0 \tag{3.24}$$

Note the great similarity to (3.8) and (3.9) of the social planning problem. Then it is not surprising that the solution is also very similar:

$$P^* = \frac{\beta}{\beta - 1}(\rho - \mu)K \tag{3.25}$$

We also have

$$B_1 - B_0 = -\frac{P^{*1-\beta}}{\beta(\rho - \mu)} \tag{3.26}$$

or, using (3.19),

$$B_0 = \frac{P^{*1-\beta} - \bar{P}^{1-\beta}}{\beta(\rho - \mu)} \tag{3.27}$$

The remarkable property of the solution is that the entry trigger

P^* is totally independent of the barrier $\bar{P}$ on the price process.[2] Of course, for the whole exercise to be meaningful, we need $\bar{P} \geqslant P^*$. But so long as this is true, the exact level of the barrier is irrelevant.

Similarly, we see from (3.26) that the difference between B_1 and B_0 is independent of the barrier. Or, from (3.19) and (3.27), the barrier affects B_1 and B_0, and therefore the value functions $V_1(P)$ and $V_0(P)$, equally.

A rough verbal intuition is as follows. Calculation of the optimal entry trigger involves trading off the benefit of entering rightaway against the benefit of investing a little later. Shifts in the barrier of the price process affect the profitability of these two actions equally, leaving the desirability of waiting unaffected.[3]

Now consider a competitive industry of identical firms. In its (rational expectations) equilibrium, the price process conjectured by each firm should be the self-confirming aggregate result of their individually optimal actions. In other words, the ceiling $\bar{P}$ should equal the entry trigger P^*. Then (3.25) gives the common value of the two prices in terms of all the exogenous parameters of the problem.

Setting $\bar{P} = P^*$ in (3.26) verifies another intuitive property of competitive equilibrium with identical firms. We get $B_0 = 0$, and therefore $V_0(P)$ becomes identically zero.[4]

But the uncertainty does make an important difference: P^* does not equal $(\rho - \mu)K$, as it would in a textbook Marshallian equilibrium; it exceeds the Marshallian level by the factor $\beta/(\beta - 1)$. We found a similar property for the social planning problem, and interpreted it in terms of option values. For a small firm in a competitive industry, the same argument applies but the expected present values of both alternatives – investing at once and waiting – are lowered by equal amounts.

For an alternative explanation, consider what would happen if firms entered as soon as the price hit the level $\hat{P}$ defined by $\hat{P}/(\rho - \mu) = K$. Then $\hat{P}$ would become the upper barrier on the price process. However, price could fall to lower levels if subsequent demand shocks were adverse. Starting at $\hat{P}$, the firm's expected net worth with an unrestricted price process is only $\hat{P}/(\rho - \mu) - K = 0$. With the barrier, the expected net worth must be negative. Thus entry cannot be optimal. The higher equilibrium ceiling P^* ensures just the right mixture of periods of supernormal and subnormal profits to ensure a normal return on average.

To complete the analysis, note that the left-hand side of (3.10) is the social marginal utility that induces the social planner to install a marginal increment to capacity, while that of (3.25) is the market price that induces a new competitive firm to enter. The right-hand sides of (3.10) and (3.25) are identical. Therefore the socially optimal investment policy is replicated in the competitive equilibrium. This is an explicit verification of the kind of general proposition proved in Lucas and Prescott (1974).

How big is the multiple $k \equiv \beta/(\beta - 1)$ that measures the option value of waiting? The answer will vary from one context to another depending on the parameters μ and σ that are appropriate to the industry. As an illustration, suppose the industry is the natural resource sector, for example copper or oil, in a less developed country. For these commodities, a proportional standard deviation (coefficient of variation) of 25 percent over one year is quite common. Then $\sigma = 0.25$. Take $\mu = 0$ for simplicity, and set $\rho = 0.05$. The quadratic equation (3.6) gives $\beta(\beta - 1) = 2\rho/\sigma^2 = 1.6$. Then $\beta = 1.86$, and $\beta/(\beta - 1) = 2.16$. Price would have to be more than twice the textbook Marshallian level before new investment would occur. Thus the difference made by the option effect can be quantitatively quite dramatic.

To examine the sensitivity of the multiple k to variations in the underlying parameters in greater detail, write equation (3.6) as

$$\xi(\xi - 1) + m\xi - r = 0$$

where

$$m = 2\mu/\sigma^2 \qquad \text{and} \qquad r = 2\rho/\sigma^2$$

Thus there are two independent parameters, m and r. Now β is a root of this equation, and $\beta/(\beta - 1) = k$, or $\beta = k/(k - 1)$. Substituting, we have

$$r = \frac{k}{(k - 1)^2} + \frac{m}{k - 1}$$

Figure 3.2 shows the contours of (m, r) that correspond to several particular values of the multiple k. The convergence condition $\rho > \mu$ becomes $r > m$; thus the region below the 45° line is irrelevant. The

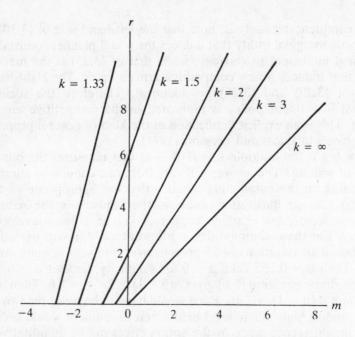

Figure 3.2 Sensitivity of option value multiple to parameters.

particular example of the previous paragraph corresponds to the point in the figure on the vertical axis with $m = 0$ and $r = 1.6$. We see that large regions of the parameter space have values of the multiple k quite substantially larger than 1; this reinforces the argument for paying careful attention to the value of waiting in situations of irreversible decisions under uncertainty.

An increase in ρ corresponds to an increase in r for fixed m. Figure 3.2 shows that such a change reduces the multiple. As the future becomes less important, the value of waiting decreases. An increase in μ corresponds to an increase in m for fixed r. This increases the multiple. Here the reason is that, with a positive trend, the effects of a small change in the initial condition are likely to be magnified over time. Therefore it is more valuable to wait for further information and reduce the risk of an error. Finally, an increase in σ corresponds to equiproportional decreases in r and m. In the figure this corresponds to a radial move toward the origin; we see that it implies a larger multiple. The intuition is that greater uncertainty means a larger value of waiting.

4 Abandonment

Perhaps the most important extension of the above simple model is the introduction of partial reversibility. In the simple model, there is no variable cost and the operating profit for each firm is always nonnegative. Therefore a firm never wants to suspend operation or shut down. More generally, we should allow a positive variable cost v per unit output. If the price falls to a sufficiently low level, some firms may wish to exit the industry temporarily or even permanently. I shall consider the case where any exit must be permanent, for example because unused capital "rusts" very quickly.[5] Similarly, a social planner may want to reduce the installed capacity. Let J be the cost of abandoning a unit of capacity. This generally consists of severance payments etc. But if part of the initial investment cost can be recouped upon exit, J can be negative, as long as there is a part that is sunk, or $-J < K$.

Social disinvestment will be triggered when a critical lower boundary $X = L(Q)$ is hit. The differential equation (3.4) for the social value of capacity Q was derived assuming no local change in Q; therefore it is valid only in the region $L(Q) < X < H(Q)$. Now the limiting argument as $X \to 0$ cannot be made, and we must retain all three terms in (3.5). To compensate, we have conditions such as (3.8) and (3.9), namely $W_Q = -J$ and $W_{QX} = 0$, at the lower boundary. The four equations, two at each boundary, determine the functions $A(Q)$, $B(Q)$ and the boundaries $H(Q)$, $L(Q)$ themselves. Written out in full, we have

$$\frac{H(Q)U'(Q)}{\rho - \mu} + A'(Q)H(Q)^{\alpha} + B'(Q)H(Q)^{\beta} = K \quad (3.28)$$

$$\frac{U'(Q)}{\rho - \mu} + \alpha A'(Q)H(Q)^{\alpha-1} + \beta B'(Q)H(Q)^{\beta-1} = 0 \quad (3.29)$$

$$\frac{L(Q)U'(Q)}{\rho - \mu} + A'(Q)L(Q)^{\alpha} + B'(Q)L(Q)^{\beta} = -J \quad (3.30)$$

$$\frac{U'(Q)}{\rho - \mu} + \alpha A'(Q)L(Q)^{\alpha-1} + \beta B'(Q)L(Q)^{\beta-1} = 0 \quad (3.31)$$

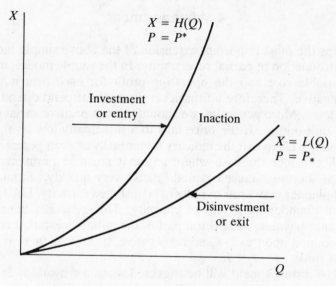

Figure 3.3 Investment and abandonment.

The system (3.28)–(3.31) does not have closed-form solutions like (3.10), but some of the properties of the solutions are easy to see. I shall merely state them; figure 3.3 illustrates the outcome.[6]

Just as the upper boundary $H(Q)$ was defined in (3.10) by a critical upper value P^* of the marginal utility or the price $P = X U'(Q)$, so is the lower boundary $L(Q)$ defined by a critical lower value P_* of the price. Moreover, we now find

$$\frac{P^*}{\rho - \mu} - \frac{v}{\rho} > K \qquad \frac{P_*}{\rho - \mu} - \frac{v}{\rho} < -J \qquad (3.32)$$

This says that investment is not made unless the expected present value of its marginal contribution net of variable costs exceeds the cost of investment, and is not retired unless the expected present value of the marginal loss from continued operation exceeds the cost of abandonment. The latter has an option value interpretation very like the former: it is optimal to accept some current loss to keep alive the option of continuing, because future prospects might improve.

In the simplest case where $\mu = 0$ and $J = 0$, (3.32) becomes

$$P^* > v + \rho K \qquad P_* < v \qquad (3.32')$$

This contrasts well with the textbook Marshallian criteria. The first inequality says that new investment is triggered only when the current price exceeds the Marshallian long-run price or full cost. Similarly, the second says that capacity is not abandoned even when the current price is a little below variable cost.

The rational expectations equilibrium again coincides with the social optimum. The demand shock process (3.1) induces a similar price process (3.14) as long as the number of firms is constant. Entry of new firms places an upper reflecting barrier on the price process at P^*, and exit induces a lower reflecting barrier at P_*.

Once again, for plausible parameter values, it is quite easy to find examples where the option value effect is numerically very large. Contemplate a full cost of 100, split between variable cost $v = 75$ and normal return on capital $\rho K = 25$. It is easy to find plausible parameters that make $P^* = 150$. This means that the current return to capital must be *three times* the normal return, or the mark-up of the current price above marginal cost must be 100 percent, before new investment occurs.

5 Interpretation

This analysis has developed a stochastic dynamic picture of a competitive industry that contrasts with the textbook notions in some important respects. It yields some new lessons for policy makers; here I shall mention a few of these.

In the stochastic dynamic picture, the industry is continuously hit by shocks. Firms know only the probabilities and not the actual paths of these shocks. Sufficiently favorable shocks bring forth new investment, and sufficiently unfavorable ones, disinvestment. The industry price fluctuates between limits determined by the entry and exit processes.

New entry does not occur unless the current price is sufficiently above the Marshallian long-run cost, and therefore *a fortiori* above the marginal cost. But the coexistence of supernormal current profit potential and a lack of new entry does not mean a market failure or any irrationality on the part of the potential entrants. Nor does it imply any excessive profit or exercise of monopoly power by the established firms. Similarly, exit does not occur unless the current price falls sufficiently below variable cost, but the firms selling at this low price are not engaged in any predatory dumping. In both cases, price-taking firms are rationally preserving the options to wait a little longer to make a better decision on the basis of more information by observing some more shocks. A planner maximizing social welfare would act no differently.

A policy maker must learn to view the evolution of the industry as an organic process. Inferences drawn from a snapshot at an instant can be misleading, in many plausible numerical calculations quite dramatically so.

Of course, the coincidence of the socially optimal investment policy and the market equilibrium is the result of some special features of the model: the absence of any externalities (discrepancies between private and social costs or benefits), price-taking rational expectations, and risk neutrality (or, more generally, the existence of efficient markets for risk bearing). The theory of stochastic industry dynamics is relatively new, and it has naturally started with the simplest idealized cases. Future research will increasingly tackle the harder problems that arise when one or more of these assumptions fail, and reasons for social intervention in the target mechanism can be identified.[7] But I hope even the tamest model developed above illustrates how far our conventional thinking must be changed when we recognize the pervasive and ongoing uncertainty of economic life.

Notes

Research support from the National Science Foundation under grant SES-8803300 is gratefully acknowledged.

1 One such extension is outlined in section 4. Others include cost uncertainty, risk-aversion, competing projects with different degrees of flexibility, and so on. For a survey of the literature, see Pindyck (1991).

2 And the solution is the same as for the case where there is no barrier on the price process at all, as for a monopolist who faces no entry of competing firms; see equation (23) of Dixit (1989). This was first observed by Leahy (1990).

3 Alternatively, we can see this as a manifestation of Bernanke's (1983)

"bad news principle of irreversible investment," namely that "of possible future outcomes, only the unfavorable ones have a bearing on the current propensity to undertake a given project."

4 Alternatively, we could have made it a definition of competitive equilibrium that an idle firm must have zero value; then the smooth pasting condition (3.22) would have emerged as a property that holds in equilibrium.

5 See McDonald and Siegel (1985) for the case of temporary suspension.

6 The mathematical details of a very similar problem are in Dixit (1989).

7 A very recent exploration along these lines, written after this chapter was completed, is in Dixit and Rob (1992).

References

Arrow, Kenneth J. and Fisher, A. C. 1974: Environmental preservation, uncertainty, and irreversibility. *Quarterly Journal of Economics*, 88 (2), 312–20.

Bernanke, Ben S. 1983: Irreversibility, uncertainty, and cyclical investment. *Quarterly Journal of Economics*, 98 (1), 85–106.

Chakravarty, Sukhamoy 1987: *Development Planning: The Indian Experience*, Oxford: Clarendon Press.

Dixit, Avinash 1989: Entry and exit decisions under uncertainty. *Journal of Political Economy*, 97 (3), 620–38.

—— 1991: Irreversible investment with price ceilings. *Journal of Political Economy*, 99 (3), 541–57.

——and Rob, Rafael 1992: Switching costs and sectoral adjustments in general equilibrium with uninsured risk. *Journal of Economic Theory*, forthcoming.

Dumas, Bernard 1988: Pricing physical assets internationally. NBER Working Paper 2569.

Edleson, Michael and Osband, Kent 1989: Competitive markets with irreversible investment. Working Paper, Rand Corporation.

Harrison, J. Michael 1985: *Brownian Motion and Stochastic Flow Systems*, New York: Wiley.

Henry, Claude 1974: Option values in the economics of irreplaceable assets. *Review of Economic Studies*, 41, 89–104.

Leahy, John 1990: Optimality, competitive equilibrium, and the entry and exit decisions of firms. Working Paper, Princeton University.

Lippman, Stephen A. and Rumelt, R. P. 1985: Demand uncertainty and investment in industry-specific capital. Working Paper, UCLA Graduate School of Management.

Lucas, Robert E., Jr and Prescott, Edward C. 1974: Equilibrium search and unemployment. *Journal of Economic Theory*, 7, 188–209.

Malliaris, Anastasios and Brock, William A. 1983: *Stochastic Methods in Economics and Finance*, Amsterdam: North-Holland.

McDonald, Robert L. and Siegel, Daniel R. 1985: Investment and the valuation of firms when there is an option to shut down. *International Economic Review*, 26, 331–49.

Merton, Robert C. 1973: The theory of rational option pricing. *Bell Journal of Economics and Management Science*, 4, Spring, 141–83.

Pindyck, Robert 1988: Irreversible investment, capacity choice, and the value of the firm. *American Economic Review*, 78 (5), 969–85.

—— 1991: Irreversibility, uncertainty, and investment. *Journal of Economic Literature*, 29 (3), 1110–52.

4

On specifying the parameters of a development plan

Prajit K. Dutta

1 Introduction

Much of Sukhamoy Chakravarty's work in the theory of development planning was directly inspired by his knowledge of the "real" problems that any actual planning exercise encounters and his deep desire to have theory and application mutually inform each other. In Chakravarty (1987) he writes of the general philosophy:

> Theoretical understanding at a given point in time, based on the perception of objectives and constraints, led to the formulation of concrete action schemes or plan directives. In turn, these action schemes, with some delay, led to the emergence of conjunctures not always anticipated, which in turn led planners and policy-makers to rethink their objectives and strategies.

An important choice variable for any planning exercise is the length of the plan horizon (and the associated choice of a final period capital stock). There are well-known theoretical arguments that suggest that the relevant horizon, especially for national planning, should be infinite (Pigou, 1920; Rawls, 1971, pp. 271–5).[1] Chakravarty was clearly convinced of the theoretical content of this argument (see, for example, the discussion in his *Capital and Development Planning* (1969), especially on pages 19–21). Yet he also believed that, given the lack of information about technologies and preferences in the distant future as well as political considerations, "for applied work on intertemporal planning, a finite horizon model with terminal capital-stock provision strikes one as the most acceptable (approach)" (Chakravarty, 1967, p. 160). However, any particular choice of horizon is arbitrary (and indeed there is no logical manner in which to select it optimally without reverting to the infinite horizon problem). Hence the question: (when) are optimal choices and maximized values robust to the actual specification of plan horizon (and terminal stock)? This was the focus of Chakravarty (1962b, 1966, 1969). Armed with the benefit of twenty-five years of hindsight, it is also the focus of this paper.

There are really two related questions of interest: are finite horizon optimal investment plans, and the associated level of maximized utility, close to each other for different specifications of horizon length? This I will call the insensitivity question. On the other hand, the continuity question is: is each finite horizon optimal plan close to some infinite horizon optimum? In turn, the insensitivity and continuity questions are examples of a broader set of questions in comparative dynamics – the changes in solutions to dynamic problems on account of changes in underlying parameters of the problem, like preferences or production relationships. In his 1969 survey, Chakravarty had this to say on the importance of these questions: "the outstanding question would seem to be the question of sensitivity, especially if we are interested in making practical policy recommendations. Sensitivity . . . should also cover questions relating to changes in parametric representations of the utility or production relationships. . . . Hence, we must be careful about distinguishing between relatively invariant properties of optimal consumption paths and merely accidental features" (p. 252).

Chakravarty's own work focused only on the insensitivity question and, although he was appreciative of the general analytical problem, his discussion was limited to numerical simulations on some simple computable stationary aggregative examples (indeed this was also true of contemporaneous studies such as those of Maneschi (1966) and Sen (1961)).[2] The literature that I primarily review in this chapter has since addressed both insensitivity and continuity questions, analytically and (in some cases) in nonstationary and multisectoral models. Not surprisingly, some of the early results and intuitions have had to be modified, or even completely abandoned, but in some other cases Chakravarty's preliminary results and intuitions have been richly rewarded. I shall also discuss, more briefly, some recent results in comparative dynamics.

The plan of the chapter is as follows. In section 2, I develop the general model. Section 3 will review the results from the aggregative, or one-sector, model while section 4 will do likewise for the multisectoral model. In section 5, I collect together some recent results on comparative dynamics. Throughout, technical details will be kept to a minimum and the emphasis will be on the intuition underlying the various results; in particular, no proofs of general theorems will be offered and the reader is invited to consult the relevant references directly for such proofs.

2 The intertemporal allocation model

Let $\mathbb{R}^n$ be n-dimensional real space with $\| \cdot \|$ denoting the max norm on this space ($\mathbb{R}^n_+$ will denote the nonnegative orthant). A correspondence or set-valued mapping Γ from $X \in \mathbb{R}^n$ to $Y \in \mathbb{R}^n$ is said to be upper semicontinuous (usc) at $x \in X$ if $\Gamma(x) = \phi$ and, for each sequence $x_n \to x$ and an associated sequence y_n where $y_n \in \Gamma(x_n)$, we have a convergent subsequence whose limit $y \in \Gamma(x)$. Γ is usc on X if it is usc at each $x \in X$. Similarly, Γ is said to be lower semicontinuous (lsc) at x if $\Gamma(x) \neq \phi$ and for each sequence $x_n \to x$ and $y \in \Gamma(x)$ there is a sequence $y_n \to y$ with $y_n \in \Gamma(x_n)$. Again, Γ is lsc on X if it is lsc at all $x \in X$. If Γ is both usc and lsc on X, it will be said to be continuous on X.

Production relations in the intertemporal model are specified by (time-indexed) nonempty production correspondences, $(F_t)_{t>0}$, $F_t: \mathbb{R}^n_+ \to \mathbb{R}^n_+$. $F_t(x)$ is the set of feasible outputs in period t that is consistent with an input x in period $t - 1$. Note that in a multisectoral model the feasible output possibilities are better described by a correspondence rather than a (single-valued) production function, since different combinations of the many commodities may be producible from the same input. Also note that it is not required that all commodities be essential for production. Finally, we take the production correspondences to be time dependent so that (certain kinds of) technological progress can be accommodated.

A special case of the above framework is the aggregative or one-sector model. Traditionally, production relations in that model are described by (time-dependent) production functions $(f_t)_{t \geq 0}$, where $f_t(x)$ is the maximum output of the single commodity available in period $t + 1$, given an investment of x in period t. Given a free disposal assumption (that I will make in the immediate sequel), a production correspondence can be derived in the aggregative case by writing $F_t(x) = \{0 \leqslant y \leqslant f_t(x)\}$. Incidentally, (inelastically supplied) labor can be straightforwardly incorporated in both the aggregative and multisectoral models; indeed, since the production relations (as well as the utility functions that follow) are time dependent, some patterns of growth in population are admissible as well.

The following assumptions on the production correspondences are standard. Each of the results that follow will employ some subset of these assumptions. Additional, less standard, assumptions will be introduced and discussed when needed.

(F0) (Null production) No output is producible from zero inputs;
$F_t(0) = \{0\}$
(F1) (Continuity) F_t is a continuous correspondence for all t
(F2) (Free disposal) $y \in F_t(x) \to y' \in F_t(x')$ if $x' \geqslant x$, $0 \leqslant y' \leqslant y$
(F3) (Convexity) The production possibility set $\{(x, y) \in \mathbb{R}^{2n}_+:$ $y \in \Gamma(x)\}$ is convex for all t
(F4) (Boundedness) $\exists \; \beta > 0$ such that $\|x\| > \beta \Rightarrow \|y\| \leqslant \|x\|$, for all $y \in F_t(x)$ and for all t.

The last two assumptions warrant brief comments. The convexity assumption rules out increasing returns to scale everywhere. Since increasing returns to scale are of central concern in a growth context, a number of authors have explored the basic questions without this assumption; consequently, several of the results that follow will not invoke (F3). The boundedness assumption asserts that strictly positive growth is, eventually, impossible – that the "marginal product" of capital is less than or equal to unity for large capital stocks. (F0)–(F4) imply that in the aggregative model the production functions f_t satisfy $f_t(0) = 0$ and are increasing, continuous, concave and have a maximum sustainable stock.

A finite horizon intertemporal allocation problem, or planning problem, is characterized by a parameter triple $\xi \equiv (x, a, T)$ where $x \in \mathbb{R}^n_+$ is the initial capital stock, $a \in \mathbb{R}^n_+$ is the target stock and T is the plan horizon. Much of the analysis that follows will involve alternative specifications of the horizon T for fixed (x, a). Writing c_t for the consumption in period t, we can define a ξ-feasible plan or program as $(x_t, c_t)_{t=0}^T$ satisfying

$$x_0 + c_0 \in F_0(x) \tag{4.1}$$

$$x_t + c_t \in F_t(x_{t-1}) \qquad t = 1, ..., T \tag{4.2}$$

$$x_T \geq a \tag{4.3}$$

$$x_t \geq 0 \qquad c_t \geq 0 \qquad t = 0, ..., T \tag{4.4}$$

An *infinite horizon feasible plan* is $x, c \equiv (x_t, c_t)_{t=0}^{\infty}$ such that (4.1), (4.2) and (4.4) are satisfied for all $t \geq 0$. Note that I shall refer to the investment (consumption) of the ith commodity in period t as x_t^i (c_t^i).

The preference structure is defined by a sequence of time-dependent utility functions $(u_t)_{t \in N}$, where $u_t \colon \mathbb{R}_+^n \to \mathbb{R}$. There are, of course, well-known problems with defining a social welfare function that aggregates individual preferences in a "consistent" fashion (I refer here to the Arrow impossibility theorem and related results). Since social choice issues are peripheral to the immediate concerns of development planning, I shall follow other writers in assuming that either a social welfare function can be defined or that u_t is some convex combination of individual utility functions. Utility is defined on consumption alone. The following assumptions are made on the utility functions:

(U1) (Continuity) u_t is a continuous function, for all t
(U2) (Monotonicity) $c' \geq c \to u_t(c') \geq u_t(c)$, for all t
(U3) (Concavity) u_t is a strictly concave function, for all t

The finite horizon optimization problem is to choose a ξ-feasible plan $[x_t^T(a), c_t^T(a)]_{t=0}^T$ such that

$$\sum_{t=0}^T u_t [c_t^T(a)] \geq \sum_{t=0}^T u_t(c_t) \tag{4.5}$$

for all ξ-feasible $(x_t, c_t)_{t=0}^T$. Note that this optimization problem is trivially equivalent to maximizing the average utility, i.e.

$$\max \frac{1}{T+1} \sum_{t=0}^T u_t(c_t)$$

over ξ-feasible plans. Denote the maximized utilities or value function $V_T(x)$ (with $v_T(x)$ for the average value).

There are several different ways in which infinite horizon preferences can be specified and each way is a response to the problem of defining an order on infinite utility streams. (A discussion of this problem is incidental to the objectives of this chapter but it is possibly worth pointing out that the second major capital theoretic contribution of Chakravarty's was precisely related to this question; see Chakravarty (1962a).) In this chapter I confine attention to, and employ, two of the more popular alternatives.

Infinite-sum utility functions

The obvious extension of finite horizon preferences is to define infinite horizon utility as

$$U(x, c) = \sum_{t=0}^{\infty} u_t(c_t) \qquad (x_t, c_t)_{t>0} \qquad (4.6)$$

The problem with (4.6) is of course that the infinite sum may not be well defined, or finite, for all feasible programs. If it is, then optimality is defined in the usual manner and we shall denote the associated value function $V(x)$. The best-known example of well-defined preferences under this criterion is that of discounted utilities: $u_t = \delta^t u$, where $\delta \in [0, 1)$.

Catching-up preferences

Alternatively, one can define a binary order. We say that (x^*, c^*) catches up to another feasible plan (x, c) if

$$\overline{\lim_{T \to \infty}} \sum_{t=0}^{T} [u_t(c_t) - u_t(c_t^*)] \leq 0 \qquad (4.7)$$

An optimal program is one that catches up to all other programs. Clearly, optimality under the first criterion implies optimality under the catching-up.

In the next two sections, I discuss the aggregative and multisectoral models respectively. It will be useful to distinguish between the two since the results, and the underlying intuition, will turn out to be quite different in the two cases.

3 Sensitivity and continuity in the aggregative model

The one-sector planning model was the exclusive focus of the early literature on sensitivity analysis. For instance, Chakravarty (1962b) analyzed the following model: the utility function is time independent and linearly homogeneous, i.e. $u_t(c) = u(c) = (1 - v)^{-1}c^{1-v}$, $v \in [0, 1)$, whereas the (time-independent) production function is linear, i.e. $f_t(x) = f(x) = bx$ where $b \geqslant 1$. This specification of utility and production has the convenient feature that the optimal solutions can be explicitly computed for different specifications of the plan horizon and terminal capital stock (as Chakravarty indeed did do, in a continuous-time framework). For the parameter values that he examined, he showed that consumption in early periods of the plan was more sensitive to the specification of horizon length and less sensitive to the specification of terminal capital stock. He surmised that these results would hold qualitatively for more general models. That some caution was called for in arriving at such a conclusion was suggested by the computations of Maneschi (1966) who in the same model showed that the result on insensitivity to terminal capital specifications was overturned for parameter specifications other than those investigated by Chakravarty.

The inconclusiveness of the debate was largely explained by the fact that the analyses were based on numerical solutions. Furthermore, this early work strongly hinted at the need for a general analytical examination of the problem. Brock (1971) was the first to do this; he examined both the investment sensitivity and continuity issues in a general convex aggregative model.[3]

Brock proved two main results relevant to the insensitivity question. The first established a strong investment monotonicity property for finite horizon optimal plans when the terminal stock requirement is zero. To be precise, the result showed that if the length of the plan horizon is increased, say from T to T', but the size of initial capital stock remains unchanged, then the optimal plan for the T' horizon maintains a higher investment level than the T horizon optimal plan in every period between 0 and T. An immediate implication of this property is that consumption is initially lower under the T' optimal plan, although it may be eventually higher. This monotonicity property is the critical intermediate result that implies insensitivity of optimal plans. Brock used it to show that, if the horizons are appropriately long, then the investment (and consequently consumption) choices in the early periods will be quite similar, i.e. that optimal plans are (initially) insensitive to horizon specification; for example, the choices in the first three periods are approximately invariant over horizon T or T', provided that both are "long enough." This last result is of great practical usefulness since a planner may not be sure at the outset of planning whether the "correct" horizon is T or T'.

I present here Brock's results under hypotheses somewhat weaker than those employed in his original discussion. The results are due to Mitra (1983). Recall that $[x_t^T(a), c_t^T(a)]_{t=0}^T$ is the notation for an optimal plan from an initial stock x (which remains fixed throughout and therefore is suppressed in the notation) to a (feasible) terminal stock a.

Theorem 1 (Brock, 1971, Mitra, 1983)

Under (F0)–(F3) and (U1)–(U3), there is a unique optimal plan $[x_t^T(a), c_t^T(a)]_{t=0}^T$ for every feasible $\xi = (x, a, T)$. Moreover, these optimal choices satisfy the following.

(i) *Horizon monotonicity*

$$x_t^{T+1}(0) \geq x_t^T(0), \text{ for all } t = 0, ..., T$$

(ii) *Horizon insensitivity* For every t, there is an $\hat{x}_t = \lim_{T \to \infty} x_t^T(0)$; consequently, for all $\varepsilon > 0$ and N, there is $\bar{T} > N$ such that whenever $T > \bar{T}$ and $T' \geq \bar{T}$

$$\|x_t^T(0) - x_t^{T'}(0)\| < \varepsilon \qquad \|c_t^T(0) - c_t^{T'}(0)\| < \varepsilon \qquad t = 0, ..., N$$

$$(4.8)$$

(iii) *Terminal stock and horizon insensitivity* There is a terminal stock $\bar{a} \geq 0$ such that, for every t, $\hat{x}_t = \lim_{T \to \infty} x_t^T(a)$ whenever $a \leq \bar{a}$.

Two additional comments are worth making. It is of some practical interest to ask how long the horizons need to be so that the investment and consumption choices are insensitive in the first three periods; equivalently, how long is $\bar{T}$ for any given N? For instance, if the choices in the first three periods are insensitive only when the horizons are at least 3 million periods long, such insensitivity would be of very limited practical significance. Unfortunately, such results on the "rate of convergence" are not currently available and seem likely to be very model specific. Second, the result in theorem 1(iii) shows that, for a subset of terminal stocks, insensitivity can be established jointly in horizon and final stock. Clearly, the result states that for any terminal stock less than $\bar{a}$ (4.8) can be established for an appropriate $\bar{T}$.

Mathematically inclined readers will no doubt notice that (ii) follows quite directly from the monotonicity result (i). Indeed, the assertion that investment levels are higher period by period if the horizon is longer is a very strong assertion. It will be seen shortly that this is the critical property of the aggregative model which is fragile in that it is untrue in the multisectoral model under otherwise identical hypotheses. The horizon monotonicity result follows from yet another monotonicity result which says that, for identical horizon length, an optimal plan to a higher capital stock maintains uniformly higher investment levels, i.e. if $a' \geqslant a$ then $x_t^T(a') \geqslant x_t^T(a)$ for $t = 0$, ..., T. The intuition for this monotonicity result is the following: the convexity of the model implies that marginal valuations are increasing in terminal stock, i.e. for any x', x with, say, $x' > x$, the difference in continuation values, $V^T(x'; a) - V^T(x; a)$, is increasing in a. Since optimal investment choices balance the marginal utility of immediate consumption (which is independent of terminal stock) against marginal valuations, it follows that investment levels are higher if terminal stocks are higher.

What of continuity, i.e. can one assert that the finite horizon optima are themselves close to any infinite horizon optimum? That this need not be so can be demonstrated quite easily by way of a well-known "cake-eating" example (which was first employed by Gale (1967) in a different context).

Example 1

The production and utility functions satisfy (F0)–(F3) and (U1)–

(U3). However, no finite horizon optimal plan is close to an infinite horizon optimal plan.

Suppose that $f_t(x) = f(x) = x$ and $u_t(c) = u(c)$ is any function satisfying (U1)–(U3) and further that the terminal stock $a = 0$.

It can be shown that in this example, the optimal T horizon consumption policy is to eat $1/T$ of the "cake" every period. (This relies on the fact that with a strictly concave utility a decision-maker prefers to spread consumption over time.) Clearly, then, the finite horizon optimal plans involve smaller and smaller amounts of consumption each period as T increases, and in the limit involve zero consumption every period – evidently an inoptimal plan under any specification of infinite horizon preferences.

However, this example does not settle the continuity issue since there is no infinite horizon optimal plan under, for example, the catching-up criterion. (The intuition behind this statement is the same as that driving the claim above.) So the next question is: suppose that the infinite horizon problem does have a solution. Does continuity obtain in that instance? Brock (1971) (and in his generalization, Mitra, 1983) provided the following positive answer to the continuity question.[4]

Theorem 2 (Brock, 1971; Mitra, 1983)

Suppose that (F0)–(F3) and (U1)–(U3) hold and suppose further that there is a catching-up optimal plan. Then the plan (x, c) defined as the limit of the finite horizon optima is precisely this infinite horizon optimum.

An equivalent statement of this result is that, if an infinite horizon catching-up optimal plan exists, then every finite horizon optimal plan is close to this unique optimum. Again, the proofs of Brock and Mitra, which are different, both exploit critically the terminal stock monotonicity result that I have discussed above.

Note that example 1 has also demonstrated that the insensitivity and continuity questions are distinct and a positive answer to the former does not imply a likewise positive answer to the latter. Shortly, we shall see that continuity does not imply insensitivity either.

Evidently, nonconvexities caused on the production side by, for example, increasing returns to scale and on the consumption side by externalities are particularly important in a development context. The question I now turn to is: to what extent are the conclusions of theorems 1 and 2 valid without the convexity assumptions (F3) and (U3). Majumdar and Nermuth (1983), Mitra and Ray (1984), and Amir et al. (1991) have explored this issue; in each case, the authors relaxed production convexity while retaining consumption convexity. I report here a version of theorem 1 provided by Mitra and Ray (1984).

Note that without convexity, albeit only on the production side, there is no longer uniqueness of optimal choice. A (weak) form of insensitivity is then: for every T horizon optimal plan, is there a T' horizon optimal plan close to it? Mitra and Ray prove just such a result after proving a (weak) monotonicity version of theorem 1(i). The intuition for weak monotonicity is identical to that for the stronger version in the fully convex case of theorem 1(i), i.e. that the marginal valuation of capital is increasing in the size of the target stock (and therefore the length of the horizon).

Theorem 3 (Mitra and Ray, 1984)

Suppose (F1), (F2) and (U1)–(U3) hold. Let $\xi \equiv (x, a, T)$ and $\xi' \equiv (x, a, T + 1)$. Then, we have the following.

(i) *Weak horizon monotonicity* For every ξ-optimal plan $[x_t^T(0), c_t^T(0)]_{t=0}^T$, there is a ξ'-optimal plan $[x_t^{T+1}(0), c_t^{T+1}(0)]_{t=0}^{T+1}$ such that $x_t^T(0) \leqslant x_t^{T+1}(0)$, $t = 0, ..., T$.

(ii) *Weak horizon insensitivity* There is a feasible infinite horizon plan (x, c), and a sequence of optimal finite horizon plans $[x_t^T(0), c_t^T(0)]_{t=0}^T$, $T \geqslant 0$, such that, for every t, $\hat{x}_t = \lim_{T \to \infty} x_t^T(0)$. Consequently, for all $\varepsilon > 0$ and N, there is $\bar{T} > N$ such that whenever $T \geqslant \bar{T}$ and $T' \geqslant \bar{T}$

$$\|x_t^T(0) - x_t^{T'}(0)\| < \varepsilon \qquad \|c_t^T(0) - c_t^{T'}(0)\| < \varepsilon \qquad t = 0, ..., N$$
(4.9)

(iii) *Terminal stock and horizon insensitivity* There is a terminal stock $\bar{a} \geqslant 0$ and a sequence of optimal plans $[x_t^T(a), c_t^T(a)]_{t=0}^T$ such that, for every t, $\hat{x}_t = \lim_{T \to \infty} x_t^T(a)$ whenever $a \leqslant \bar{a}$.

Majumdar and Nermuth impose the stronger assumption of differentiability on the production and utility functions. Correspondingly they establish a stronger result: they prove theorem 3(i) for all finite horizon optimal plans, i.e. they prove that any ξ'-optimal plan has higher investment levels than any ξ-optimal plan. Consequently they are able, like Brock (1971), to find a unique limiting behavior for finite horizon optimal plans as the horizons become longer.

Note that the continuity question, i.e. whether or not an analog of theorem 2 holds in the nonconvex case, is still open. (It is easy to see, however, that the method of proof employed by Mitra (1983) on the continuity question implies the following result in the Mitra–Ray nonconvex model: if there is a unique catching-up optimal plan, say (x, c), then every convergent sequence of finite horizon optimal plans has (x, c) as limit.) Also it is not known which of these results would generalize to the fully nonconvex case, i.e. when both production and utility functions can be nonconcave. My conjecture would be that the monotonicity results, and hence the insensitivity results, would *not* be robust to this generalization.

A brief recapitulation of the results for the aggregative model is in order. Chakravarty (1962a) had noted that investment and consumption levels in the early years of a plan were seemingly insensitive to the terminal capital requirement, although Maneschi then showed that sensitivity was reestablished for other terminal stock specifications. Chakravarty also conjectured that optimal choices appear to be more sensitive to the length of the horizon. Subsequent analytical investigations have identified the set of the terminal stocks on which insensitivity can be asserted and further shown that horizon insensitivity is more generally true, provided the horizons are appropriately long.

4 Sensitivity and continuity in the multisectoral model

The one-good model of intertemporal allocation is at once a convenient simplification and a significant restriction. Its simplicity allows us to test intuitions and explicitly solve some examples. However, from a practical planning viewpoint, the restriction to a single commodity is clearly unacceptable. The central issue is which of the conclusions of the aggregative model are robust to a multisectoral generalization. In this section I summarize recent results on multi-sectoral sensitivity and continuity. It is worth pointing out that the literature here is much smaller than that for the aggregative model; the papers I shall refer to are Gale (1967), Radner (1967), Nermuth (1978), Amir (1991), and Dutta (1991a).

From the perspective of sensitivity and continuity analysis, the multisectoral model turns out to be very different from the aggregative one. The principal reason for this is that the monotonicity results (theorems 1(i) and 3(i)) are invalid in such a model. (Amir (1991) shows that monotonicity results can be established for the multisectoral model as well but under much stronger conditions.) Since the insensitivity and continuity properties of the aggregative model were intimately predicated on the monotonicity results, they fail to generalize as well. We present an example to demonstrate this point.

Example 2

F_t and u_t satisfy (F0)–(F3) and (U1)–(U3) but period 0 investment is very sensitive to horizon length. In particular, $\|x_0^{T+1} - x_0^T\| = 1$, for all $T \geq 1$.

Consider a two-sector model and denote investment (consumption) in period t of the two commodities as x_t^1, x_t^2 (c_t^1, c_t^2). Suppose that

$$F_t(x_{t-1}^1, x_{t-1}^2) = \{(y^1, y^2) \in \mathbb{R}_+^2 : y^i \leq x_{t-1}^i, i = 1, 2\} \qquad t \geq 1$$
$$(4.10)$$

$$F_0(x^1, x^2) = \{(y^1, y^2) \in \mathbb{R}_+^2 : y^1 + y^2 \leq x^1 + x^2\}$$

Let $(m_t)_{t>0}$ be a strictly increasing sequence, $m_t > 0$, for all t. The preferences are defined as

$$u_t(c_t^1, c_t^2) = m_t c_t^i \qquad i = 1 \text{ if } t \text{ is odd; } i = 2 \text{ if } t \text{ is even}$$
$$u_0(c_0^1, c_0^2) \equiv 0 \qquad\qquad (4.11)$$

Finally, let the initial stock $x = (1/2, 1/2)$ and the terminal stock $a = (0, 0)$. It is easy to see from (4.10) and (4.11) that (F0)–(F3) and (U1)–(U3) are satisfied.

Claim: for T odd, the optimal period 0 investment is given by $x_0^1 = 1$, $x_0^2 = 0$ whereas, for T even, $x_0^1 = 0$, $x_0^2 = 1$.

It is easy to see that, given (4.10) and (4.11), once (x_0^1, x_0^2) has been determined, in any optimal policy the only consumption that takes place is at the terminal and penultimate dates; for instance, when T is odd $c_T^1 = x_0^1$, $c_{T-1}^2 = x_0^2$, and all other consumption is zero. But a unit of consumption yields greater utility in period T than in $T - 1$. Hence, given the substitution possibilities in period 0, the claim follows.

A major role of convexity in the aggregative model (in production and especially in consumption) was to generate investment monotonicity. Since such monotonicity will not obtain, and should not be expected, in the multisectoral model even under convexity, the necessity for such assumptions is moot. In all the arguments that follow in this section I shall therefore drop the requirement of convexity and by so doing bring the theory arguably closer to the increasing returns and externality issues that are critical to the development context.

Note further that example 2 need not be a cause for despair as far as multisectoral insensitivity is concerned. Asking for investment insensitivity in the presence of the substitution possibilities that are opened up by a multisectoral specification is asking for too much in any case. Besides, from a planner's point of view, the relevant question would appear to be whether the level of maximized utility is insensitive to the specification of plan horizon. A partial intuition for a positive answer to this question is that a substantial wedge between the values for T and $T + 1$ period plans would imply that we would be strictly better off by choosing one of the two plans in both cases.

Of course, for this question to be meaningful we have to normalize the sum of utilities appropriately, for different values of T. The most obvious normalization is to take averages. Recall that $v_T(x)$ is the average maximized utility from initial state x. The value insensitivity question I now analyze is: under what conditions are $v_T(x)$ and $v_{T'}(x)$ close, for long but distinct plan horizons T and T'?[5]

I present now a positive result on value insensitivity. For this result I need three new assumptions and one additional piece of notation. For $x, x' \in \mathbb{R}^n$, we say that $x' > x$ if $x' \geq x$ and $x' \neq x$. Recall the productivity bound β which has been defined by (F4).

(F5) (Uniform productivity) For all x such that $0 < x < (\beta, ..., \beta)$,
       there is a $y(x) \in F_t(x)$ satisfying $x < y(x)$, for all t
(F6) (Limiting technology) On the compact set $\{x \in \mathbb{R}^n : 0 \leq x \leq$

$(\beta, \ldots, \beta)\}$, as $t \to \infty$ the production correspondences F_t converge uniformly to a production correspondence F^*

U4) (Limiting preferences) On the compact set $\{c \in \mathbb{R}^n: 0 \leqslant c \leqslant (\beta, \ldots, \beta)\}$, the utility functions u_t converge uniformly to a function u^* as $t \to \infty$

F5) is a standard assumption in intertemporal allocation models. The limiting assumptions (F6) and (U4) are less standard (but trivially satisfied if the model is time independent or discounted stationary). If the average values are to satisfy some limiting behavior (as I will report that they do), it must be the case that the environments of planning (the production and utility relationships) also satisfy some limiting behavior. Indeed, in example 3 below, I show that without (F5) and (U4) the value insensitivity result fails.

Consider any infinite horizon feasible plan (x, c) and define its long-run average utility as

$$u(x, c) = \lim_{T \to \infty} \frac{1}{T} \sum_{t-0}^{T-1} u_t(c_t)$$

The long-run average value, for initial state x, is then defined as $v(x)$ = sup $u(x, c)$, (x, c) feasible from x.

Theorem 4 (Dutta, 1991a)

Suppose that (F0)–(F2) and (F4)–(F6) hold on the production side and (U1), (U2), and (U4) hold on the consumption side. Then, there is a v^* such that

(i) $v^* = \lim_{T \to \infty} v_T(x)$ $\qquad 0 < x \leqslant (\beta, \ldots, \beta)$ $\qquad$ (4.13)

ii) v^* is the long-run average value, for all $0 < x \leqslant (\beta, \ldots, \beta)$. In particular, average values are insensitive to the length of the plan horizon (and initial nonzero stock) provided the horizon is sufficiently long: $\forall \varepsilon > 0$ and $0 < x, x' \leqslant (\beta, \ldots, \beta)$, there is $\hat{T} < \infty$ such that $|v_T(x) - v_{T'}(x')| < \varepsilon$ whenever $\min(T, T') \geqslant \hat{T}$.

Theorem 4 implies that even if the investment and consumption choices from two different horizons, T and T', are very different, the associated values per period are very similar. This has the following useful implication for planning: suppose the planner is unsure of the exact horizon length but learns about this as time passes and consequently adjusts his investment levels appropriately. Such an "adaptive planning" framework yields average utilities that are approximately the same as those that would have been generated had the planner known the correct horizon with certainty at period 0.

I now present a brief example to show that the limiting assumptions (F6) and (U4) were necessary for theorem 4.

Example 3

Technology and preferences satisfy (F0)–(F5), (U1)–(U3) but average values are sensitive to the horizon.

$$f_t = f(x) = \begin{cases} 2x & x \leq 1/2 \\ 1 & x > 1/2 \end{cases} \qquad (4.14)$$

Let $\bar{u}_t$ be any equicontinuous sequence of functions that are individually continuous (C^∞ even), strictly increasing, and strictly concave and which satisfy the following property:

$$\overline{\lim_{T \to \infty}} \frac{1}{T} \sum_{t=0}^{T-1} \bar{u}_t\left(\frac{1}{2}\right) > \underline{\lim_{T \to \infty}} \frac{1}{T} \sum_{t=0}^{T-1} \bar{u}_t\left(\frac{1}{2}\right) \qquad (4.15)$$

Now define

$$u_t(c) = \begin{cases} \bar{u}_t(c) & c \leq 1/2 \\ \bar{u}_t(1/2) & c > 1/2 \end{cases} \qquad (4.16)$$

It is clear that with initial state $x = 1$ (and hence $f(x) = 1$) the optimal T-period plan is $x_t = c_t = 1/2$, $t = 0, ..., T$. But then (4.15) implies that average values are sensitive to the horizon.

I turn now to the continuity question: is every finite horizon optimal plan (for some admissible set of terminal stocks) "closer" to *some* infinite horizon optimal plan, for long but finite horizons? Similarly, is the value, or maximized utilities, continuous at horizon length infinity? From example 1 we know that some conditions, in ddition to the basic assumptions (F0)–(F2) and (U1), (U2), will need to be placed in order to obtain affirmative answers to these questions. In the aggregative convex model, recall that it suffices to know that there exists an optimal plan in the infinite horizon problem. I now show that in the multisectoral model we need a somewhat stronger condition: we need a condition which *guarantees* that an optimum exists in the infinite horizon problem.

I present here only one positive result and the reader can consult Dutta (1991a) for other results. The common intuition for these results is the following: think of the finite and infinite horizon planning problems as special cases of the same family of problems, differentiated only by the fact that a relevant parameter, the plan horizon, varies. As the parameter varies in a continuous fashion – the horizon goes from finite to infinite – under some restrictions on technology and preferences, the associated optimal choices should vary continuously as well.

Theorem 5 (Dutta, 1991a)

Suppose that (F1), (F2) and (U1), (U2) hold and further that, on the set of feasible infinite horizon plans from initial state x, $\Sigma_{t=0}^{\infty} u_t(c_t)$ is finite and upper semicontinuous (with respect to the product topology). Then we have the following.

(i) *Value continuity* As $T \to \infty$, $V_T(x)$ approaches the infinite horizon value function $V(x)$.

(ii) *Investment–consumption continuity* If the horizon is appropriately long, each finite horizon optimal plan has an infinite horizon optimal plan close to it, i.e. for all $\varepsilon > 0$ and $T < \infty$, there is a $\bar{T}$ such that whenever $T' > \bar{T}$, for any T' optimal program $[x^{T'}(0), c^{T'}(0)]$ to target stock zero, there is an infinite horizon optimal plan (x^*, c^*) satisfying

$$\|x_t(T') - x_t^*\| < \varepsilon \qquad t = 0, ..., T$$
$$\|c_t(T') - c_t^*\| < \varepsilon \qquad t = 0, ..., T$$

Remark

Nermuth (1978) sought to prove the same theorem under a considerably stronger condition on infinite horizon preferences but for a larger set of terminal stocks. Although the theorem is not true under the hypotheses he examined (see Dutta, 1991a, example 4.3), he did pioneer an analytical approach to the continuity problem which has proved very useful in general. It should also be noted that an early value-continuity result is to be found in Radner (1967). In that paper, theorem 5(i) was shown to hold in a multisectoral model with continuity–monotonicity assumptions much like the ones employed here and the additional assumption that the model is discounted stationary ($F_t \equiv F$ and $u_t \equiv \delta^t u$). (Some additional technical restrictions were also placed.) The discounting feature implies that the distant future is (relatively) unimportant and drives the conclusion of continuity in that paper.

Finally, I present an example to show that even if it is known that there is an infinite horizon optimum, under the catching-up criterion, it does not follow that finite horizon optima are close to it even if the finite horizons are "long." (Contrast this with the Brock result for the aggregative case reported in theorem 2.)

Example 4

There is a unique catching-up optimal plan (x^*, c^*) and unique finite horizon optimal plans $[x^T(0), c^T(0)]$. However, no finite horizon optimal plan is close to the infinite horizonal optimum. In particular, $\|c_0^T(0) - c_0^*\| = 1$, for all T.
$n = 2$. Let $x = (1/2, 1/2)$,

$$F_0(x) = \{(y^1 + y^2 \leq x^1 + x^2\}$$

$$F_t(x) = \{(y^1, y^2): y^1 \leq f(x^1), y^2 \in Q_t(x^2)\} \tag{4.17}$$

$$f(x^1) = \begin{cases} 2x^1 & x^1 \leq 1 \\ 2 & x^1 > 2 \end{cases} \tag{4.18}$$

$$Q_t(x^2) = \begin{cases} 0 & x^2 < Q_{t-1} \\ [0, Q_t] & x^2 \geq Q_{t-1} \end{cases} \tag{4.19}$$

and Q_{t-1} is an increasing sequence such that $Q_t > t$, $Q_{-1} = 1$. Finally,

$$u_t(c^1, c^2) = c^1 + c^2 \tag{4.20}$$

Essentially the two commodities are perfectly substitutable in production in period 0 and thereafter follow totally independent processes. Moreover, for commodity 2's production to get off the ground, the sum of the commodities has to be used in the second production process. So the choices are (a) only produce commodity 1 from period 1 onwards (and then the catching-up optimal policy is $x_t = c_t = 1$, for all t) or (b) switch to commodity 2 and the discrete alternatives are $x = (1, Q_0, Q_1, ..., Q_T, 0, 0, ...)$ with an associated $c = (0, 0, ..., 0, Q_T, 0)$. Since $Q_t > t$, the finite horizon optimum is (b), for $T = T'$. But clearly the unique catching-up optimum is $c_t^1, c_t^2 = 1$, 0, for all t.

To summarize, I have argued that some of the strong results regarding investment monotonicity do not carry over from the aggregative to the multisectoral models given the substitution possibilities inherent in the latter. However, value insensitivity and investment–consumption continuity can still be demonstrated under quite general conditions on production and preference. It is worth pointing out that, in the stationary convex multisectoral model, an early result of Gale (1967) elegantly demonstrated that both insensitivity and continuity did hold. However, his approach relied very heavily on the underlying convexities.

5 Other comparative dynamics topics

In this section, I shall briefly discuss some other comparative dynamics questions that arise in the theory of intertemporal allocation. A planner is typically unsure about preferences and technologies in the future. This is particularly so, the further away are the relevant periods. On the technological side, the lack of information relates to how much technological progress there will be and how fast, what the likely menu of commodities available in the future will be, what the prospects are for future resource discoveries, etc. On the preference side, a current planner can only approximate actual social preferences in the future. All of this is self-evident and so is the first theoretical query that is suggested by it: how robust are the qualitative features of optimal plans to different specifications of technology and preferences?

The literature on comparative dynamics with respect to production and utility is limited. Feldman and McLennan (1990) and Dutta et al. (1991) are two recent papers which address aspects of this problem. Both these papers are set in a framework much more general than the intertemporal allocation problem that I have discussed here. Within a very general dynamic programming problem, Dutta et al. establish conditions under which optimal choices and value functions will vary continuously with the underlying parameters that index technology and preferences. Feldman and McLennan are interested in differentiable changes in optimal choices (under correspondingly stronger restrictions on the dependence of technology and preferences on unknown parameters).

One particular aspect of intertemporal preference, whose effect on optimal choices has been examined in great detail, is the discount factor. In our discussion above, if we take $u_t = \delta^t u$, for some discount factor $\delta \in [0, 1)$ and the horizon $T = \infty$, then we are in the standard infinite horizon discounted model. A greater value of the discount factor places a bigger weight on the utilities of future consumption, and in this sense implies an increase in "patience." Several authors (Becker, 1983, 1985; Dutta, 1987; Amir et al., 1991) have explored the following question in the context of the aggregative model: does an increase in patience imply higher investment out of a given capital stock? I present a result from Amir et al. The result establishes capital deepening along the optimal discounted plans by exploiting the fact that the marginal continuation valuations are increasing in the rate of patience, for every fixed level of capital stock.

Theorem 6 (Amir et al., 1991)

Suppose that (F0)–(F2), (F4), and (U1)–(U3) hold and suppose further that $\delta' \geq \delta$. Then, for every δ-optimal plan $[x_t(\delta), c_t(\delta)]_{t=0}^{\infty}$, there is a δ'-optimal plan $[x_t(\delta), c_t(\delta)]_{t=0}^{\infty}$ such that $x_t(\delta) \leq x_t(\delta')$, $t \geq 0$.

A different aspect of the comparative dynamics of discounting is the following question: under what circumstances can we treat the two cases of discounting and no discounting ($\delta = 1$) as special instances of the same general problem? In particular, do the optimal solutions under discounting converge to optimal solutions under no discounting? In general, the undiscounted case creates many problems for the definition of infinite horizon preferences and the establishment of the existence of optima. Dutta (1991b) has recently shown that, under some general conditions like convexity and in the presence of uncertainty, in many economic models the discounted and undiscounted cases can indeed be analyzed as special cases of the same unified problem.

6 Conclusions

This chapter reported some recent results on a research question which Sukhamoy Chakravarty pioneered and considered to be a theoretical question of central importance for development planning. For both sensitivity and continuity questions, strong characterizations are now available in the one-sector model when both preferences and technologies are convex. A modified version of the insensitivity result also holds when preferences are convex (although technologies need not be so). In the multisectoral nonconvex model, a framework of particular interest in developing planning, the results are necessarily less striking. However, even here value insensitivity and investment continuity hold under reasonably general conditions.

Many interesting questions remain to be explored. Clearly, uncertainty, particularly in production, is an important feature of any planning problem. Majumdar and Zilcha (1987) have investigated the sensitivity question in the aggregative model with production uncertainty; an inquiry in the multisectoral model remains to be done. Furthermore, all of the analyses deal with technological progress in virtually an exogenous manner; the production correspondence and utility functions have arbitrary time dependence. However, not all forms of technological growth are feasible or even desirable. Moreover, such growth it itself determined by the rate and composition of capital accumulation and hence needs to be substantively endogenous to the model.

Notes

This chapter is dedicated to the memory of Sukhamoy Chakravarty, one of the true pioneers in development planning. I have benefited from helpful conversations with Mukul Majumdar, Tapan Mitra, and Itzhak Zilcha as well as the detailed comments of Tapan Mitra on an earlier draft.

1 Pigou and Rawls argued against a finite horizon for social planning problems because it reflects a bias against the consumption of future generations. Indeed, Pigou dismissed the time preference exhibited by

individuals as "habitual myopia" motivated perhaps by the finiteness of lifetimes. Since the lifetime of a nation has no logical terminal date and since the interests of current and future generations should be *a priori* identical from a social welfare viewpoint, the Pigou–Ramsey approach advocated an infinite horizon–zero discount rate framework for planning.

2 An exception is Radner (1967). See the discussion in section 4.

3 Although Brock was the first to discuss investment insensitivity analytically, an earlier discussion of value insensitivity is contained in Radner (1967). Since Radner's framework accommodates the multisectoral model, his result is discussed in detail in section 4.

4 Actually Mitra's result only requires that there exist a "weakly maximal" plan; any catching-up optimal plan is definitionally also weakly maximal. (For a definition of the weak maximality criterion, see Mitra (1983).)

5 An alternative definition of value and insensitivity was proposed by Mirrlees and explored in Hammond and Mirrlees (1973) and Hammond (1975) – see also McKenzie (1974). For a fixed infinite horizon plan (x, c) and an initial length of time N, let $V_T(x; N)$ denote the maximum utility that can be generated in a T-period planning problem, starting from initial stock x, if in the first N periods investment (and consumption) has to be identical to that specified by (x, c). The finite horizon optimum plans are said to be value insensitive, agreeable in the terminology of these papers, if there is a plan (x, c) and a sufficiently long horizon $\bar{T}$ such that $V_T(x; N)$ and $V_{T'}(x; N)$ are appropriately close to each other whenever T and T' are greater than $\bar{T}$ (and this is true for all N). This concept of value insensitivity is interesting; however, the literature was largely inconclusive in that the authors were able to derive results on questions like the existence of agreeable plans, their relation to optimality etc. only in very special cases. This literature is not detailed in this survey.

References

Amir, R. 1991: Sensitivity analysis of multi–sector optimal economic dynamics. Mimeo, SUNY Stonybrook and CORE, Louvain.

——, Mirman, L. and Perkins, W. 1991: One-sector nonclassical optimal growth: optimality conditions and comparative dynamics. *International Economic Review*, 32, 625–44.

Becker, R. 1983: Comparative dynamics in the one-sector optimal growth model. *Journal of Economic Dynamics and Control*, 6, 99–107.

—— 1985: Comparative dynamics in aggregate models of optimal capital accumulation. *Quarterly Journal of Economics*, 22, 1235–55.

Brock, W. 1971: Sensitivity of optimal growth paths with respect to a change in target stocks. *Zeitschrift für Nationalökonomie*, Supplementum 1, 73–89.

Chakravarty, S. 1962a: The existence of an optimum savings program. *Econometrica*, 30, 178–87.

—— 1962b: Optimal savings with a finite planning horizon. *International Economic Review*, 3, 338–55.

—— 1966: Reply. *International Economic Review*, 7, 119–21.

—— 1967: Alternative preference functions in problems of investment planning on the national level. In E. Malinvaud and M. Bacharach (eds), *Activity Analysis in the Theory of Planning and Growth*, London: St Martin's Press, 150–69.

—— 1969: *Capital and Development Planning*. Cambridge, MA: MIT Press.

—— 1987: *Development Planning: The Indian Experience*. Oxford: Clarendon Press.

Dutta, P. 1987: Capital deepening and impatience equivalence in a stochastic aggregative growth model. *Journal of Economic Dynamics and Control*, 11, 519–30.

—— 1991a: Finite horizon optimization: sensitivity and continuity in multisectoral models. *Journal of Mathematical Economics*, forthcoming.

—— 1991b: What do discounted optima converge to? A theory of discount rate asymptotics in economic models. *Journal of Economic Theory*, 55, 64–94.

——, Majumdar, M. and Sundaram, R. 1991: Parametric continuity in dynamic programming problems. Mimeo, California Institute of Technology, Pasadena, CA.

Feldman, M. and McLennan, A. 1990: Comparative statics in dynamic programming problems. Mimeo, University of Minnesota, Minneapolis, MN.

Gale, D. 1967: On optimal development in a multi-sector economy. *Review of Economic Studies*, 34, 1–18.

Hammond, P. 1975: Agreeable plans with many capital goods. *Review of Economic Studies*, 42, 1–14.

—— and Mirrlees, J. 1973: Agreeable plans. In J. Mirrlees and N. Stern (eds), *Models of Economic Growth*. London: Macmillan, 283–99.

Majumdar, M. and Nermuth, M. 1983: Dynamic optimization in nonconvex models with irreversible investment: monotonicity and turnpike results. *Zeitschrift für Nationalökonomie*, 42, 339–62.

—— and Zilcha, I. 1987: Optimal growth in a stochastic environment: some sensitivity and turnpike results. *Journal of Economic Theory*, 43, 116–33.

Maneschi, A. 1966: Optimal savings with finite planning horizon: a note. *International Economic Review*, 7, 109–13.

Mckenzie, L. 1974: Turnpike theorems with technology and welfare functions variable. In J. Los and M. W. Los (eds), *Mathematical Models in Economics*, New York: Elsevier.

Mitra, T. 1983: Sensitivity of optimal programmes with respect to changes in target stocks: the case of irreversible investment. *Journal of Economic Theory*, 29, 172–84.

—— and Ray, D. 1984: Dynamic optimization on a non-convex feasible set: some general results for non-smooth technologies. *Zeitschrift für Nationalökonomie*, 44, 151–75.

Nermuth, M. 1978: Sensitivity of optimal growth paths: with respect to a change in target stocks or in the length of the planning horizon in a multi-sector model. *Journal of Mathematical Economics*, 5, 289–301.

Pigou, A. 1920: *The Economics of Welfare*. London: Macmillan.

Radner, R. 1967; Dynamic programming of economic growth. In E. Malinvaud and M. Bacharach (eds), *Activity Analysis in the Theory of Planning and Growth*, London: St Martin's Press, 150–69.

Rawls, J. 1971: *A Theory of Justice*. Cambridge, MA: Belknap Press, Harvard.

Sen, A. 1961: On optimizing the rate of savings. *Economic Journal*, 71, 479–90.

5

Comparative dynamics and chaos in capital accumulation models

Mukul Majumdar and Tapan Mitra

1 Introduction

We remember Sukhamoy Chakravarty of the 1960s: a researcher at the frontier of capital theory whose extraordinary range of scholarship inspired his students at Presidency College and Delhi School of Economics. His contributions reflected a concern for facing up to the deeper logical issues that escape from a routine application of some mathematical technique to analyze an economic model. Equally pervasive was his concern for using economic models to make practical policy recommendations. Thus, in *Capital and Development Planning* (1969, p. 246) he observed that the

> discussion of intertemporal planning problems has followed two principal lines. One of those is concerned primarily with the elucidation of certain conceptual issues that are relatively invariant with regard to the degree of aggregation that is postulated. The other is concerned with the problem of generating computable models that might give explicit directions to policy.

In his contributions on intertemporal economics, two themes figured prominently: (a) the need to settle the question of *existence* of a "best" or optimal policy particularly when a dynamic optimization problem is attacked by the techniques of calculus of variations; (b) the need for *sensitivity analysis* (either qualitatively or numerically) to gain insights into the response of an optimal policy with respect to changes in the parameters of the model.

Our chapter is primarily related to the second theme mentioned above, which can be traced back to the suggestions of Samuelson in his *Foundations of Economic Analysis* (1947) on developing a theory of *comparative dynamics* which would include comparative statics but cover "a much richer terrain, even the majestic problems of economic development." In comparative dynamics (or sensitivity analysis) the central notion is that we change a parameter and "we investigate the effect of this change on the whole motion or behavior over time of the economic process under consideration."[1] For aggregative models of dynamic optimization, Chakravarty's pioneering efforts led to several insightful qualitative results.[2] We should perhaps stress that such models have subsequently found wide applications at both micro and macro levels, even though the usefulness of models to describe national planning is questionable in the atmosphere of the 1990s. In any event, the attraction of a mathematical model is enhanced if it can yield significant qualitative predictions.

The last two decades have witnessed major developments in understanding the global behavior of nonlinear processes and the complexities that apparently "simple" processes can generate. Progress in mathematical analysis (as well as computational facilities) has, in turn, led to applications in dynamic economics. It is perhaps too early to judge whether the implications are positive or negative, but several leading scholars appear to welcome these developments. Richard Goodwin (1990) (one of the earliest explorers of nonlinear models in economics, which generate "cycles") has remarked that if one is looking for "a system capable of endogenous, irregular, wavelike growth," the "discovery and elaboration of chaotic attractors seemed to me to provide the kind of conceptualization that we economists need." It is by now clear that highly complex or chaotic behavior can be displayed by simple nonlinear models arising in a variety of contexts in dynamic economics. Such models throw light on the scope of comparative dynamics and the difficulties of making qualitative predictions (and numerical computations) of the trajectories of the process. It is now possible to classify alternatives that may emerge when a dynamic process does not converge to a steady state or a limit cycle.

This chapter is primarily expository. In sections 2 and 3 we collect some basic definitions and results from the theory of chaotic dynamics and bifurcations. In section 4 we indicate how these results can be applied to capital accumulation models. For other applications, the interested reader can turn to a number of surveys from different perspectives (see, for example, Collet and Eckmann, 1980b; Grandmont, 1985, 1986; Baumol and Benhabib, 1989; Day and Pianigiani, 1991; Saari, 1991). Section 5 concludes the chapter with a few informal speculative comments.

2 Chaotic dynamics

2.1 Definitions

Let X be a closed interval $[\alpha, \beta]$ of the real line (with $\alpha < \beta$) and let h be a map from X to X. We refer to X as the *state space*, and to h as the *law of motion* of the state variable $x \in X$. The pair (X, h) is called a *dynamical system*. Thus, if $x_t \in X$ is the state of the system in time period t (where $t = 0, 1, 2, \ldots$) then $x_{t+1} = h(x_t) \in X$ is the state of the system in time period $t + 1$.

We write $h^0(x) = x$ and, for any integer $k \geq 1$, $h^k(x) = h[h^{k-1}(x)]$. If $x \in X$, the sequence $\tau(x) \equiv [h^j(x)]_{j=0}^{\infty}$ is called the *trajectory* from (the initial condition) x. The *orbit* from x is the set $\gamma(x) \equiv \{y: y = h^j(x)$ for some $j \geq 0\}$. The asymptotic behavior of a trajectory from x is described by the *limit set*, which is defined as the set of all limit points of $\tau(x)$ and is denoted by $\omega(x)$.

A point $x \in X$ is a *fixed point* of h if $h(x) = x$. A point $x \in X$ is called *periodic* if there is $k \geq 1$ such that $h^k(x) = x$. The smallest such k is the *period* of x. (In particular, if $x \in X$ is a fixed point of h, it is a periodic point with period 1.) We denote the set of periodic points in X by $P(X)$. Its complement in X, the set of nonperiodic points in X, is denoted by $N(X)$.

Note that if $x \in X$ is a periodic point, then $\omega[h^j(x)] = \gamma(x)$ for every $j = 0, 1, \ldots$. A periodic point $\bar{x} \in X$ is *stable* if there is an open interval V (in X) containing $\bar{x}$ such that $\omega(x) = \gamma(\bar{x})$ for all $x \in V$. (In this case we also say that the periodic orbit $\gamma(\bar{x})$ is stable.) If h is continuously differentiable on X, and $\bar{x}$ is a periodic point of period k, then a sufficient condition for $\bar{x}$ to be stable is that $|Dh^k(\bar{x})| < 1$. If $|Dh^k(\bar{x})| > 1$, then $\bar{x}$ is not stable.

Let $h: X \to X$ be continuously differentiable. Then, for any $x \in X$, the *Lyapunov exponent* $\xi(x)$ is defined as

$$\xi(x) = \lim_{t \to \infty} \frac{1}{t} \ln|Dh^t(x)|$$

For sufficiently large t and small $\varepsilon > 0$, the Lyapunov exponent satisfies (approximately) the relation

$$\varepsilon \exp[t\xi(x)] \approx |h^t(x + \varepsilon) - h^t(x)|$$

The right-hand side indicates how far apart x and $x + \varepsilon$ are under t iterates of h. Thus, when $\xi(x) > 0$, initially nearby points are stretched (by the successive iterations of h) at a positive exponential rate.

Related to the above phenomenon is the following concept due to Guckenheimer (1979). The dynamical system (X, h) has *sensitive dependence on initial conditions* if there is a set $Y \subset X$ of positive Lebesgue measure and an $\varepsilon > 0$ such that, given any $x \in Y$ and any neighborhood U of x, there is $y \in U$ and $n \geqslant 0$ such that $|h^n(x) - h^n(y)| > \varepsilon$.

Let $\mathscr{S}$ be the Borel σ-field of X, and ν a probability measure on $\mathscr{S}$. Thus, $(X, \mathscr{S}, \nu)$ is a probability space. If h is $\mathscr{S}$-measurable, then ν is called *invariant* under h if $\nu(E) = \nu[h^{-1}(E)]$ for all E in $\mathscr{S}$; ν is called *ergodic* if "$E \in \mathscr{S}$ and $h^{-1}(E) = E$" implies $\nu(E) = 0$ or 1.

2.2 *Topological chaos*

A basic result characterizing the behavior of the dynamical system (X, h) has been given by Li and Yorke (1975), and may be stated as follows.

Theorem 1 (Li–Yorke)

Let α, β be in $\mathbb{R}$, with $\alpha < \beta$. Suppose that $X = [\alpha, \beta]$ and $h: X \to X$ is continuous. If there is $x^* \in X$ such that

$$h^3(x^*) \leqslant x^* < h(x^*) < h^2(x^*) \tag{L–Y}$$

then

(i) for every integer $k \geqslant 1$ there is a periodic point $x_k \in X$ with period k;

(ii) there is an uncountable set $W \subset N(X)$ satisfying the following conditions:

(a) if $x, y \in W$ with $x \neq y$, then

$$\overline{\lim_{k \to \infty}} \, |h^k(x) - h^k(y)| > 0$$

and

$$\underline{\lim_{k \to \infty}} \, |h^k(x) - h^k(y)| = 0$$

(b) if $x \in W$ and $y \in P(X)$ then

$$\overline{\lim_{k \to \infty}} \, |h^k(x) - h^k(y)| > 0$$

The dynamical system (X, h) is said to exhibit *topological chaos* if conditions (i) and (ii) of theorem 1 are satisfied. Thus, the Li–Yorke condition (L–Y) is a sufficient condition for topological chaos; its simplicity makes it easily verifiable. For example if $X = [0, 1]$, and $h(x) = 4x(1 - x)$ for $x \in X$, then it can be easily checked that (L–Y) is satisfied by the point $x^* = (\sqrt{2} - 1)/2\sqrt{2}$.

The Li–Yorke theorem leads naturally to two questions regarding the prediction of the long-run behavior of trajectories, one qualitative and the other quantitative. We elaborate below on each question in turn.

Qualitative prediction

Suppose we knew exactly the dynamical system (X, h) and wanted "qualitatively" to predict the asymptotic behavior of the trajectory starting from a given initial state, i.e. without actually computing the trajectory for very long time periods. Then it would certainly be useful to know whether the limit set of a "typical" trajectory was independent of the initial state. Further, if the limit set was indeed invariant for trajectories from almost all initial states, we would want to know the nature of this limit set: specifically, whether (for instance) it consisted of a finite number of states or whether it was a set of states with positive Lebesgue measure. These would clearly have quite different consequences for the scope and meaning of long-run prediction (in the deterministic sense). We note, however, that for all "practical" purposes, periodic orbits with very long periods may be indistinguishable from aperiodic orbits.

Quantitative prediction

The "quantitative" problem of prediction may be posed as follows. Suppose, again, that we knew the dynamical system (X, h) exactly and we were actually willing to compute the trajectories from given initial states (at least for long periods of time). What would be the long-run error in prediction if there was a "small" (observational) error in the specification of the initial state? If the initial state is in the set W of "chaotic" states, then the Li–Yorke theorem indicates that such errors can be significant, since a trajectory starting from an initial state in W stays bounded away from any trajectory from a different initial state infinitely often. Again, this prediction problem has to be taken seriously when the Lebesgue measure of W is positive, for then such prediction errors will actually be observed.

Providing precise answers to the above questions turns out to be fairly difficult, in general. For the purpose of this review, we shall survey some results which give at least partial answers for the specific family of dynamical systems where the law of motion belongs to the "quadratic family" which we introduce below.

2.3 The quadratic family

Let $X = [0, 1]$ and $I = [1, 4]$. The *quadratic family of maps* is then defined by

$$h(x, \mu) = \mu x(1 - x) \text{ for } (x, \mu) \in X \times I$$

We interpret x as the *variable* and μ as the *parameter* of the map h.

A few observations about the quadratic family are useful at this point. Note that, for each parameter specification $\mu \in I$, the state space is the same. Thus we can conveniently examine a family of dynamical systems $(X, h(., \mu))$ parametrized by μ.

For each $\mu \in I$, $h(x, \mu)$ has exactly one *critical point* (i.e. a point where $D_1 h(x, \mu) = 0$), and this critical point (equal to 0.5) is independent of the parameter μ.

The role of the parameter $\mu \in I$ will become clear as we proceed with the review. In the next two sections we shall consider particular members of the quadratic family to establish the *possibility* of asymptotically perodic or aperiodic behavior of trajectories. In subsequent sections, we shall be studying situations in which we are less interested in the nature of the limit set of trajectories at a specific value of μ and more in such limit sets for a range of values of μ, with the objective of assessing the *robustness* or asymptotic periodic or aperiodic behavior of trajectories.

2.4 Stable periodic orbits

Even though there may be an infinite number of periodic orbits for a given dynamical system (as in the Li–Yorke theorem), a striking result, due to Julia and Singer,[3] informs us that there can be *at most one* stable periodic orbit.

Theorem 2 (Julia–Singer)

Let $X = [0, 1]$, $I = [1, 4]$; given some $\mu \in I$, define $h(x) = \mu x(1 - x)$ for $x \in X$. Then there can be at most one stable periodic orbit. Furthermore, if there is a stable periodic orbit, then $\omega(0.5)$, the limit set of $x^* = 0.5$, must coincide with this orbit.

Suppose, now, that we have a stable periodic orbit. This means that the asymptotic behavior (limit sets) of trajectories from all initial states "near" this periodic orbit must coincide with the periodic orbit. But what about the asymptotic behavior of trajectories from other initial states? If one is interested in the behavior of a "typical" trajectory, a remarkable result, due to Misiurewicz (1983), settles this question. Let λ denote the Lebesgue measure on (the Borel σ-field of) $[0, 1]$.

Theorem 3 (Misiurewicz)

Let $X = [0, 1]$, $I = [1, 4]$; given some $\mu \in I$, define $h(x) = \mu x(1 - x)$ for $x \in X$. Suppose there is a stable periodic orbit. Then for λ-almost every $x \in [0, 1]$, $\omega(x)$ coincides with this orbit.

Combining the above two results, we have the following scenario. Suppose we do have a stable periodic orbit. Then there are no other stable periodic orbits. Furthermore, the (unique) stable periodic orbit "attracts" the trajectories from almost every initial state. Thus we can make the qualitative prediction that the asymptotic behavior of the "typical" trajectory will be just like the given stable periodic orbit.

Following Guckenheimer (1979, theorem 3.1) it can also be checked that, in this scenario, sensitive dependence on initial conditions is not possible and so the "quantitative prediction problem" discussed above does not occur.

Theorem 4 (Guckenheimer)

Let $X = [0,1]$, $I = [1,4]$; given some $\mu \in I$, define $h(x) = \mu x(1 - x)$ for $x \in X$. Suppose there is a stable periodic orbit. Then the dynamical system does not have sensitive dependence on initial conditions.

It is important to note that the above scenario (existence of a stable periodic orbit) is by no means inconsistent with condition (L–Y) of the Li–Yorke theorem (and hence with its implications). Let us elaborate on this point following Devaney (1989) and Day and Pianigiani (1991). Consider $\mu = 3.839$, and define $h(x) = \mu x(1 - x)$ for $x \in X$. Choosing $x^* = 0.1498$, it can be checked then that there is $0 < \varepsilon < 0.0001$ such that $h^3(x)$ maps the interval $U \equiv [x^* - \varepsilon, x^* + \varepsilon]$ into itself, and $|Dh^3(x)| < 1$ for all $x \in U$. Hence, there is $\hat{x} \in U$ such that $h^3(\hat{x}) = \hat{x}$, and $|Dh^3(\hat{x})| < 1$. Thus, $\hat{x}$ is a periodic point of period 3, and it can be checked (by choice of the range of ε) that $h^3(\hat{x}) = \hat{x} < h(\hat{x}) < h^2(\hat{x})$ so that condition (L–Y) of theorem 1 is satisfied. Also, $\hat{x}$ is a periodic point of period 3 which is *stable*, so that theorem 3 is also applicable. Then we may conclude that the set W of "chaotic" initial states in theorem 1 must be of Lebesgue measure zero. In other words, topological chaos exists but is *not* "observed" when $\mu = 3.839$.

2.5 Aperiodic behavior and ergodic chaos

Quite a different asymptotic behavior of a typical trajectory (from that discussed in the previous section) may be observed when there is no stable periodic orbit, a situation which occurs when there is "ergodic chaos."[4]

The dynamical system (X, h) exhibits *ergodic chaos* if there is an ergodic invariant measure v that is absolutely continuous with respect to the Lebesgue measure (i.e. if E is a set in the Borel σ-field of X, and $\lambda(E) = 0$, then $v(E) = 0$). In this case, v is called an *ergodic measure* of h.

If v is an ergodic measure of h, then the *ergodic theorem*[5] informs us that for every v-integrable function ϕ on X we have

$$\lim_{T \to \infty} \frac{1}{T} \sum_{k=1}^{T} \phi[h^k(x)] \to \int \phi \, dv$$

for v-almost every $x \in X$. Denoting the density of v by ρ, we then have for any v-measurable set A,

$$\lim_{T \to \infty} \frac{1}{T} (\text{cardinality}\{k < T: h^k(x) \in A\}) = \int \rho \, d\lambda$$

for v-almost every $x \in X$. That is, for any v-measurable set A, $v(A)$ measures the fraction of the time a trajectory from x spends in the set A, for almost every x in the support of the measure v.

Note that when a dynamical system (X, h) has a stable periodic orbit from $\bar{x}$ (with period k), as in section 2.4, then the fraction of the time a typical trajectory spends in a small open interval containing $h^j(\bar{x})$ ($j = 0, 1, ...$) is $1/k$. Thus, the density of the empirical distribution of $\{x, h(x), h^2(x), ..., h^T(x)\}$, as $T \to \infty$, will appear as "spikes" (more precisely, delta functions) at k distinct points of X, for almost every initial state $x \in X$. Contrast this with the situation in which (X, h) exhibits ergodic chaos with an ergodic measure v. Here, for v-almost every $x \in X$ (and hence on a set of $x \in X$ of positive Lebesgue measure), the trajectory from x will "fill up" the support of the measure v. Thus, ergodic chaos is sufficient to rule out the presence of a stable periodic orbit, which is the reason to focus on it in studying asymptotically *aperiodic* behavior.

There are several sufficient conditions for ensuring that a dynamical system exhibits ergodic chaos. The one which is most easily applicable to the quadratic family of maps is given in the following result, due to Misiurewicz (1981), where some iterate of the critical point is mapped to an "unstable" fixed point.

Theorem 5 (Misiurewicz)

Let $X = [0, 1]$, $J = [3, 4]$; given some $\mu \in J$, define $h(x) = \mu x(1 - x)$ for $x \in X$. Suppose that there is some $k \geqslant 2$ such that $y = h^k(0.5)$ satisfies $h(y) = y$ and $|Dh(y)| > 1$; then (X, h) exhibits ergodic chaos.

A well-known example of a dynamical system (X, h) exhibiting ergodic chaos is one where $X = [0,1]$ and $h(x) = 4x(1 - x)$ for all $x \in X$. (Here $h^2(0.5) = 0$, $h(0) = 0$, and $|Dh(0)| = 4 > 1$, and so theorem 5 is directly applicable.) For this example, the density ρ of the ergodic measure v has been calculated to be

$$\rho(x) = \frac{1}{\pi[x(1 - x)]^{1/2}} \qquad \text{for } 0 < x < 1$$

Thus, the support of v is X, and every point $y \in [0, 1]$ is a limit point of the trajectory from λ-almost every $x \in X$; i.e. for λ-almost every $x \in X$, $\omega(x) = [0, 1]$, so that the asymptotic behavior of a typical trajectory resembles the realization of a stochastic process, although the sequence of iterates $[h^j(x)]_{j=0}^{\infty}$ is determined by a purely deterministic system. "Qualitative prediction," in the deterministic sense, of the long-run behavior of trajectories is futile in this case.

The Lyapunov exponent of this dynamical system is in fact seen to be independent of $x \in X$ and is given by

$$\xi = \xi(x) = \ln 2 > 0 \qquad \text{for all } x \in X$$

Finally, sensitive dependence on initial conditions can be shown for this example on the set Y where Y is the set of points $x \in X$ such that every point $y \in X$ is a limit point of the trajectory from x. (From the above discussion, the Lebesgue measure of Y is 1.) This is done by demonstrating (following Guckenheimer, 1979, theorem 2.6) that the set of points which are mapped to the critical point 0.5 by some iterate of h is dense in $[0, 1]$ (i.e. the set $M = \cup_{k=0}^{\infty} (x \in X : h^k(x) = 0.5)$ is dense in X). Now, pick any $0 < \varepsilon < 1/2$. For $x \in Y$, 2ε is a limit point of the trajectory from x. Also, given any neighborhood U of x, there is some $y \in M \cap U$, since M is dense in X. But the trajectory from y gets eventually mapped to 0.5, and so to 1 and then 0, which is a fixed point. Hence, there is a k large enough for which $|h^k(x) - h^k(y)| > \varepsilon$. Thus, the dynamical system (X, h) exhibits sensitive dependence on initial conditions, so that the problem of "quantitative prediction" will also arise.

2.6 Robustness of ergodic chaos

In the last two sections, we have noted the nature of limit sets of typical trajectories for some specific members of the quadratic family of maps. We have demonstrated that, for some values of μ, there may be no practical problems of long-run prediction even when there is topological chaos. For other values of μ, leading to ergodic chaos, both qualitative and quantitative prediction problems can arise.

Let us now consider a situation in which we do not know the dynamical system (X, h) exactly. Specifically, the state space X and the set of parameters $J = [3, 4]$ are known, and the form (quadratic) of h is known, but the exact value of μ is not known. There then arises the question of the "relative frequency" of periodic and aperiodic asymptotic behavior of trajectories. Formally, let $\nabla = \{\mu \in J : [X, h(., \mu)]$ has a stable periodic orbit$\}$. We checked that $\mu = 3.893$ belongs to ∇, and the argument used there clearly shows that for an open interval, containing $\mu = 3.839$, there is a stable periodic orbit of period 3. In fact, the "window" of values of μ for which there exists a stable period-3 cycle can be calculated (see May, 1976) to be (3.8284, 3.8415). In particular, then, ∇ has positive Lebesgue measure.

Let $\Delta = \{\mu \in J : [X, h(., \mu)]$ exhibits ergodic chaos$\}$. Then a natural question to ask is whether the set Δ also has positive Lebesgue measure. For, if the set Δ is "negligible" (in the sense that it has Lebesgue measure zero) then one could argue that the problems of long-run prediction, noted in section 2.5, might not be observed in practice, and a typical dynamical system is "well-behaved" even though for some accidental cases the system might be chaotic.

The conjecture that the set Δ has positive Lebesgue measure, so that the quadratic family of maps displays "robust" ergodic chaos, was one of the outstanding mathematical problems in chaotic dynamics, until it was resolved by Jakobson (1981).[6]

Theorem 6 (Jakobson)

Let $X = [0, 1]$, $J = [3, 4]$, and $h(x, \mu) = \mu x(1 - x)$ for $(x, \mu) \in X \times J$. Then the set $\Delta = \{\mu \in J: [X, h(., \mu)]$ exhibits ergodic chaos$\}$ has positive Lebesgue measure.

As Jakobson remarks, the construction of the proof of his theorem also implies that there is a set $\Delta' \subset \Delta$, of positive Lebesgue measure, such that for all $\mu \in \Delta'$ the dynamical system $[X, h(., \mu)]$ exhibits sensitive dependence on initial conditions.[7] Thus, Jakobson's theorem and remark indicate that the qualitative and quantitative problems of long-run prediction occur for a nonnegligible set of parameter values; they cannot be dismissed as "accidental."[8]

In fact, more can be said. Consider the interval $J_\eta = [4 - \eta, 4]$ for $0 < \eta \leqslant 1$. Denote by λ_η the Lebesgue measure of the set of μ in J_η for which the dynamical system $[X, h(., \mu)]$ exhibits ergodic chaos. (Formally, $\lambda_\eta = \lambda(J_\eta \cap \Delta)$.) Then, given any $\varepsilon > 0$, there is $0 < \eta < 1$ such that

$$\lambda_\eta / \eta > 1 - \varepsilon$$

Thus, as η gets smaller (so that all parameter values in J_η are close to 4) *most* of the values of the parameter μ lead to ergodic chaos. Jakobson refers to this as follows: $\mu = 4$ is a "one-sided Lebesgue point" of Δ.

3 Bifurcation theory and sensitivity analysis

In this section we wish to review results which tell us how the typical asymptotic behavior of trajectories reacts to *perturbations* in the dynamical system. The motivation for studying this may be explained as follows. Suppose our dynamical system is a model of some real-world phenomenon. It is then plausible to consider the situation that the model captures the "real-world" dynamical system not exactly, but only approximately. We would then feel fairly confident in making predictions about the long-run behavior of actual trajectories based on those of our model, if the dynamical system was not very "sensitive" to perturbations. If it was very sensitive, then small errors in modeling could lead to large errors in prediction. Thus, the situation is similar to that explained in section 2.2, where we argued that sensitivity of prediction with respect to perturbation of the initial state needs to be explored carefully. Here, we are arguing for a study of the sensitivity of prediction to perturbation of the dynamical system itself.

This is a forbidding task, and rather than deal with it at the most general level we rephrase the sensitivity problem in more specific terms. Let us, for this purpose, take as given that the law of motion of the dynamical system we are dealing with is given by the quadratic family of maps introduced in section 2.3. The state space $X = [0, 1]$ and the parameter space $I = [1, 4]$ are known, as is the form (quadratic) of the law of motion $h(x, \mu)$. However, we allow for the fact that there might be a "specification error" with respect to the parameter μ. We would then like to see whether a small discrepancy in μ can lead to significantly different limit sets of the typical trajectory.

3.1 Period doubling route to chaos

Bifurcation theory applied to the quadratic family of maps gives us a fairly complete answer to the problem posed above. It can be summarized in the following result.[9]

Theorem 7

Let $X = [0, 1], I = [1, 4]$. Let $h(x, \mu) = \mu x(1 - x)$ for $(x, \mu) \in X \times I$. Then there is a sequence $(\mu_k)_{k=0}^{\infty}$ such that

(i) $\mu_0 = 1$, $\mu_k < \mu_{k+1}$ for $k = 0, 1, 2, 3, \ldots$;
(ii) $\mu_k \to \mu_\infty$ as $k \to \infty$, where $\mu_\infty \approx 3.569946$;
(iii) for $\mu \in (\mu_k, \mu_{k+1})$, there is a stable periodic point $x(\mu)$, with period 2^k, such that for almost every $x \in X$, $\omega(x) = \gamma[x(\mu)]$.

We see from the result that as the parameter changes, for instance, from $1 < \mu < \mu_1$ to $\mu_1 < \mu < \mu_2$, the asymptotic behavior of a typical trajectory changes from convergence to a stable fixed point of $h(x, \mu)$ to convergence to a stable periodic orbit with period 2. The dynamical system experiences a "bifurcation" (a distinct qualitative change in asymptotic behavior) as the parameter μ crosses the value μ_1. The same is true of other "bifurcation values" μ_k for $k > 1$. Notice that each successive bifurcation value gives rise to a stable periodic point of a period which is double that at the previous bifurcation value.

The first few values of μ_k are collected below.

$$\mu_1 = 3 \qquad \mu_5 = 3.568759$$
$$\mu_2 = 3.449499 \qquad \mu_6 = 3.569692$$
$$\mu_3 = 3.544090 \qquad \mu_7 = 3.569891$$
$$\mu_4 = 3.564407 \qquad \mu_8 = 3.569934$$

These values appear to converge to the limit μ_∞ in a geometric progression as

$$\mu_k \approx \mu_\infty - \frac{\theta}{\mathscr{F}^k} \qquad (5.1)$$

where $\theta = 2.63267$, $\mathscr{F} = 4.669202$. Feigenbaum (1978) noted that this pattern of period doubling is quite a universal phenomenon, and for a very large class of maps the constant $\mathscr{F}$ (the Feigenbaum constant) has the same value. For practical purposes, it provides the possibility of making a prediction of μ_∞ as soon as the first few period doubling values are known. For example, take $\mu_2 = 3.4495$ and $\mu_3 = 3.5541$ in our case. Then using (5.1) we have

$$\mu_\infty \approx \frac{\mathscr{F}\mu_3 - \mu_2}{\mathscr{F} - 1} = 3.5699$$

which is correct to four decimal places.

The period doubling scenario described above leads to the following observation regarding the sensitivity of limit sets of typical trajectories to "specification errors" of μ. Suppose that 0.005 is a plausible specification error of μ. Thus if the actual value of μ is, say, 3.562 one might actually be working with a specification of 3.567. Then, while the actual limit set of a typical trajectory will be a period-8 periodic orbit, the model will predict a period-16 periodic orbit.

More generally (and now relying on the fact that the "window" of parameter values (μ_k, μ_{k+1}), for which a periodic orbit of period 2^k is stable, shrinks to zero as k becomes large), given any specification error $\varepsilon > 0$, we can find an integer k^* such that $|\mu_{k+1} - \mu_k| < \varepsilon$ for all

$k \geq k^*$. Then if the actual value of μ is in (μ_{k^*}, μ_∞), a specification error of ε can lead to a prediction of the period of the stable periodic orbit which will be (at most) half or (at least) double the actual period.

3.2 Periodic versus aperiodic behavior

The sensitivity with respect to a change in the parameter μ is more striking in the "chaotic regime" $C = [\mu_\infty, 4]$ than in the regime $B = (1, \mu_\infty)$. What is possible in this regime is that the actual asymptotic behavior of trajectories is aperiodic, but because of a specification error of the parameter μ the model could predict that the limit set of the typical trajectory would coincide with a stable periodic orbit.

To illustrate this, suppose that 0.05 is a plausible specification error of μ. Assume that the actual value of the parameter μ^* (more precisely, the real positive solution to the equation $(\mu - 2)^2(\mu + 2) = 16$) is 3.6785735. Then, as Ruelle (1977) demonstrates, the *third* iterate of $h(., \mu^*)$ is mapped to the fixed point y of $h(., \mu^*)$ given by $y = 1 - (1/\mu^*)$. Further, $|D_1 h(y; \mu^*)| > 1$, so that by applying theorem 5 the dynamical system $[X, h(., \mu^*)]$ displays ergodic chaos. Because of a specification error, suppose the model uses a value of $\mu = 3.6285735$. This value of μ is actually in the "window" of a stable periodic point of period 6. Using theorem 3, from almost all initial states, the limit set of trajectories coincides with the orbit of the above periodic point. Thus, our prediction would be asymptotically periodic behavior from Lebesgue-almost all initial states, whereas from a set of initial states of positive Lebesgue measure the actual trajectories are aperiodic. This extreme sensitivity of limit sets to parameter changes can be confirmed by computer simulations of the densities of the invariant measures associated with the law of motion in each case (see, for example, Hoppensteadt and Hyman, 1977; Collet and Eckman, 1980b).

Is the sensitivity problem noted above a "rare phenomenon"? Certainly, if the set of μ in the parameter set $I = [1, 4]$, for which there is some stable periodic point, is dense in I, then given any $\varepsilon > 0$ the sensitivity problem will arise for all $\mu \in I$ for which there is ergodic chaos. By theorem 6, and the remarks following it, this set has positive Lebesgue measure, and so the sensitivity problem would be robust.

Although it has been conjectured that such a result ought to be true for the quadratic family and, indeed, for a larger class of unimodal maps (see, for example, Collet and Eckmann, 1980b; Misiurewicz, 1983), there is, unfortunately, no theorem that has been reported along this line. We note, however, that in the course of proving the result of Jakobson (1981) via a different route, Benedicks and Carleson (1985) demonstrate the following result. There is $\eta > 0$ small enough such that the set $V_\eta = \{\mu \in [4 - \eta, 4]:$ $[X, h(., \mu)]$ has a stable periodic point$\}$ is dense in the set $J_\eta = [4 - \eta, 4]$.

If we combine this result with our remarks following theorem 6 (Jakobson's result), we have the following scenario. There is $0 < \eta_0 < 1$ with η_0 small enough such that the set $J_{\eta_0} = [4 - \eta_0, 4]$ has both the following properties: (a) the set of $\mu \in J_{\eta_0}$, for which there is ergodic chaos, has positive Lebesgue measure; (b) the set of $\mu \in J_{\eta_0}$, for which there is a stable periodic orbit, is dense in J_{η_0}. Thus, on J_{η_0}, the "sensitivity problem" noted above is indeed robust. It is worth pointing out, though, that if the stable periodic orbits (for μ in J_{η_0}) have very long periods, then this sensitivity will not be observed in actual computations.

4 Capital accumulation models

That chaotic behavior can arise in a variety of contexts is well recognized. It is consistent with intertemporal equilibrium conditions (see Benhabib and Day, 1982) as well as intertemporal optimization with convex structures (see Boldrin and Montrucchio, 1986; Deneckere and Pelikan, 1986). The literature has examples of simple "disequilibrium" models like the classical *tâtonnement* even with just two goods (see Saari, 1985; Bala and Majumdar, 1990), as well as purely "descriptive" models of capital accumulation which exhibit chaos. We shall present only two illustrations and indicate how the mathematical results on robustness and bifurcation can be directly invoked.

4.1 *A descriptive growth model*

We shall follow the model of a "Ricardian system" discussed by Bhaduri and Harris (1987) (for other examples of descriptive accumulation models leading to chaotic dynamics, see Godwin, 1990).

Suppose that the total product of "corn" (Y) as a function of "labor" (N) is given by

$$Y_t = aN_t - bN_t^2/2$$

Hence, the average product of labor (AP_t) is given by

$$\mathrm{AP}_t = \frac{Y_t}{N_t} = a - \frac{bN_t}{2}$$

The "rent" R_t in period t emerges as

$$R_t = \left(\frac{Y_t}{N_t} - \frac{\mathrm{d}Y_t}{\mathrm{d}N_t}\right)N_t = \frac{bN_t^2}{2}$$

"Profit" P_t is the residual after payment of rent and replacement of the wage fund W_t advanced to employ labor. Thus,

$$P_t \equiv Y_t - R_t - W_t$$

Bhaduri and Harris focus on the dynamics of the wage fund as representing the process of accumulation. The size of the wage fund governs the amount of labor that can be employed on the land. At a given wage rate $w > 0$ we have

$$W_t = wN_t$$

Accumulation of the wage fund comes from the reinvestment of profits accruing to the capitalists. If there is no consumption out of profit income we have

$$W_{t+1} - W_t = P_t$$

This leads to

$$N_{t+1} - N_t = \frac{P_t}{w} = \frac{a}{w}N_t - \frac{b}{w}N_t^2 - N_t$$

or, upon simplification,

$$N_{t+1} = \frac{a}{w} N_t - \frac{b}{w} N_t^2$$

Since the positivity of the marginal product of labor requires $a > bN_t$, corresponding to all meaningful employment levels, Bhaduri and Harris define $n_t \equiv bN_t/a < 1$ and obtain

$$n_{t+1} = \frac{a}{w} n_t - \frac{a}{w} \frac{b^2 N_t^2}{a^2} = \frac{a}{w} n_t(1 - n_t)$$

Thus, the basic equation governing the dynamics of the Ricardian system is

$$n_{t+1} = \mu n_t(1 - n_t) \tag{5.2}$$

where $\mu = a/w$.

We are now in a position to use the results of sections 2 and 3 on the quadratic family to examine the "robustness" of ergodic chaos, and the scope of comparative dynamics in the Ricardian system. The detailed interpretation is left to the reader.

We now turn to the more difficult question of consistency of chaotic behavior when the accumulation rules are derived from a utility maximization exercise in a "convex environment." Here we follow Majumdar and Mitra (1922a, b) and sketch our main results.

4.2 Dynamic optimization with wealth effects

Our analysis deals with a discrete-time aggregative model of "discounted" dynamic optimization where the one-period return or "felicity" function depends on both consumption and capital stock. The need for studying such a model has been stressed in the theory of optimal growth and also in the economics of natural resources (see, for example, Koopmans, 1967; Kurz, 1968; Arrow and Kurz, 1970; Dasgupta, 1982). The "standard" aggregative model of capital accumulation in which felicity is derived solely from consumption is a special case of our framework. In this "standard" model, optimal programs exhibit *monotone* behavior over time; in fact, this feature continues to hold even when the technology exhibits increasing returns (see Majumdar and Mitra, 1982; Dechert and Nishimura, 1983; Mitra and Ray, 1984) and investment is irreversible (see Majumdar and Nermuth, 1982). Thus, it is often suggested that a one-sector optimal growth model can only display "simple dynamics." Our exploration indicates that even in the aggregative framework the presence of a "wealth" or "stock" effect opens up the possibilities of "complex dynamics."

Consider an economy E specified by a *gross output function* f: $\mathbb{R}_+$ $\to \mathbb{R}_+$, a *felicity (return) function* w: $\mathbb{R}_+^2 \to \mathbb{R}_+$ and a *discount factor* $\delta \in (0, 1)$. The following assumptions on f are used.

(F1) $f(0) = 0$; f is continuous on $\mathbb{R}_+$.
(F2) f is nondecreasing and concave on $\mathbb{R}_+$.
(F3) There is some $K > 0$ such that $f(x) > x$ when $0 < x < K$ and $f(x) < x$ when $x > K$.

To describe some of the remaining assumptions as well as our results, it is convenient to define a set $\Omega = \{(x, z) \in \mathbb{R}_+^2 : z \leq f(x)\}$. The following assumptions on w are used.

(W1) $w(x, c)$ is continuous on $\mathbb{R}_+^2$.
(W2) $w(x, c)$ is nondecreasing in x given c, and nondecreasing in c given x on $\mathbb{R}_+^2$. Furthermore, if $x > 0$, $w(x, c)$ is strictly increasing in c on Ω.
(W3) $w(x, c)$ is concave on $\mathbb{R}_+^2$. Furthermore, if $x > 0$, $w(x, c)$ is strictly concave in c on Ω.

A *program* from $x > 0$ is a sequence $(x_t)_0^\infty$ satisfying

$$x_0 = x, \quad 0 \leq x_{t+1} \leq f(x_t) \qquad \text{for } t \geq 0$$

The consumption sequence $(c_{t+1})_0^\infty$ is given by

$$c_{t+1} = f(x_t) - x_{t+1} \qquad \text{for } t \geq 0$$

It is easy to verify that for *every* program $(x_t)_0^\infty$ from $x \geq 0$ we have

$$(x_t, c_{t+1}) \leq K(x) \equiv \max(K, x) \qquad \text{for all } t \geq 0$$

In particular, if $x \in [0, K]$, then $x_t, c_{t+1} \leq K$ for all $t \geq 0$.

A program $(\hat{x}_t)_0^\infty$ from $x \geqslant 0$ is *optimal* if

$$\sum_{t=0}^\infty \delta^t w(\hat{x}_t, \hat{c}_{t+1}) \geqslant \sum_{t=0}^\infty \delta^t w(x_t, c_{t+1})$$

for every program $(x_t)_0^\infty$ from x.

Monotonicity: simple dynamics

It is often convenient to look at the ("reduced-form utility") function $u: \Omega \to \mathbb{R}$ defined by

$$U(x, z) \equiv w[x, f(x) - z] \tag{5.3}$$

A compactness argument can be used to show that given any $x \geqslant 0$ there is some optimal program $(\hat{x}_t)_{t=0}^\infty$ from x. Furthermore, the optimal program is unique. We can define a *value function* $V: \mathbb{R}_+ \to \mathbb{R}$ by

$$V(x) = \sum_{t=1}^\infty \delta^t w(\hat{x}_t, \hat{c}_{t+1}) \tag{5.4}$$

and the *optimal transition function*

$$h(x) = \hat{x}_1 \tag{5.5}$$

where $\{\hat{x}_t\}$ is the optimal program from $x \geqslant 0$. The properties of V and h are summarized in the following.

Theorem 8

(i) The value function V is the unique continuous real-valued function on $[0, K]$ satisfying the functional equation of dynamic programming

$$V(x) = \max_{(x,z)\in\Omega} [u(x, z) + \delta V(z)] \tag{5.6}$$

Further, V is concave and nondecreasing on $\mathbb{R}_+$.

(ii) The transition function h satisfies the following property: for each $x \in \mathbb{R}$, $h(x)$ is the unique solution to the constrained maximization problem

$$\text{maximize } u(x, z) + \delta V(z)$$
$$\text{subject to } (x, z) \in \Omega$$

Furthermore, h is continuous on $\mathbb{R}_+$.

The problem of identifying conditions under which the function h is monotone nondecreasing has been much discussed (see, for example, Benhabib and Nishimura, 1985; Amir et al., 1991). Instead of presenting the most general technical conditions (which involve the notion of "supermodular" functions studied by Topkis, 1968) we present a set of sufficient conditions in the "differentiable" case.[10]

Theorem 9

Suppose f is continuously differentiable on $\mathbb{R}_{++}$ and w is twice continuously differentiable on the interior of Ω (denoted by Ω°) and

$$-w_{22}(x, c) f'(x) \geq w_{12}(x, c) \qquad \text{for all } (x, c) \in \Omega^\circ \quad (5.7)$$

Then h is nondecreasing on $\mathbb{R}_+$.

Observe, finally, that if w depends *only* on c, $w_{12} = 0$, so that (5.7) is satisfied if $w_{22} < 0$. Hence, theorem 9 leads to the consumption turnpike theorem if we assume that $f'(x)$ increases to infinity as x tends to zero (since this assumption rules out the possibility that the optimal $(\hat{x}_t)_0^\infty$ from $x > 0$ converges to zero).

Complex dynamics
We consider a class of economies indexed by a parameter μ (where $\mu \in I = [1, 4]$). Each economy in this family has the same *gross output function* (satisfying (F1)–(F3)) and the same *discount factor* $\delta \in (0, 1)$. The economies in this family differ in the specification of their *felicity or one-period return functions*: $w: \mathbb{R}_+^2 \times A \to \mathbb{R}_+$ (w depending on the parameter μ). For a fixed $\mu \in [1, 4]$, the one-period return function $w(., ., \mu)$ can be shown to satisfy (W1)–(W3).

In specifying the class of economies in this particular way, we are following a direction of research that Chakravarty (1969, p. 248) considered particularly important. According to him, sensitivity analysis in intertemporal optimization models should "cover questions relating to changes in parametric representations of the utility or production relationships. *The former are especially important, since they refer to questions of valuation rather than fact*" (italics ours).

The numerical specifications are as follows:

$$f(x) = \begin{cases} (16/3)x - 8x^2 + (16/3)x^4 & \text{for } x \in [0, 0.5) \\ 1 & \text{for } x \geq 0.5 \end{cases}$$

$$\delta = 0.0025$$

The function w is specified in a more involved manner. To ease the writing, denote $L \equiv 98$, $a \equiv 425$, $X \equiv [0, 1]$; recall the family

$$h(x, \mu) = \mu x(1 - x) \qquad \text{for } x \in X, \mu \in I$$

and define $u: X^2 \times I \to \mathbb{R}$ by

$$u(x, z, \mu) \equiv ax - 0.5Lx^2 + zh(x, \mu) - 0.5z^2$$
$$- \delta\{az - 0.5Lz^2 + 0.5[h(z, \mu)]^2\}$$

Define $D \subset X^2$ by

$$D = \{(c, x): c \leq f(x)\}$$

and a function $w: D \times I \to \mathbb{R}_+$ by

$$w(c, x, \mu) = u[x, g(x) - c, \mu] \qquad \text{for } (c, x) \in D, \mu \in I$$

The definition of $w(., ., \mu)$ can be extended to the domain Ω as follows: for $(c, x) \in \Omega$ with $x > 1$ (so that $f(x) = 1$, $c \leq 1$) define

$$w(c, x, \mu) = w(c, 1, \mu)$$

Finally, define $w(., ., \mu)$ on $\mathbb{R}_+^2$ as follows: for $(c, x) \in \mathbb{R}_+^2$ with $c > f(x)$, let

$$w(c, x, \mu) = w[f(x), x, \mu]$$

It can be shown (see Majumdar and Mitra, 1992b) that the optimal transition function for this family is

$$h(x, \mu) = \mu x(1 - x) \qquad \text{for } x \in X, \mu \in I$$

The results of sections 2 and 3 can now be used to study the sensitive dependence of optimal programs on initial stocks, as well as the sensitivity of the asymptotic behavior of optimal programs to changes in the felicity parameter.

5 Concluding comments

In his *Capital and Investment Planning*, Chakravarty emphasized that model-building in the area of investment planning involved

> three sets of considerations. There is the *empirical* part, which refers to the collection and processing of data pertaining to the particular economy we are interested in. There is the *theoretical* part, which tells us what the appropriate design of a model is and the nature of the relevant economic consideration. And finally, there is the *computational* part of working out actual numerical solutions in the light of the first two considerations.

The book was concerned with the *theoretical* part of model-building work, which reflected the author's conviction that "the normative theory of capital, as well as the theory of multisectoral growth processes as developed in recent years, can provide some general insights into the question of planning investment decisions" of particular importance to developing economies.

Our very select review of some of the results from dynamical systems is intended to highlight problems of predicting the behavior of even highly aggregative economic models arising in capital theory. "Convexity" and "optimizing behavior" may not yield "meaningful theorems" in comparative dynamics. This difficulty suggests the need for looking at models with more structures in which the primitives are restricted to reflect a better appreciation of the relevant data. The unreasonably low values of the discount factor δ (very high rates of "impatience") that have typically been used to produce chaotic dynamics in optimizing models in economics is a case in point. Some recent work (see, for example, Sorger, 1992) seems to indicate that, at least for a class of dynamic optimization problems, for discount factors which are more "reasonable," some of the unimodal maps commonly used to display chaotic dynamics can be disqualified as optimal transition functions.

Notes

Research support from the National Science Foundation is gratefully acknowledged. We dedicate this paper to Sukhamoy Chakravarty who taught Mukul Majumdar at Presidency College and Tapan Mitra at Delhi School of Economics. We would like to thank Professors P. Holmes and J. Guckenheimer for helpful conversations.

1 See Samuelson (1947, chs X, XI and appendix B).
2 See Chakravarty (1962) for the basic results on the subject.
3 Julia proved the result for the quadratic family. Singer extended it to the broader class of unimodal maps having "negative Schwarzian derivative"; for details, see Singer (1978).
4 We caution the reader that "ergodic chaos" does not always occur when there is no stable periodic orbit. See, especially, Collet and Eckmann (1980b) and Guckenheimer (1987) for discussions of other possibilities.
5 See Lanford (1983) and Day and Shafer (1987) for discussions of the ergodic theorem.
6 Subsequently, alternatively approaches to the theorem of Jakobson can be found in the work of Benedicks and Carleson (1985), Rychlik (1988), and Johnson (1989).
7 This result has subsequently been proved, following a different approach, by Guckenheimer (1987). Also, Collet and Eckmann (1980a) have proved the result for a somewhat different family of functions. It is worth observing that sensitive dependence on initial conditions does not imply ergodic chaos: for an example, see Johnson (1987).
8 More recent work indicates that the set of parameter values for which the dynamical system exhibits positive Lyapunov exponent also has positive Lebesgue measure (for details, see especially Benedicks and Carleson, 1991; Ruelle, 1989).
9 The exposition of this section relies on Lauwerier (1986) and Devaney (1989).
10 See Ross (1983) for an exposition of the basic result of Topkis.

References

Amir, R., Mirman, L. J. and Perkins, W. R. 1991: One sector neo-classical optimal growth: optimality conditions and comparative dynamics. *International Economic Review*, 32, 625–44.

Arrow, K. J. and Kurz, M. 1970: *Public Investment, The Rate of Return and Optimal Fiscal Policy*. Baltimore, MD: Johns Hopkins University Press.

Bala, V. and Majumdar, M. 1990: Chaotic tâtonnement. *Economic Theory*, 2, 437–46.

Baumol, W. J. and Benhabib, J. 1989: Chaos: significance, mechanism and economic applications. *Journal of Economic Perspectives*, 3, 77–105.

Benedicks, M. and Carleson, L. 1985: On iterations of $1 - ax^2$ on $(-1, 1)$. *Annals of Mathematics*, 122, 1–25.

—— and —— 1991: The dynamics of the Henon map. *Annals of Mathematics*, 133, 73–169.

Benhabib, J. and Day, R. 1982: A characterization of erratic dynamics in the overlapping generations model. *Journal of Economic Dynamics and Control*, 4, 37–55.

—— and Nishimura, K. 1985: Competitive equilibrium cycles. *Journal of Economic Theory*, 35, 284–306.

Bhaduri, A. and Harris, D. J. 1987: The complex dynamics of the simple Ricardian system. *Quarterly Journal of Economics*, 102, 893–901.

Boldrin, M. and Montrucchio, L. 1986: On the indeterminacy of capital accumulation paths. *Journal of Economic Theory*, 40, 26–39.

Chakravarty, S. 1962: Optimal savings with a finite planning horizon. *International Economic Review*, 3, 338–55.

——1969: *Capital and Development Planning*. Cambridge, MA: MIT Press.

Collet, P. and Eckmann, J. P. 1980a: On the abundance of aperiodic behaviour for maps of the interval. *Communications in Mathematical Physics*, 73, 115–60.

—— and —— 1980b: *Iterated Maps on the Interval as Dynamical Systems*. Boston, MA: Birkhauser.

Dasgupta, P. S. 1982: *The Control of Resources*. Oxford: Blackwell.

Day, R. H. and Pianigiani, G. 1991: Statistical dynamics and economics. *Journal of Economic Behavior and Organization*, 16, 37–84.

—— and Shafer, W. 1987: Ergodic fluctuations in deterministic economic models. *Journal of Economic Behavior and Organization*, 8, 339–61.

Dechert, W. D. and Nishimura, K. 1983: A complete characterization of optimal growth path in an aggregated model with a non-concave production function. *Journal of Economic Theory*, 31, 332–54.

Deneckere, R. and Pelikan, S. 1986: Competitive chaos. *Journal of Economic Theory*, 40, 13–25.

Devaney, R. L. 1989: *An Introduction to Chaotic Dynamical Systems*. New York: Addison-Wesley.

Feigenbaum, M. 1978: Quantitative universality for a class of nonlinear transformations. *Journal of Statistical Physics*, 19, 25–52.

Goodwin, R. 1990: *Chaotic Economic Dynamics*. Oxford: Clarendon Press.

Grandmont, J. M. 1985: On endogenous competitive business cycles. *Econometrica*, 53, 995–1045.

—— 1986: Periodic and aperiodic behavior in discrete one dimensional dynamical systems. In W. Hildenbrand and A. MasColell (eds), *Contributions to Mathematical Economics in Honor of Gerard Debreu*, New York: North-Holland.

Guckenheimer, J. 1979: Sensitive dependence to initial conditions for one dimensional maps. *Communications in Mathematical Physics*, 70, 133–60.

—— 1987: Renormalization of one dimensional mappings and strange attractors, *Lefschetz Centennial Conference*, Part III, 1984, edited by V. Verjovsky. *Contemporary Mathematics*, 58, 143–60.

Hoppensteadt, F. C. and Hyman, J. M. 1977: Periodic solutions of a logistic difference equation. *SIAM Journal of Applied Mathematics*, 32, 73–81.

Jakobson, M. V. 1981: Absolutely continuous invariant measures for one-parameter families of one-dimensional maps. *Communications in Mathematical Physics*, 81, 39–88.

Johnson, S. 1987: Singular measures without restrictive intervals. *Communications in Mathematical Physics*, 110, 185–90.

—— 1989: Continuous measures in one dimension. *Communications in Mathematical Physics*, 122, 293–320.

Koopmans, T. C. 1967: Objectives, constraints and outcomes in optimal growth models. *Econometrica*, 35, 1–15.

Kurz, M. 1968: Optimal economic growth and wealth effect. *International Economic Review*, 9, 348–57.

Lanford, O. E. 1983: Introduction to the mathematical theory of dynamical systems. In G. Iooss, R. H. G. Hellerman, and R. Stora (eds) *Chaotic Behavior of Deterministic Systems*, Amsterdam: North-Holland.

Lauwerier, H. A. 1986: One dimensional iterative maps. In A. V. Holden (ed.), *Chaos*, Princeton, NJ: Princeton University Press, 39–57.

Li, T. and Yorke, J. A. 1975: Period three implies chaos. *American Mathematical Monthly*, 82, 985–92.

Majumdar, M. and Mitra, T. 1982: Intertemporal allocation with a non-convex technology: the aggregative framework. *Journal of Economic Theory*, 27, 101–36.

—— and —— 1992a: Periodic and chaotic programs of optimal intertemporal allocation in an aggregative model with wealth effect. *Economic Theory*, forthcoming.

—— and —— 1992b: Robust ergodic chaos in discounted dynamic optimization models. *Economic Theory*, forthcoming.

—— and Nermuth, M. 1982: Dynamic optimizations in non-convex models with irreversible investments: monotonicity and turnpike results. *Zeitschrift für Nationalökonomie*, 42, 339–62.

May, R. M. 1976: Simple mathematical models with very complicated dynamics. *Nature*, 261, 459–67.

Misiurewicz, M. 1981: Absolutely continuous measures for certain maps of an interval. *Publications Mathematiques*, 53, 17–51.

—— 1983: Maps of an interval. In G. Iooss, R. H. G. Hellerman, and R. Stora (eds), *Chaotic Behavior of Deterministic Systems*, Amsterdam: North-Holland.

Mitra, T. and Ray, D. 1984: Dynamic optimization on a non-convex feasible set: some general results for non-smooth technologies. *Zeitschrift für Nationalökonomie*, 44, 151–75.

Ross, S. M. 1983: *Introduction to Stochastic Dynamic Programming*. New York: Academic Press.

Ruelle, D. 1977: Applications conservant une mesure absolument continue par rapport à dx sur [0, 1]. *Comunications in Mathematical Physics*, 55, 47–52.

—— 1989: *Chaotic Evolution and Strange Attractors*. Cambridge: Cambridge University Press.

Rychlik, M. 1988: Another proof of Jakobson's theorem and related results. *Ergodic Theory and Dynamical Systems*, 8, 93–110.

Saari, D. G. 1985: Iterative price mechanisms. *Econometrica*, 53, 1117–31.

—— 1991: Erratic behavior in economic models. *Journal of Economic Behavior and Organization*, 16, 3–36.

Samuelson, P. A. 1947: *Foundations of Economic Analysis*. Cambridge, MA: Harvard University Press.

Singer, D. 1978: Stable orbits and bifurcations of maps of the interval. *SIAM Journal on Applied Mathematics*, 35, 260.

Sorger, G. 1992: On the minimum rate of impatience for complicated optimal growth paths. *Journal of Economic Theory*, 56, 160–79.

Topkis, D. 1968: Minimizing a submodular function on a lattice. *Operations Research*, 26, 305–21.

PART II

Development and Welfare

6

A note on the theory of
cost–benefit analysis in the small

Roy Radner

1 Introduction and summary

Cost–benefit analysis is a familiar technique for determining whether a proposed project is economically desirable. In this chapter I shall provide a theoretical justification of this technique in the case in which the project is "small" in a precise sense that will be defined below and certain "regularity" conditions are satisfied. Roughly speaking, the latter conditions will require that market equilibria vary "smoothly" with the data of the problem.

For the purposes of this chapter, a *project* determines a change in the total supply of goods and services – commodities – available for consumption, currently and/or in the future. A project is a *potential Pareto improvement* if the new supply can be allocated among the consumers in such a way as to make everyone better off – or at least someone better off and no one worse off.

Let z^h denote the change in the supply of commodity h that is determined by the project, and let $z = (z^h)$ be the vector with coordinates z^h. Positive coordinates correspond to net outputs, and negative ones to net inputs. The vector z is sometimes called the "net-output vector" for the project, and for our purposes we may identify z with the project.

A common test to determine whether a project z is a potential improvement involves the following steps.

1 Determine a "correct" set of prices p^h for those commodities for which the corresponding coordinates of z are not zero, i.e. for those commodities that actually appear as inputs and/or outputs of the project. For those inputs or outputs that occur in the future, the corresponding prices are to be interpreted as *discounted* prices, with the discounting done according to some "correct" rates of interest.

2 Calculate the total "net benefit," $p \cdot z = \Sigma_h p^h z^h$, for the project z. Accept the project if the total net benefit is positive. If the project involves future inputs and/or outputs, then the total net benefit is also called the *present value*. The positive terms $p^h z^h$ are the (discounted) *benefits* of the project, and the negative terms are the (discounted) *costs*. (In the formula for total net benefit, the prices and quantities of *all* the commodities appear, but for those commodities that do not appear as inputs or outputs in the project, i.e. those commodities h for which z^h is zero, it clearly does not matter how the prices are determined.)

In this chapter I shall consider the situation in which the initial supply of commodities has been allocated according to a market equilibrium that is competitive on the consumers' side, and where (p^h) are the equilibrium prices. (In other words, the initial supply is given by some mechanism, the consumers are price-takers, and the prices are market clearing.) I shall also assume that the consumers have "textbook preferences" (this will be made precise in subsequent sections).

It is well known that, even in this situation, a project that passes the net-benefit test need not be a potential Pareto improvement.[1] This problem is illustrated in figure 6.1. There are two commodities, corresponding to the two axes in the figure. The point x represents the initial total supply. The curve C represents the *community indifference curve*,[2] namely, the set of total supplies that can be efficiently allocated in such a way as to make every consumer exactly as well off as in the initial equilibrium allocation. The relative prices corresponding to the initial equilibrium are determined by the slope of the straight line L that is tangent to C at the point x. Points that are above and to the right of C represent total supplies that are potentially Pareto superior to x. On the other hand, points that are above and to the right of L have a higher value than x does at the initial equilibrium prices (p^h). In the northwest quadrant of the

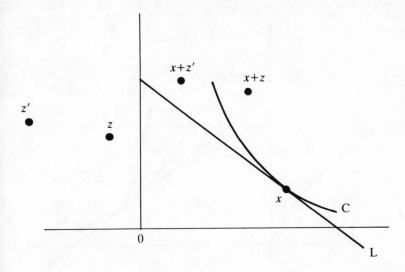

Figure 6.1 The net-benefit test in the large does not always work.

figure, the points z and z' represent two different projects, both of which use commodity 1 as a net input and produce commodity 2 as a net output. Corresponding to z, we have the new total supply $x + z$ in the northeast quadrant, and corresponding to z' is the new total supply $x + z'$. We see that both z and z' have a positive net benefit, whereas only $x + z$ is potentially Pareto superior to x.

To deal with this problem, let us expand the concept of a project. A "project" usually can be built at different scales. Let $\zeta(s)$ denote the corresponding net-output vector if the "project" is built at scale s, where $0 \leq s \leq S$; of course, $\zeta(0) = 0$. In figure 6.2, the broken curve in the northwest quadrant is traced out by $\zeta(s)$ as s varies from 0 to S, whereas the broken curve in the northeast quadrant is traced out by $x + \zeta(s)$. Suppose that the coordinates of $\zeta(s)$ vary "smoothly" with s, and let $\zeta'(0)$ denote the vector of derivatives of the coordinates of $\zeta(s)$ with respect to s, evaluated at $s = 0$. In figure 6.2, $\zeta'(0)$ is represented by the arrow emanating from the point x and tangent to the curve $x + \zeta(s)$ at x. Since $\zeta'(0)$ points upward and to the right of the line L, we see that $p\zeta'(0) > 0$. Furthermore, we see that for some *entire interval of positive scale values s, the new supply $x + \zeta(s)$ is potentially superior to the initial supply x.*

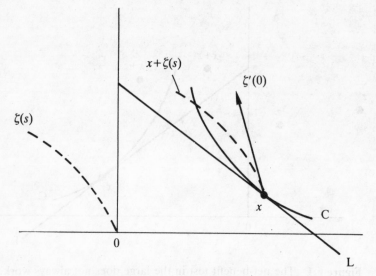

Figure 6.2 The net-benefit test in the small.

Figure 6.2 suggests the following reformulation of the net-benefit test. A *project* is a function ζ from an interval $[0, S]$ to the commodity space; $\zeta(s)$ represents the net-output vector of the project if it is adopted at scale s. We shall say that the project passes the net-benefit test if $p\zeta'(0) > 0$. The main result of this chapter is that, under certain regularity conditions that will be described below, if a project passes the net-benefit test, then at some positive scale s^* the net-output vector $\zeta(s)$ is a potential Pareto improvement for all s such that $0 < s \leqslant s^*$. The actual argument will be analytical, rather than geometrical as above. This will enable me to elucidate conditions under which an allocation of the new supply is an actual – not just potential – improvement, and also to make precise the related idea of "consumer surplus in the small."

Sections 2 and 3 set out the model and show how to calculate the changes in consumers' welfares that result from a new allocation. Section 4 states and proves the main result. Section 5 shows how changes in wealth (income) can be used to realize a potentially superior improvement, and elucidates the concept of "consumer surplus in the small."

The main result makes use of quite strong "smoothness" assumptions. No attempt has been made here to justify these assumptions in terms of more primitive assumptions about the consumers' preferences and consumption sets. The tools for such a justification would be found in the book by Mas-Colell (1985). Nor have I attempted to relate this chapter to the (now vast) literature on cost–benefit analysis, beyond providing a few citations in the notes.

In fact, the immediate origins of this chapter were lecture notes for a course in microeconomic theory that I gave at the University of California, Berkeley, during the 1960s and 1970s. They were part of my attempts to illustrate how the abstract (and, to the students, often boring) constructs of utility and demand theory might be applied to practical problems, a goal which seems particularly appropriate to pursue in a volume dedicated to the memory of Sukhamoy Chakravarty.

2 Allocations and projects

Consider an economy with I consumers, and a vector x of quantities of H commodities allocated among the m consumers. Call x the *total supply*. An *allocation* of x is an I-tuple (x_i) such that $\Sigma_i x_i = x$. Given an allocation (x_i) of x, suppose that it is proposed to replace x by x', another vector of total supplies. We are interested in determining whether or not the proposed total supply x' represents an "improvement." The difference $z \equiv x' - x$ may be interpreted as a *project*; typically, some of the coordinates of z will be positive and some will be negative.[3]

The proposed total supply x' will be called *potentially superior* to the allocation (x_i) if there is an allocation of x' that is Pareto superior to the allocation (x_i); equivalently, in this case we shall call the project z a *potential improvement* with respect to the allocation (x_i). (Recall that an allocation (x_i') is Pareto superior to an allocation (x_i) if, for every i, x_i' is at least as good as x^i for consumer i and, for at least one i, consumer i strictly prefers x_i' to x_i.)

As noted in section 1, instead of a single project we shall consider a one-parameter family of vectors $\zeta(s)$, where s is interpreted as the "scale" of the project and $x' = x + \zeta(s)$ is the new total supply if the project is adopted at scale s. Here s is a nonnegative real number; I shall assume that $\zeta(s)$ is defined for s in some interval $[0, S]$, that the coordinates ζ^h of ζ are continuously differentiable functions on that interval, and that $\zeta(0) = 0$. Let $\zeta'(s)$ denote the vector of derivatives of the coordinates of ζ with respect to s; then $\zeta'(0)$ will be called the *direction of change of the total supply* at $s = 0$.

In order to formulate the net-benefit test precisely, I introduce the concept of a valuation equilibrium. An allocation is a valuation equilibrium with respect to a price vector p if, for each consumer i, any consumption vector that i strictly prefers to his own allocation would cost more at the given prices. Suppose now that the initial allocation (x_i) of the initial supply x is a valuation equilibrium with respect to p. For any two vectors $y = (y^h)$ and $z = (z^h)$ let $y \cdot z$ denote, as usual, the inner product

$$\sum_h y^h z^h$$

I shall say that the project $\zeta(.)$ passes the net benefit test if

$$p \cdot \zeta'(0) > 0 \tag{6.1}$$

In what follows I shall show that, under certain "regularity" conditions, *if ζ passes the net-benefit test, then there is some positive scale s^* such that $\zeta(s)$ is a potential Pareto improvement for all s such that $0 < s < s^*$.*

3 Changes in consumer utility

Let us represent the preferences of consumer i by a numerical utility function, say u_i. It is to be understood that all consumption vectors are nonnegative. I shall assume that each consumer's utility function is concave and continuously differentiable. (Further regularity assumptions will be made as appropriate.) I shall also make the assumption of nonsatiation for each consumer i, i.e. for each consumer i and each consumption vector x_i, there is another consumption vector that consumer i strictly prefers to x_i.

Using the notation that has just been introduced, an allocation (x_i^*) is a valuation equilibrium with respect to a price vector p if, for every consumer i and every nonnegative consumption vector x_i, $p \cdot x_i \leq p \cdot x_i^*$ implies $u_i(x_i) \leq u_i(x_i^*)$.

Suppose that (x_i) is an allocation of the initial supply x and is a valuation equilibrium with respect to the price vector p. For each i, let $W_i = p \cdot x_i$ denote the *wealth* of consumer i. The consumption x_i can be characterized as maximizing consumer i's utility subject to the "budget constraint" that the cost of consumption not exceed his wealth. I shall assume that the valuation equilibrium satisfies, for each i, the familiar first order ("marginal") conditions for such a constrained maximum: there is a number m_i such that[4]

$$D_h u_i(x_i) = m_i p^h \qquad h = 1, ..., H \qquad (6.2)$$

$$\sum_h p^h x_i^h = W_i \qquad (6.3)$$

The assumption of nonsatiation implies that, for each i, $m_i > 0$.

As a consequence of the prevailing economic and social policy, if the project were adopted at scale s, then the new supply $x + \zeta(s)$ would be allocated in some way which we may write (without loss of generality) in the form $[x_i + \zeta_i(s)]$, where

$$\sum_i \zeta_i(s) = \zeta(s) \qquad (6.4)$$

Consumer i's utility at this new allocation would then be

$$V_i(s) \equiv u_i[x_i + \zeta_i(s)] \qquad (6.5)$$

Assume now that, for each i, ζ_i is continuously differentiable, and that $\zeta_i(0) = 0$. Then the derivative of consumer i's utility with respect to the scale of the project is, from (6.5),

$$V_i'(s) = \sum_h D_h u_i[x_i + \zeta_i(s)]D\zeta_i^h(s) \qquad (6.6)$$

Setting $s = 0$ in (6.6), and using (6.2), we get

$$V_i'(0) = \sum_h D_h u_i(x_i)D\zeta_i^h(0)$$

$$= m_i \sum_h p^h D\zeta_i^h(0)$$

$$= m_i p \cdot \zeta_i'(0). \qquad (6.7)$$

If we use the suggestive notation

$$\mathrm{d}u_i \equiv V_i'(0) \qquad \mathrm{d}x_i \equiv \zeta_i'(0) \qquad (6.8)$$

then (6.7) can be rewritten as

$$\mathrm{d}u_i = m_i p \cdot \mathrm{d}x_i \qquad (6.9)$$

4 The net-benefit test

I shall now prove the main result concerning the validity of the net-benefit test. Recall the definition of a *competitive equilibrium* in the case of pure exchange. For each i, let ε_i be i's *endowment vector* (in $\mathbb{R}^H$), and let $\varepsilon \equiv \Sigma_i \varepsilon_i$. A competitive equilibrium (CE) relative to (ε_i) is an $(I + 1)$-tuple $[(\alpha_i), \varphi]$ such that

1 (α_i) is an allocation of ε;
2 (α_i) is a valuation equilibrium with respect to φ;
3 for each i, $\varphi \cdot \alpha_i \leq \varphi \cdot \varepsilon_i$.

Let (k_i) be H strictly positive numbers summing to 1, and for each scale s define (with a slight abuse of the previous notation)

$$\varepsilon_i(s) = x_i + k_i \zeta(s) \qquad (6.10)$$

where – as in sections 2 and 3 – (x_i) is the initial allocation and $\zeta(s)$ is the project at scale s. For each s let $[\alpha_i(s), \varphi(s)]$ be a CE relative to $[\varepsilon_i(s)]$. Assume that φ and (α_i) are continuously differentiable, with $\varphi(0) = p$ and $\alpha_i(0) = x_i$ for all i. I shall show that, *if $p \cdot \zeta'(0) > 0$, then there is an $s^* > 0$ such that the allocation $[\alpha_i(s)]$ is strictly Pareto superior to (x_i) for all s such that $0 < s < s^*$*.

Define $\zeta_i(s) \equiv \alpha_i(s) - x_i$. By (6.7) it is sufficient to show that, for each i, $p \cdot \zeta_i'(0) > 0$. By the assumption of nonsatiation, for each i and s,

$$\varphi(s) \cdot \alpha_i(s) = \varphi(s) \cdot \varepsilon_i(s)$$

$$\varphi(s)[x_i + \zeta_i(s)] = \varphi(s) \cdot [x_i + k_i \zeta(s)]$$

$$\varphi(s) \cdot \zeta_i(s) = k_i \varphi(s) \cdot \zeta(s)$$

Differentiating both sides of this last equation with respect to s and setting $s = 0$ we get

$$\varphi'(0) \cdot \zeta_i(0) + \varphi(0) \cdot \zeta_i'(0) = k_i[\varphi'(0)\zeta(0) + \varphi(0)\zeta'(0)]$$

But $\zeta_i(0) = \zeta(0) = 0$ and $\varphi(0) = p$, so that

$$p \cdot \zeta_i'(0) = k_i p \cdot \zeta'(0) > 0$$

5 Wealth, prices, and consumer surplus in the small

In section 4, the achievement of a Pareto-superior allocation was accomplished by giving each consumer his initial allocation plus a share of the *physical* net output of the project, and then letting the consumers trade in a corresponding competitive pure exchange equilibrium. In many (if not most) applications, it will be more natural to suppose that the net benefits of the project are distributed in the form of *monetary wealth*, followed by a corresponding change in equilibrium prices and consumptions (allocations). In this section, using standard demand theory, I shall characterize the directions of change in the wealth distribution that are consistent with both a Pareto improvement and an equilibrium of supply and demand.[5]

As in section 2, we start with an allocation (x_i) of an initial supply x that is a valuation equilibrium with respect to a price vector p. Consumer i's initial "monetary wealth" is $W_i \equiv p \cdot x_i$. We suppose further that if the project is adopted at scale s, then consumer i would dispose of a monetary wealth $\omega_i(s)$, where $\omega_i(0) = W_i$. Let ξ_i denote consumer i's demand function, i.e. if his wealth were $\bar{W}_i$ and prices were $\bar{p} = (\bar{p}^h)$, then his demand (vector) would be $\xi_i(\bar{W}_i, \bar{p})$. Accordingly, if the project were adopted at scale s, the equilibrium price vector $\varphi(s)$ would be determined by the equation

$$\sum_i \xi_i[\omega_i(s), \varphi(s)] = x + \zeta(s) \tag{6.11}$$

This actually represents H equations in the H unknowns $\varphi^h(s)$.

If the individual demand functions are sufficiently "well-behaved," then we can change the wealth functions $\omega_i(.)$ arbitrarily – at least in some neighborhood of the original functions – and still get solutions to (6.11), thus obtaining a variety of different allocations of the net output of the project.

Returning to the case in which the wealth functions are fixed, at scale s consumer i will receive, in equilibrium, the allocation

$$\alpha_i(s) \equiv \xi_i[\omega_i(s), \varphi(s)] \qquad (6.12)$$

and his resulting utility will be

$$V_i(s) \equiv u_i[\alpha_i(s)] \qquad (6.13)$$

We wish to study the first derivatives of the functions V_i in the neighborhood of $s = 0$. To this end, we write down the first-order conditions that determine the demand functions at each scale s, corresponding to (6.2): for each i there is a positive number $\mu_i[\omega_i(s), \varphi(s)]$ such that

$$D_h u_i[\alpha_i(s)] = \mu_i[\omega_i(s), \varphi(s)]\varphi^h(s) \qquad h = 1, \ldots, H \quad (6.14)$$

Also, corresponding to the budget constraint (6.3) we have

$$\varphi(s) \cdot \alpha_i(s) = \omega_i(s) \qquad (6.15)$$

Assume that the functions ζ_i and μ_i are continuously differentiable, as well as the functions ζ, ω_i, and φ (and hence α_i); in particular,

$$\zeta(0) = 0 \qquad \omega_i(0) = W_i$$
$$\alpha_i(0) = x_i \qquad \varphi(0) = p \qquad (6.16)$$
$$\mu_i(W_i, p) = m_i$$

Differentiating (6.13) with respect to s:

$$V_i'(s) = \sum_h D_h u_i[\alpha_i(s)] D\alpha_i^h(s)$$

By (6.14),

$$V_i'(s) = \mu_i[\omega_i(s), \varphi(s)] \sum_h \varphi^h(s) D\alpha_i^h(s)$$

$$= \mu_i[\omega_i(s), \varphi(s)]\varphi(s) \cdot \alpha_i'(s) \qquad (6.17)$$

By (6.15),

$$\omega_i'(s) = \frac{d}{ds}[\varphi(s)\cdot\alpha_i(s)]$$
$$= \varphi'(s)\cdot\alpha_i(s) + \varphi(s)\cdot\alpha_i'(s)$$

$$\varphi(s)\cdot\alpha_i'(s) = \omega_i'(s) - \varphi'(s)\cdot\alpha_i(s) \tag{6.18}$$

Hence, from (6.17),

$$V_i'(s) = \mu_i[\omega_i(s), \varphi(s)][\omega_i'(s) - \varphi'(s)\cdot\alpha_i(s)] \tag{6.19}$$

Setting $s = 0$ and recalling (6.16) we have

$$V_i'(0) = m_i[\omega_i'(0) - \phi'(0)\cdot x_i] \tag{6.20}$$

If we use the suggestive notation

$$du_i \equiv V_i'(0) \qquad dW_i \equiv \omega_i'(0) \qquad dp \equiv \varphi'(0) \tag{6.21}$$

then (6.20) can be rewritten as

$$du_i = m_i(dW_i - x_i\cdot dp) \tag{6.22}$$

Recall the standard result of demand theory that m_i is the "marginal utility of wealth" for consumer i at his original allocation. That is, define

$$U_i(W_i, p) = u_i[\xi_i(W_i, p)]$$

to be the maximum utility in the optimization problem corresponding to (6.2)–(6.3); then

$$m_i = \frac{\partial}{\partial W_i}U_i(W_i, p) \tag{6.23}$$

(The function U_i is the consumer's *indirect utility function*.) It follows from (6.22) that, for small s, consumer i's change in utility will be approximately $sm_i\, d\bar{W}_i$, where

$$d\bar{W}_i \equiv dW_i - x_i\cdot dp \tag{6.24}$$

Thus $sd\bar{W}_i$ is the change in the amount of i's wealth that would lead approximately to a change sdu_i in utility, provided there were no concomitant change in prices. We are therefore justified in calling $d\bar{W}_i$ consumer i's consumer surplus in the small corresponding to the project ζ.

Let $dx_i \equiv \alpha_i'(0)$; from (6.22) we see that

$$\frac{du_i}{m_i} = d\bar{W}_i \equiv dW_i - x_i dp \qquad (6.25)$$
$$= p \cdot dx_i$$

Hence

$$\sum_i \bar{W}_i = \sum_i \frac{du_i}{m_i} = p \cdot dx \qquad dx \equiv \zeta'(0) \qquad (6.26)$$

We see from (6.26) that, if we can achieve a Pareto improvement at small scale s with some new wealth distribution (and the corresponding equilibrium allocation), then the total net benefit $p \cdot dx$, which is the same as the total surplus, must be strictly positive. Conversely, if the total net benefit is strictly positive, then as was shown indirectly in section 4 there is some distribution of wealth that makes every consumer's surplus $d\bar{W}_i$ positive, i.e. results in a Pareto improvement. There will, in general, be many such wealth distributions.

Equation (6.24) tells us what information will enable us to estimate a given consumer's surplus generated by a small project: his preproject consumption, and the changes in his wealth and in prices induced by the adoption of the project. The changes in prices can possibly be estimated from knowledge of aggregate demand functions, but the other data are about individual consumers. One typically tries to overcome this last problem by dividing the consumers into a small number of groups (e.g. by wealth, location, etc.), in the hope that wealth changes and demands will be approximately constant within the groups.

Notes

I am grateful for comments by M. K. Majumdar and A. Mas-Colell on an earlier draft. The views expressed here are those of the author, and not necessarily those of AT&T Bell Laboratories.

1 See Chipman and Moore (1973). Material on cost–benefit analysis can be found in Little and Mirrlees (1969) and in Drèze and Stern (1987).
2 See Debreu (1959, p. 97, note 1). This concept of the community indifference curve is apparently due to Scitovsky (1942).
3 The present paper deals only with projects whose inputs and outputs are consumer goods and services (including labor). Many projects (such as an irrigation system or a steel mill) produce only outputs that are inputs into further production. The present analysis can be extended to such situations but considerable additional care is needed to ensure that the prices used reflect the actual rates of transformation in production.
4 I shall use the following notation for partial derivatives. If f is a function of H variables, say $z_1, \ldots, z_H$, then $D_h f(z)$ will denote the partial derivative of f with respect to the hth variable, evaluated at the particular point $z = (z_h)$. If f is a function of one variable, then the derivative will be denoted by Df or f'.
5 For a related discussion, see Milleron (1970).

References

Chipman, John S. and Moore, James C. 1973: Aggregate demand, real national income, and the compensation principle. *International Economic Review*, 14, 153–81.
Debreu, Gerard 1959: *Theory of Value*. New York: Wiley.
Drèze, Jean and Stern, Nicholas 1987: The theory of cost–benefit analysis. In A. J. Auerbach and M. Feldstein (eds), *Handbook of Public Economics*, vol. II, New York: Elsevier, ch. 14, 909–89.
Little, I. M. D. and Mirrlees, James A. 1969: *Manual of Industrial Project Analysis in Developing Countries*. Paris: OECD.
Milleron, Jean-Claude 1970: Distribution of income, social welfare functions, and the criterion of consumer surplus. *European Economic Review*, 2, 45–77.
Scitovsky, Tibor 1942: A reconsideration of the theory of tariffs. *Review of Economic Studies*, 9, 89–110.

7

Trade and development in the presence of an informal sector: a four-factor model

M. Ali Khan

1 Introduction

In a 1951 essay on Tolstoy, Isaiah Berlin distinguished between two types of thinkers: those "who relate everything to a single central vision – a universal, organizing principle – in terms of which they understand, think and feel [and] in terms of which alone all that they are and say has significance"; as opposed to those "who pursue many ends, often unrelated and even contradictory, connected, if at all, only in some *de facto* way [and whose] thought is scattered or diffused [and moves] on many levels."[1]

At first pass, it is easy to place Sukhamoy Chakravarty within this classification. He was nothing if not a development planner, and the development and planning theme dominates his entire *oeuvre*. It was development planning that took him to Ramsey, von Neumann and Mahalanobis, and through them to Mill and Marshall on the one hand, and to Marx and Schumpeter on the other.[2] It was again development planning and problems concerning intertemporal allocation of resources that took him to Tinbergen,[3] and to Samuelson,[4] his two great mentors. In his 1973 essay in honor of Tinbergen, he appraised development planning, and in his last published article, in 1991, he reappraised development planning. There is a chapter on the von Neumann model in his first book, and an interpretation of this model in his last one. His entries in *The New Palgrave* were on Mahalanobis and Tinbergen, development planners *par exellence*, and on cost–benefit analysis and optimal savings. He himself was very clear about his genealogy.

> It is worth emphasizing that the capital theoretic schema underlying the Mahalanobis Model is descended from Marx and includes the much more elaborate models associated with the names of Leontief, von Neumann, Morishima and many others. The only alternative to this schema is the neo-Austrian theory of Hicks whose operational significance . . . is too early to judge.[5]

A deeper examination, however, reveals the superficiality of such a unitary conception of Chakravarty's work. Chakravarty was interested in development planning because he was interested in development economics, and development economics is a subject that is all-embracing, too multi-faceted and too nuanced for a serious student to be wedded to one single-minded vision. He was forced to formulate questions such as:

> What is the character of East Asian economies? Does it provide the way out of endemic poverty for other countries in Asia such as India and China? Does it deliver a final blow to the conceptual presuppositions of Marxist economic theory? Does it rehabilitate neoclassical theory as a theory of economic development?

These questions led him to formulate others:

> Should LDCs maintain an outward-looking orientation throughout their rapid growth phase? Should they maintain a very hospitable climate for foreign investment? Should they "keep prices right" which is to say that they keep a relatively low real price of labor, a relatively high interest rate and "realistic" exchange rates?[6]

It is these questions that led the master of the subject to become a puzzler,[7] and revealed the hedgehog to be, in part, a fox. They led him to the study of the English "enclosure movement" and to explore the idea of agricultural involution,[8] to relationships between agrarian power structures and productivity;[9] to catastrophe theory and the idea of morphogenesis;[10] to Veblen and the evolutionary point of view;[11] to Morishima's emphasis on the role of Confucian ethics as a contrast to Weber's emphasis on the Protestant ethic;[12] to biology and to Goldschmidt's successful monster;[13] to a Hegelian evolutionary approach and to the Bukharin–Preobrazhensky debate;[14] to the difference in the order that emerges in a "crystal" as opposed to a living system,[15] and, more generally, to classical mechanics and to disequilibrium thermodynamics.[16] They forced him to evaluate the entire planning experience of independent India,[17] and to appreciate the importance of time[18] and irreversibility – he quotes with approval Lukacs' prescription to view present as history.[19]

In short, Chakravarty was both a hedgehog and a fox; he juggled many balls but also gave a superb display of virtuosity with one little ball;[20] he was an insider as well as an outsider; his interests were both pure and applied; his research was both internally and externally propelled;[22] he questioned the canon as he extended it; he was as much at home in the intricacies of mathematical economics[23] as in the difficult judgment calls required for policy prescriptions; his career spanned both academia[24] and ministries of planning.[25] In the words of Paul Samuelson,

> Here is a case of water rising above its own source: Interested in the dualisms of Tolstoy as in those of linear programming, Dr Chakravarty is that rare specimen of an almost empty set – namely, the logical intersection of C. P. Snow's two cultures.[26]

In this tribute to the memory of Sukhamoy Chakravarty, nothing if not a great South Asian economist, I present, with some diffidence, a multisectoral model and use it, first, to shed light on the intellectual context in which he worked and the thinkers he admired, and second, to begin an investigation of two questions which dominated his thinking towards the end of his life. I refer, of course, to the "agriculture first" strategy and to the question of the optimal degree of "openness" for an economy.[27] I end the chapter with three concluding remarks.

2 The model

I work with a model of an economy with four factors of production. Three of these – land, labor, and capital – are primary factors, whereas the remaining one, henceforth to be referred to as an informal input, is a produced means of production. The economy is segmented into a rural and an urban region and the latter is further subdivided into a formal and an informal sector. The relevant variables of the rural region are subscripted by r but those of the urban region carry the subscript u or i depending on whether they pertain to the formal or the informal sector.

Since the informal input is produced within the economy, it is also an output. In addition to it, there are three other outputs. One of these is produced in the rural region and can be usefully thought of as a composite agricultural commodity, while the other two are produced in the formal sector of the urban region and constitute the manufacturing sector of the economy.

The technologies for all of this are summarized by

$$X_r = F_r(L_r, T)$$

$$X_{uj} = F_{uj}(L_{uj}, X_{ij}, K_{uj}) \qquad j = 1,2 \qquad (7.1)$$

$$aX_i = L_i \qquad a > 0$$

where T represents land, L and K, suitably subscripted, represent the amount of labor and capital input, while X, again suitably subscripted, represents both outputs and inputs, reflecting the fact that the output of the informal sector is also used as an intermediate input in the formal sector. The material balance condition $X_{i1} + X_{i2} = X_i$ eliminates any ambiguity on this score.

The aggregate resources of the economy are summarized by exogenously given and homogeneous amounts of land $\mathscr{T}$, labor $\mathscr{L}$, and capital $\mathscr{K}$. The demand for land T is equated to its supply $\mathscr{T}$, and the remaining material balance equations are given by

$$K_{u1} + K_{u2} = \mathscr{K} \qquad L_{u1} + L_{u2} + L_r + L_i = \mathscr{L} \qquad (7.2)$$

I shall assume that F_{uj} and F_r are continuously differentiable and exhibit constant returns to scale and diminishing marginal productivity to each factor. There is a single technique in the informal sector and $1/a$ represents both the average and the marginal productivity of informal labor.

I shall assume that the rural and urban formal output is internationally traded at prices which cannot be influenced by the production decisions made in the economy – this is the traditional small-country assumption. I shall use p, again suitably subscripted, to denote the relevant international price. I shall not assume that the informal output is internationally traded – its price p_i is determined in equilibrium.

I shall not go into the details of the definition, characteristics, magnitude, and importance of the informal sector,[28] and shall justify its formalization as a nontraded intermediate input.[29] I have in mind particularly the case prevalent in many less developed countries in which certain labor-intensive stages of production are subcontracted from the formal to the informal sector.

> By [an] informal sector, I [simply] mean the set of economic activities often, but not exclusively, carried out in small firms or by the self employed, which elude government requirements such as registration, tax and social security obligations, and health and safety rules. Informal activities are often illegal, but not necessary clandestine since lack of coordination between state agencies, lax enforcement and other types of official connivance can permit informally run enterprises to flourish openly.[30]

It is worth noting, however, that a relatively large share of the informal input compared with the share of formal labor thus allows for the possibility of some degree of direct substitution between the informal input and formal labor and indirect substitution between informal and formal labor.[31]

I shall assume that wages in the urban formal sector are exogenously given by $\bar{w}_u$. This is a standard assumption and it takes special force in my context since it is used as one of the defining characteristics of the informal sector.[32]

> Classical economists could be content with a subsistence wage theory, writing at a time when labour was abundant. The Western economies have outlived this state; the minimum subsistence theory of wages is surely outmoded there. Yet there is a large part of the world where even today distress selling of labour is a common feature. In India, for example, even in the so-called formal sector where there are trade unions to bargain in the labour market, one is not sure if the prevailing wage rate is at all above what, by any reasonable standard, one could recognize as minimum subsistence. Outside the formal sector conditions are much worse.[33]

I now turn to the equilibrating condition in the labor market. Analytically, what makes my informal sector worthy of its name is that wages are the lowest in this sector and that employment is automatic for all who do not obtain a job in the highest wage formal sector. Since urban labor has two options for employment, the Harris–Todaro hypothesis can be reformulated so that the guaranteed rural wage is equated to a weighted sum of the two urban wages, the weights λ and $1 - \lambda$ being the employment rates in the two sectors and representing proxies for the probability of finding employment in the two sectors. More formally, the equilibrium condition in the labor market is given by

$$w_r = \frac{L_{u1} + L_{u2}}{L_{u1} + L_{u2} + L_i} \bar{w}_u + \frac{L_i}{L_{u1} + L_{u2} + L_i} w_i \equiv \lambda \bar{w}_u + (1 - \lambda) w_i$$

(7.3)

where w, suitably subscripted, represents wage rates and λ the proportion of informal employment to the urban labor force.

I shall assume universal marginal productivity pricing. Given the constant returns to scale assumption, this allows me to represent the "price equals unit cost" condition as

$$p_r = C_r(w_r, \tau) \qquad p_{uj} = C_{uj}(\bar{w}_u, p_i, R) \qquad j = 1, 2 \qquad p_i = aw_i$$

(7.4)

where τ and R denote the rentals to land and capital. The properties of the unit-cost functions are by now well understood.[34]

The specification of my model is now complete. I have to determine the allocation of capital, K_{u1} and K_{u2}, and informal input, X_{i1} and X_{i2}, among the two formal sectors in the urban region; the allocation of labor, L_{u1}, L_{u2}, L_r, and L_i among all the four sectors in the economy; the probability λ of urban formal employment; the returns to land, capital, and rural and informal labor, τ, R, w_r, and w_i; the price p_i of informal output; and, finally, the four outputs X_{u1}, X_{u2}, X_r, and X_i. I also have to guarantee that the demand for land T equals its supply $\mathscr{T}$. My parameters are the factor endowments $\mathscr{T}$, $\mathscr{K}$, and $\mathscr{L}$; the international prices p_r, p_{u1}, and p_{u2}; the technologies a, $F_r(.,.)$, $F_{u1}(.,.,.)$, and $F_{u2}(.,.,.)$, and the formal sector wage $\bar{w}_u$. I have to determine nineteen unknowns in terms of the fourteen equations explicitly stated above, and five equations which are implicit in the unit-cost functions.[35]

3 Other settings

I now view my model from the vantage point of other models in the trade and development literature. I do this to get insight into the strengths and weaknesses of the setting in which I work, as well as into the settings in which Chakravarty worked. This can lead to the formulation of other questions and is instructive in other regards as well. If my model contains as a special case other canonical models whose structure is well analyzed and well understood, I can rely on this for pointers on how to analyze the 19 × 19 matrix that I confront in the comparative statics analysis to follow.

I begin with the Heckscher–Ohlin–Samuelson (HOS) model[36] of trade theory, and with the simple observation that this 2 × 2 setting is embedded in my model. If there is no rural sector, if the formal wage is flexible rather than a parameter, and if the formal sector does not require informal output as an input in production and there is a consequent lack of urban informal production, I obtain the HOS model. More specifically, my equations reduce to those of the HOS model if

$$a = 1 \qquad F_r(.,.) = 0 \qquad \bar{w}_u = w_1$$

$$F_{uj}(L_{uj}, X_{ij}, K_{uj}) = F_j(X_{ij}, K_j) \qquad j = 1, 2$$

and everything else is kept unchanged. However, what needs to be emphasized is that the decomposition property[37] of the HOS model does not fully hold in my setting, subsystem (7.4) notwithstanding.

One does not have to look far for the reason for the absence of this decomposition – it lies in the inclusion of land as a factor of production in agriculture. It is this that allows me to move away from the universal assumption of constant returns to scale technologies and introduce a neoclassical element into my formulation. The point is that the 2 × 3 Ricardo–Viner (RV) model, another canonical setting of trade theory,[38] is also embedded in my model. If the formal wage is equated to the rural wage, and if the formal sector in the urban region is not disaggregated and does not require informal output as an input in production, I obtain the RV model. More specifically, my equations reduce to those of the RV model if

$$a = 0 \qquad F_{u1}(.,.,.) = 0 \qquad \bar{w}_u = w_r$$

$$F_{u2}(L_{u2}, X_{2j}, K_{u2}) = F_2(L_2, K_2)$$

Indeed, I can push the analogy with the neoclassical non-HOS setting a little further and consider the disaggregated version of the RV model considered by Gruen and Corden (GC). If there is no production of informal output and no use of it as an input into the formal manufacturing sector, and if the formal wage is identical to the rural wage, an unknown to be determined rather than a parameter, I obtain the GC model.[39] More specifically, my equations reduce to those of the GC model if

$$a = 0 \qquad \bar{w}_u = w_r \qquad F_{uj}(L_{uj}, X_{uj}, K_{uj}) = F_j(L_j, K_j) \qquad j = 1, 2$$

In all of the above three special cases of my model, wages are identical between the two sectors and fully flexible. I now turn to a specialization which is distinguished by a sector-specific exogenously given rigid wage. In such a case, if there is an absence of an intermediate goods informal sector in the urban region, I obtain a disaggregated version of the Harris–Todaro model. This reduces to the conventional two-sector version if the formal urban sector is aggregated, as when

$$a = 0 \qquad F_{u1}(L_{u1}, X_{i1}, K_{u1}) = F_1(L_1, K_1) \qquad F_{u2}(L_{u2}, X_{i2}, K_{u2}) = 0$$

However, note that this Harris–Todaro setting is one without intersectoral capital mobility, i.e. the neoclassical RV incarnation rather than the HOS one.[40] It is of some interest that the HOS version of the Harris–Todaro model – one in which capital is mobile between the rural and urban regions – is not covered by the model that I study in this chapter.

So, far, in each of the cases that I have considered, the presence of the informal sector is ignored. This is also generally true of the theoretical literature[41] in this area, and I shall mention two recent attempts to remedy this deficiency. Chandra's model[42] is identical to the one presented here except for the fact that capital is mobile among the urban and rural regions. As such, her model is relevant for a land-surplus rather than a land-scarce economy.[43] However, given the degree of aggregation in these models, I am more comfortable with the shiftable/nonshiftable distinction than one formulated in terms of the surplus or scarcity of land, and Chandra's model can be viewed as the shiftable capital HOS cousin of the nonshiftable RV version presented here. Grinols' model, on the other hand, does allow for the nonshiftability of capital but between the formal and informal sectors rather than between the urban and rural regions,[44] and his setting can be usefully seen as the GC rendering of the issues modeled here.[45]

I would now like to focus on this reinterpretation of land $\mathcal{T}$ as another kind of capital, and on the consequent emphasis on the shiftable/nonshiftable dichotomy that the competing HOS and RV versions highlight. This is particularly warranted in a chapter honoring Chakravarty, a recognized authority on a model whose distinguishing characteristic lies precisely in its emphasis on the sectoral nonshiftability of capital – I refer, of course, to the Fel'dman–Mahalanobis model. Chakravarty was very clear as to its importance.

> The Indian planners at the time of formulating the Second Five Year Plan had to find practical answers to the questions of how much to invest, where to invest and in what forms to invest.[46] Despite the fact that the Mahalanobis model is a severely rigid construct, it has one important virtue. This lies in its recognition of the fact that capital equipment once installed in any specific producing sector of the economy may not be shiftable.[47] While such non-shiftability is an important factor in any economy, its degree of importance is clearly much greater for an underdeveloped economy with a relatively inadequate capital base. For some small-sized underdeveloped countries with specially favourable foreign trade situations, non-shiftability is again a feature of relative unimportance. However, for a very large number of underdeveloped countries, foreign trade positions seem to be difficult enough to make "non-shiftability" a matter of relative concern from the planning point of view.[48]

It was precisely the idea of *irreversibility* that Chakravarty chided Marshall for neglecting[49] and one that he singled out in his tribute to Suzy Paine's work on migration and foreign investment.[50] However, in his later writing he began to take a broader and more pervasive view.

> Dynamic systems with evolutionary elements are characterized by problems of persistence of memory and several other forms of irreversibility.[51] Societies grow in historical time characterized by irreversibilities.[52]

What is somewhat of a puzzle in this context is that Chakravarty did not emphasize, not even take note of, the reorientation of the pure theory of international trade that was currently under way at the hands of Jones and Samuelson.[53] Such a reorientation hinged precisely on the consequences of nonshiftability for the HOS setting.

Chakravarty used HOS as an adjective synonymous with "neoclassical" and did not take account, to my knowledge, of the differences in
the implications arising out of the RV and GC models from their
HOS counterparts.

> Maintenance of an outward-looking framework of economic policy
> has indeed been an important feature of the growth process [of
> Korea], but it is not at all clear that industrial development has
> conformed particularly closely to the Heckscher–Ohlin–Samuelson
> model of international trade, especially during the last ten years or so.
> In that respect, it is possible that Taiwan's policy has been closer to
> the dictates of the neoclassical theory of comparative advantage.[54]

> The relative difference in factor intensities between the consumer
> goods and capital goods industries which alone would otherwise
> justify two-sector exercises does not seem to be empirically very
> important.[55] We should possibly reorient the study of international
> economics from its preoccupation with problems of comparative
> advantage based on internationally-immobile primary factors, to-
> wards a study of processes based on internationalization of capital,
> changes in income distribution and the resulting variations in sectoral
> productivity levels. Such a reorganization . . . will have possibly
> greater explanatory power than conventional trade theory structured
> as a general equilibrium system on Heckscher–Ohlin–Samuelson
> lines.[56]

What adds to the puzzle is that in his 1987 review[57] of *optimal
savings*, he chose to ignore all of the Massachusetts Institute of
Technology and Yale work[58] on optimal savings under nonshiftability of capital, a literature inspired by his 1967 paper and particularly
enriched by the contributions of the succeeding generation of Indian
economic theorists.

My discussion of nonshiftability and irreversibility has carried me
into dynamics and growth theory, and thereby somewhat away from
the principal concerns of my model. These fall squarely within the
Marshallian tradition of partial equilibrium analysis.[59] However, it is
fair to say that this aspect of Marshall's work did not particularly
appeal to Chakravarty – even when working in the mainstream
theoretical tradition, his focus was primarily on "issues connected
with 'viability or reproducibility' of economic configurations rather
than with issues connected with the misallocation of resources in the
narrower sense of the term."[60] For him, Marshall loomed larger as a
precursor of Solow.[61] It is not clear to me to what extent he

considered static efficiency to be prior to and a prerequisite for dynamic efficiency,[62] and whether one ought to be involved, at least at first pass, with models such as the one I have presented here.[63]

There is no such tension in his writing on the utility and importance of simple constructs. Commenting on the first Mahalanobis model, he wrote

> To my mind, . . . the very simplicity of the model constitutes its great merit, not merely because it is easy to understand a simple model but also because simple models are often much more robust than the complicated constructs which are overlaid with a whole host of highly tenuous assumptions.[64]

There is another way in which my model is not at total variance with the thrust of Chakravarty's work – this consists in my neglect of demand and in my exclusive emphasis on production structures.

> The major difference between the classical and the neoclassical streams of theorizing lies in ignoring the treatment of consumer choice as subject to *useful* economic theorizing. Marx in particular was fully willing to admit the assumption of "optimizing" choices on the part of capitalist producers. Von Neumann's model rests on the assumption of optimizing choices on the part of producers in a *dynamic* context, but not on the part of consumers. . . . Both are rooted in the production process, although realized through a system of generalized exchange.[65]

So far, I have totally ignored inter-industry flows as well as the recursive nature of the production process. It is in the production of informal output by labor and the production of manufacturing output by the combination of labor, informal output, and capital that introduces inter-industry flows in my setting. The input–output table underlying my model and presented as table 7.1 is instructive in this regard. If I ignore the diagonal entries in the upper block of this table, I obtain a standard input–output matrix of the Leontief variety. The diagonal entries emphasize the lack of joint production, and the lower block brings out the dependence on non-produced means of production. In both these respects, my model differs from that of von Neumann.[66]

In terms of Sraffa's work, table 7.1 reveals a production structure somewhat intermediate between the S1 and S2 versions identified by Peter Newman.[67] If the outputs X_{u1}, X_{u2}, and X_r are ploughed back into the system to produce X_i, the zero entries in the X_i column are

Table 7.1 The input–output table

	X_{u1}	X_{u2}	X_r	X_i
X_{u1}	1	0	0	0
X_{u2}	0	1	0	0
X_r	0	0	1	0
X_i	$-C_{u1}^2(\bar{w}_u, p_i, R)$	$-C_{u2}^2(\bar{w}_u, p_i, R)$	0	1
$\mathscr{L}$	$-C_{u1}^1(\bar{w}_u, p_i, R)$	$-C_{u2}^1(\bar{w}_u, p_i, R)$	$-C_r^1(w_r, \tau)$	$-a$
$\mathscr{K}$	$-C_{u1}^3(\bar{w}_u, p_i, R)$	$-C_{u2}^3(\bar{w}_u, p_i, R)$	0	0
$\mathscr{T}$	0	0	$-C_r^2(w_r, \tau)$	0

replaced by the input amounts, the entries $-C_{uj}^2(\bar{w}_u, p_i, R)$ are replaced by $-C_{uj}^2(\bar{w}_u, p_i, R)X_{uj}$, and the lower block is ignored, I obtain the S1 version. On the other hand, if there is only one non-produced means of production, say labor, rather than three as in my model, I obtain the S2 version. A much more direct relationship is obtained by considering Samuelson's embedding of Sraffa's inequalities in a generalized von Neumann model.[68]

What is missing in my version, as well as in Newman's S1 version of Sraffa, is any conception of time-phasing. Intermediate goods are instantly produced and in time to be used as production of formal output. If I allow a one-period lag in production and constrain the production of formal urban output by the amount of informal intermediate input produced last year, I am in a drastically simplified version of Malinvaud's 1953 world. This version represents the Solow–Wicksell world[69] in which labor produces machines and then is combined with machines to produce output. However, I now enter a Scandinavian–Austrian domain into which Chakravarty did not venture.[70]

Finally, I would like to mention the disaggregated versions of the Fel'dman–Mahalanobis model that were presented by Mahalanobis, Raj-Sen, Weitzman, and Chakravarty and Lefeber.[71] The last was an 11×11, five-year, dynamic input–output model and it is of interest for my context that it was criticized by Srinivasan precisely for its neglect of labor as a constraining non-produced means of production as well as for its assumption of a constant and uniform lag structure.[72] In any case, in all of this work, my assumption of the exogeneity of $\mathscr{T}$, $\mathscr{L}$, and $\mathscr{K}$ renders the analysis to follow the first stage of optimizing exercise whereby the Hamiltonian is defined in terms of given values of the state variables and maximized with respect to the controls. To put the matter in another less technical way, the allocation of the various inputs is optimally determined by taking the prices and stocks of the various kinds of capital as given.[73] I have, of course, built into such an exercise a variety of institutional distortions – these attenuate the Komiya critique of the Fel'dman–Mahalanobis model, something to which the Bhagwati–Chakravarty survey gave prominent attention.[74]

4 The basic analysis

I now turn to the equilibrium of my model and in particular to the nineteen equations which characterize it and which constitute my section 2. The primary and basic observation is that this equation system can be sliced so as to enable me to work with rural wages and the employment rate in the formal sector as the relevant variables. Accordingly, I shall decompose the model into two subsections, the first consisting of the labor market equilibrium condition (7.3) and the second consisting of the remaining equations. This leads me to work in the λ–w_r plane. Observe that (7.3) furnishes a linear relationship that can be represented as LL in figures 7.1 and 7.2, LL being a mnemonic device for equilibrium in the labor market. The slope of the LL curve is easily seen to be

$$\left. \frac{d\lambda}{dw_r} \right|_{LL} = \frac{1}{\bar{w}_u - w_i} \tag{7.5}$$

The LL curve is independent of p_r and changes with changes in the international prices p_{u1} and p_{u2} as a consequence of (7.4); its graph lies in the range of λ between zero and unity.

Next, I turn to the other relationship between λ and w_r. Pick a particular value of w_r. This fixes the value of L_r from the marginal productivity condition[75] $p_r F_r^L(L_r, \mathcal{T}) = w_r$ and determines the supply of labor that is available for the production of urban output, both formal and informal. Since the choice of technique in the urban region has already been determined by the international prices,[76] this supply, along with that of capital, determines both the

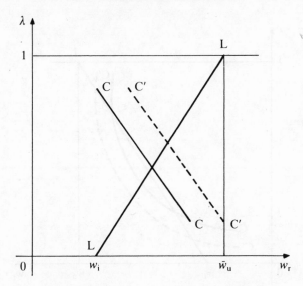

Figure 7.1 Intensity rankings conflict.

outputs and the factor inputs.[77] Since the probability of formal employment depends on L_{u1}, L_{u2} and L_r, I obtain my second relationship between λ and w_r and my second graph in the λ–w_r plane. Represent this graph by CC as in figures 7.1 and 7.2.

The interesting question, of course, concerns the slope of this curve. What I would like to emphasize is that, once w_r is given, I am in a position to exploit all the insights of the Heckscher–Ohlin–Samuelson model. Just as in the proof of Rybczynski's theorem, once the "price equals unit cost" conditions (7.4) fix the input–output coefficients, total differentiation of the material balance equations yields

$$
\begin{bmatrix} K_{u1}/L_{u1} & K_{u2}/L_{u2} \\ 1 + a(X_{i1}/L_{u1}) & 1 + a(X_{i2}/L_{u2}) \end{bmatrix} \begin{bmatrix} dL_{u1} \\ dL_{u2} \end{bmatrix} = \begin{bmatrix} d\mathscr{K} \\ d(\mathscr{L} - L_r) \end{bmatrix}
\tag{7.6}
$$

Let x_j represent the proportion of the intermediate informal input utilized in the production of the jth formal output, $j = 1, 2$, and let the determinant of the matrix be given by D. I can now present my first foothold.

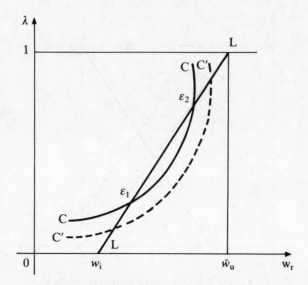

Figure 7.2   Intensity rankings coincide.

Definition 1

The first urban commodity is said to be capital intensive with respect to the second iff

$$\text{sign}(D) \iff \text{sign}\left(\frac{K_{u1}}{L_{u1} + x_1 L_i} - \frac{K_{u2}}{L_{u2} + x_2 L_i}\right)$$

Otherwise, the second urban commodity is said to be capital intensive with respect to the first.[78]

Note that in this definition, I measure the capital–labor ratio with respect to both the direct and indirect labor requirements of a particular commodity. Furthermore, as illustrated in figure 7.3, the first urban commodity can be capital intensive with respect to the second and yet $K_{u1}/L_{u1} < K_{u2}/L_{u2}$, though figure 7.4 brings out the fact that this need not necessarily be so. Even though I shall not have occasion to use these conventional but, in terms of my context, restricted factor intensities until section 8, I record the following definition.

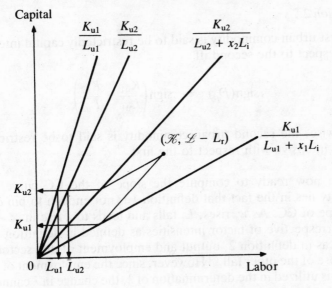

Figure 7.3 Intensities and restricted intensities conflict.

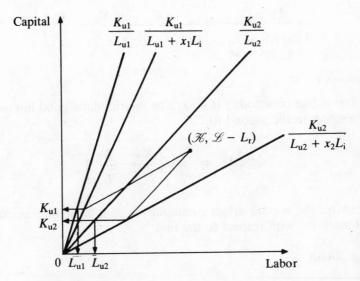

Figure 7.4 Intensities and restricted intensities coincide.

Definition 2

The first urban commodity is said to be restrictedly capital intensive with respect to the second iff

$$\text{sign}(D_\rho) \quad \Leftrightarrow \quad \text{sign}\left(\frac{K_{u1}}{L_{u1}} - \frac{K_{u2}}{L_{u2}}\right)$$

Otherwise, the second urban commodity is said to be restrictedly capital intensive with respect to the first.[79]

I am now ready to compute the slope of the CC curve. The difficulty lies in the fact that definition 1 is not enough to pin down the slope of CC. As w_r rises, L_r falls and leads to a rise in $\mathscr{L} - L_r$. Now, irrespective of factor intensities as defined in definition 1, or indeed as in definition 2, output and employment of one sector rise and those of the other fall.[80] However, since the employment of both sectors is utilized in the determination of λ, the change in λ cannot be determined without additional information relating to magnification. Thus more computation is unfortunately necessary, and it yields my second foothold.[81]

$$\frac{d \log \lambda}{d \log (\mathscr{L} - L_r)} = \frac{a\mathscr{K}}{D(L_{u1} + L_{u2})}\left(\frac{X_{i1}}{L_{u1}} - \frac{X_{i2}}{L_{u2}}\right) \qquad (7.7)$$

Definition 3

The first urban commodity is said to be intermediate good intensive with respect to the second iff

$$\text{sign}(\Delta) \quad \Leftrightarrow \quad \text{sign}\left(\frac{X_{i1}}{L_{u1}} - \frac{X_{i2}}{L_{u2}}\right)$$

Otherwise, the second urban commodity is said to be intermediate good intensive with respect to the first.[82]

I now obtain

$$\left.\frac{d\lambda}{dw_r}\right|_{CC} = -\frac{1}{p_r F_r^{LL}} \frac{a\mathscr{K}}{(\mathscr{L} - L_r)^2} \frac{\Delta}{D} \qquad (7.8)$$

which leads me to conclude that the slope of CC is positive if either urban commodity is *both* capital and intermediate good intensive with respect to the other. More comprehensively, I can state the following.

Definition 4

Factor intensities are said to conflict if one urban commodity is capital intensive but not intermediate good intensive with respect to the other, i.e. if $\text{sign}(D) \neq \text{sign}(\Delta)$. Otherwise factor intensities are said to coincide.

If factor intensities conflict, as in figure 7.1, the slope of CC is negative; and if they coincide, as in figure 7.2, this slope is positive. The two cases are pictured in figures 7.1 and 7.2, and figure 7.2 highlights the interesting possibility of multiple equilibria.[83]

A question logically prior to the conduct of comparative static exercises is the nonemptiness and the cardinality of the set of equilibria. In terms of nonemptiness, figure 7.2 illustrates how an equilibrium can be destroyed by shifting the curve CC outward. It is important to notice that this fragility also extends to the case where the factor intensities coincide – in figure 7.1, the curves LL and CC may easily intersect outside the feasible range of λ. Furthermore, even when there does exist an unspecialized equilibrium, as in figures 7.3 and 7.4, it is a very easy matter to find parameter values for which such an equilibrium can be destroyed – simply perturb $\mathscr{K}$ or $\mathscr{L}$ such that the point $(\mathscr{K}, \mathscr{L} - L_r)$ moves out of the analog of the Chipman–McKenzie cone of diversification.[84] It is only fitting that I give some prominence to this question in a chapter such as this – Chakravarty was one of the first to emphasize the importance of the existence issue in single (representative?) agent optimizing problems over an infinite-dimensional commodity space.[85] However, I give no existence theorem – given the variety of parameters involved, it would essentially reduce to a statement that equilibrium exists when it exists.

I turn next to the question of the cardinality of the set of equilibria. If the CC curve is tangent to the LL curve in figure 7.2 and the two equilibria ε_1 and ε_2 collapse to a unique equilibrium, the situation is not very propitious for comparative statics analysis. This is, of course, none other than Debreu's insistence on the existence of an unspecialized equilibrium which is robust enough for local comparative statics analysis to be meaningful.[86] This leads me to look for conditions on the parameters of my economy which prevent the occurrence of such nonrobust equilibria. Again, given the distortions in my model, it is difficult for me to conceive that any general results on this issue can be obtained. In his results on the number of equilibria of an Walrasian exchange economy, Dierker used Walras's law and assumptions on the behavior of excess demands on the boundary of the price simplex in an essential way.[87] In any case, I leave all this for future work and content myself with the following criterion.

Definition 5

An equilibrium is said to be robust iff

$$\frac{\partial \lambda}{\partial w_r}\bigg|_{LL} \neq \frac{\partial \lambda}{\partial w_r}\bigg|_{CC}$$

One final point. Note that definition 5 is of a second-order level – I have already built in the fact that my analog of the Chipman–McKenzie cone of diversification is not degenerate in the assumption that D is not equal to zero in definition 1.

5 Choice among equilibria

Dierker also showed in the context of a Walrasian equilibrium of a regular exchange economy that local asymptotic stability of the equilibrium prices in terms of the Walrasian adjustment process implies a unique equilibrium.[88] I now turn to the more conventional enquiry and ask whether there exist intuitively plausible dynamic adjustment processes, the stability of whose rest rules out some of the equilibria in the case when factor intensities coincide. Towards this end, I propose an adjustment process $\mathcal{Q}$ defined by the following differential equations:

$$DL_r = \pi\{w_r - [\lambda \bar{w}_u + (1 - \lambda)w_i]\} \qquad \pi'(.) > 0, \pi(0) = 0$$

$$D\lambda = \psi\left(\frac{L_{u1} + L_{u2}}{L_{u1} + L_{u2} + L_i} - \lambda\right) = \psi\left(\frac{L_{u1} + L_{u2}}{\mathscr{L} - L_r} - \lambda\right)$$

$$\psi'(.) > 0, \psi(0) = 0$$

Note that my process puts the brunt of the adjustment in the informal sector. If the rural wage is greater than the expected urban wage, $\mathcal{Q}$ postulates that there will be a reverse migration to the rural sector, one that releases the pressure on the informal sector and thereby lowers the rural wage and increases the informal sector wage. On the other hand, if the probability of finding a formal sector job is less than the formal sector employment as a proportion of the total urban labor force, a migrant revises upward his probability of finding a job in the formal sector.

It is difficult to place my process $\mathcal{Q}$ within the traditional Marshallian–Walrasian dichotomy. The adjustment of labor is clearly Marshallian in spirit, but that of the (formal) employment rate has Walrasian elements to the extent that it reflects a price – the expected urban wage.[89]

I can now present a theorem which states that stability of equilibrium implies and is implied by the fact that the slope of the CC curve is greater than that of the LL curve.

Theorem 1

A robust equilibrium is locally asymptotically stable under adjustment process $\mathcal{Q}$ iff

$$\left. \frac{\partial \lambda}{\partial w_r} \right|_{LL} > \left. \frac{\partial \lambda}{\partial w_r} \right|_{CC}$$

In this case the approach to equilibrium is monotonic.[90]

Note that ε_1 is locally asymptotically stable while equilibrium ε_2 is a saddle-point. For an intuition behind the result, consider, for example, a situation in which the system finds itself in the lens in figure 7.2. Since it is above the CC curve, the value of λ is more than that required for equilibrium. Hence the argument of ψ is negative and λ decreases. Analogously, since the system is below the LL curve, w_r is more than that required for equilibrium. Hence the argument of π is positive and L_r increases and leads to a decrease in w_r. The two effects in conjunction drive the system away from ε_2 and towards ε_1.

I find theorem 1 interesting when I view it in the context of previous work on the stability of equilibrium of either the HOS model with exogenously given wage differentials or the HOS version of the Harris–Todaro model. In this work, instability and other pathologies are intimately tied to conflicting factor intensities.[91] Here, it is precisely conflicting intensities that rule out multiple equilibria.

6 Project evaluation

In his entry on *cost–benefit analysis*, Chakravarty wrote

> Tinbergen [in 1958] was amongst the first set of influential economists who strongly recommended the use of "accounting prices," subsequently often referred to as "shadow prices" for the appraisal of social worthwhileness of investment projects. The leading idea behind cost–benefit analysis is that prevailing market prices involve significant distortions. These prices include the interest rate, the wage rate as well as the rate of foreign exchange. It is believed that if *suitable corrections* are made to the prices of goods and factors . . . a "proper" measure of the benefit–cost ratio for a project can be obtained.[92]

Since my model has nothing to say as regards issues connected with money or time, I do not have anything to say on the shadow interest rate or the shadow rate of foreign exchange and shall confine myself to the social opportunity costs of the three primary factors labor, land and capital. In particular, I shall ask how a loan officer, primarily interested in increasing the international value of gross national product (GNP), should price these primary factors taking into account the obvious distortions in the economy. I shall also assume that it is a "small" project that is being financed. In such a setting, this question was clearly posed by Harberger,[93] and Chakravarty himself referred to its importance more generally.

> A widely prescribed remedy, suggested by the U.N. Committee on development planning and many noted economists, is to adopt a scheme of rural public works. Either we pay labour engaged on public works the same wage rate as what would correspond to the market rate . . . or we pay him only a part of the market wage and compensate him in other ways for the labour he has put in. It is surprising that in the fairly voluminous literature that has sprung up on the question of rural public works, there is little or no discussion of these basic issues.[94]

I shall assume that all projects are evaluated in terms of what they contribute to GNP measured in international prices. Denote this by

W and note that it depends on all the parameters of my model. If I ignore the functional representatives of the rural and formal urban technologies, I can write it as[95]

$$W(\mathcal{T}, \mathcal{K}, \mathcal{L}; p_r, p_{u1}, p_{u2}; a) = p_r X_r + p_{u1} X_{u1} + p_{u2} X_{u2} \quad (7.9)$$

It is easy to see that for every particular equilibrium configuration I obtain one, and only one, value of W. However, I shall ignore Chipman's (1972) warning and assume the differentiability of W in terms of its arguments. On appealing to the marginal productivity pricing conditions that I assume to hold universally and to the material balance equations, I can rewrite W in terms of national income:[96]

$$W = R.\mathcal{K} + \tau T + w_r L_r + w_i L_i + \bar{w}_u(L_{u1} + L_{u2})$$

$$= R.\mathcal{K} + \tau T + w_r \mathcal{L} \quad (7.10)$$

Before I present my first result of this section, let me adopt the convention, to be enforced throughout the section, that by the market price of labor I mean the rural wage and that alone.

Proposition 1

The social opportunity cost of any factor is its market price adjusted by a factor reflecting the marginal change in the labor income of the urban sector, i.e. the urban employment multiplied by the marginal change in the average urban wage.

This follows from a routine differentiation of (7.10) which yields[97]

$$\frac{\partial W}{\partial \alpha} = x + (\mathcal{L} - L_r)\frac{\partial w_r}{\partial \alpha} \qquad x = \tau, R, w_r, \ \alpha = \mathcal{T}, \mathcal{K}, \mathcal{L} \quad (7.11)$$

A more interesting question is whether this proposition can be sharpened. I turn to this, beginning first with a consideration of an increase in capital. Certainly, the LL curve does not shift and I have to focus solely on the CC curve. Towards this end, note that for a given value of w_r rural employment and hence labor supply to the urban region does not change. The question then arises as to what happens to λ. This is a more straightforward computation than the one behind (7.7).

$$\frac{d \log \lambda}{d \log \mathscr{H}} = \frac{\mathscr{H}}{L_{u1} + L_{u2}} \left(\frac{dL_{u1}}{d\mathscr{H}} + \frac{dL_{u2}}{d\mathscr{H}} \right) = -\frac{a\mathscr{H}}{L_{u1} + L_{u2}} \frac{\Delta}{D} \quad (7.12)$$

But now the analysis is complete. If factor intensities conflict, λ increases and the CC curve shifts upward as shown by C'C' in figure 7.1. On the other hand, if factor intensitives coincide, λ decreases and the CC curve shifts downward as shown by C'C' in figure 7.2. Even though there is the possibility of multiple equilibria under the dynamic process $\mathcal{Q}$ leads me to focus only on the equilibrium labeled ε_2 in figure 7.2. Consequently, I have established the part of the following proposition that pertains to capital.

Proposition 2

If factor intensities conflict, the social opportunity cost of both capital and land, but not of labor, is underestimated by their market prices. If factor intensities do not conflict and the equilibrium is locally asymptotically stable, the social opportunity cost of labor, but not of capital or land, is underestimated by its market price – the rural wage which, in equilibrium, also represents the average urban wage.

The case of an increase in land or labor is more straightforward since I can rely on the computation behind (7.7) that I used to establish the slope of the CC curve. Consider an increase in labor. Again, the LL curve does not change. For a given value of w_r, rural employment also does not change and the question then reduces to the induced change in λ, which follows from (7.7). On the other hand, an increase in land leads to an increase in rural employment and hence to a fall in the labor available to the urban region, namely in $\mathscr{L} - L_r$. Again, (7.7) specifies the induced change in λ, and the full proposition can now be established.

It is well to contrast my findings with Harberger's recommendations to use the informal sector wage for projects in the urban sector.

> I have attempted to present the case for using prevailing wage levels in the . . . unprotected sector as a point of departure for estimating the social opportunity cost of labor in a given market area. With modest

qualifications and occasional adjustments (usually upward) the unprotected-sector wage stands as the basic measure of social opportunity cost. As against alternative measures, most of which are based on macroeconomic analyses of one form or another, it has the great advantage of being readily capable of reflecting the complexity and subtlety of labor-market phenomena. The approach here advocated takes the infinitely complex machinery of the economy itself as its computer and finds in the data generated by that machinery – in the form of unprotected-sector wages – the best approach to measuring the social opportunity cost of labor – by type, skill, and location.[98]

The problem with Harberger's prescription is that despite the wide-ranging and insightful discussion that is adduced in justification, it is difficult to pin down precisely the model that lies behind and articulates the several conceptions of the labor markets that he presents. Of course, what we are to do depends crucially on the conception of the economy which one has in mind.[99] In any case, under my conception, given the interconnectedness and the size of the project, the social opportunity cost is independent of location. Furthermore, the benchmark used is not the important point – it can be the rural wage or the informal wage – but rather the divergence from it. Thus I can rephrase the part of proposition 1 pertaining to labor in terms of the informal sector wage, with (7.11) rewritten as

$$\frac{\partial W}{\partial \mathscr{L}} = w_i + \lambda(\bar{w}_u - w_i)\left[1 + \left(1 - \frac{L_r}{\mathscr{L}}\right)\varepsilon_{\lambda\mathscr{L}}\right] \quad (7.13)$$

However, whether the market price overestimates or underestimates the social opportunity cost of labor depends on $\varepsilon_{\lambda\mathscr{L}}$, the elasticity of formal employment with respect to changes in the endowment of labor. For a complete treatment, this should be decomposed into more fundamental measures – a point emphasized by Stiglitz some years ago.[100] One final point in this connection: note that unlike some of Harberger's settings I do not have a separate category of urban unemployed in my model. It was precisely the provision of an underpinning in terms of livelihood for the unemployed that constituted one of my motivations for the introduction of an informal sector, but I may have swung to the other extreme.[101]

One of the insights of the generalized theory of distortions of Bhagwati, Johnson, and others,[102] is that the possibility of negative social opportunity costs of a factor of production has as its direct reflection the possibility of immiserizing growth from an increase in that factor.[103] Accordingly, I can rephrase my proposition 2 as follows.

Proposition 3

If factor intensities conflict, there is no possibility of immiserizing growth of land and capital, but population growth may be immiserizing. If factor intensities do not conflict and the equilibrium is locally asymptotically stable, there is no possibility of immiserizing growth of labor, but accumulation in land or in capital may be immiserizing.

Given the general theory, what is interesting is not the impossibility of immiserizing growth but the possibility of immiserizing growth. In any case, it is important to appreciate that, whatever novelty lies in proposition 3, it has to do with the relevance of conflicting factor intensities even when capital is intersectorally immobile. Unlike stability considerations,[104] this aspect has not been brought out before in the treatment of this question.

7 Targeting the rural sector

In one of his last articles, Chakravarty asks, and answers, the following question.

> How does one explain the persistence of poverty in India as well as in other South Asian countries despite their achievements in various other areas? In my opinion, the answer to this question has to be traced to a deeper perception of the problem. First, during the early days of planning, the agrarian structure and its possible consequences for accelerated industrialization were not adequately grasped by policymakers. Second, the agrarian structure has also not been fully perceived in terms of the interaction between physical factor endowments, knowledge of techniques of cultivation and property rights.[105]

Presumably, it is ideas such as these which lead Harcourt and Singh to write in their tribute

> In place of [the] pattern of growth led by urban middle class consumption – what Lance Taylor has called the Brazilian model – Chakravarty

put forward an "agriculture first" strategy. In this view, instead of allowing investment in car production and other consumer durables with import-intensive technologies, . . . the government should invest in agriculture, so as to spread the "green revolution" technology from Punjab and Haryana to the rest of the country.[106]

It goes without saying that my model can hardly do full justice to a discussion of this strategy. However, I can use it to derive some preliminary results pertaining to two kinds of experiments: the first is traditional agricultural development and involves infusion of resources on the input end, and the second concerns programs aimed directly at the rural population. I take each in turn.

7.1 Agricultural development

In his discussion of the new strategy of agricultural development in the Fourth Five-Year Plan, Chakravarty distinguishes four elements: a shift from major to minor irrigation works; adequate provision of "credit"; an alteration in the input base; and the development of fertilizer-sensitive varieties of grains.[107] Focusing more specifically on labor-saving technical progress, he writes

> It is sometimes added that the Green Revolution led to undue mechanization of agriculture. There is little doubt that certain types of capital goods, such as diesel and electric pump sets, increased very subtantially, and so to a lesser extent did the use of tractors. But to use A. K. Sen's felicitous expression, much of the capital was "land-esque" rather than "labour-esque". As a result, the Green Revolution did not lead to the type of labour displacement from agriculture which was predicted. In fact, the increase in capital intensity in Indian agriculture, especially during the 1970s, has helped to achieve an increase in output per unit of land as well as per agricultural worker, in the face of severe land constraint and rising agricultural population.[108]

I begin by recording a simple implication of my model.

Proposition 4

Agricultural price support programs, improvements in the quality of land, technical progress in agriculture, increases in nonshiftable agricultural capital are all equivalent from a welfare-theoretic point of view and lead to an increase in rural employment.

All the parametric changes that I consider in the proposition shift only the CC curve, and differentiation of $p_r F_r^L(L_r, \mathcal{T}) = w_r$ shows that in each case rural employment increases, i.e. all of these changes are "land-esque."

The interesting question, of course, is the effect of these parametric changes on changes in welfare. As above, an increase in rural employment decreases the labor supply available to the urban region and from (7.7) leads the CC curve to rise if factor intensities conflict and to fall if they coincide. If I refer to all of these parametric changes as a *targeting of the agricultural sector*, I can summarize this discussion by the following proposition.

Proposition 5

If factor intensities conflict, the targeting of the agricultural sector leads to an improvement in welfare. If factor intensities coincide and the equilibrium is locally asymptotically stable, the targeting of the agriculture sector leads to a deterioration in welfare.

7.2 Rural poverty programs

In his view of poverty alleviation strategies, Chakravarty describes three approaches that have been followed in India: the Minimum Needs Program (MNP);[109] large-scale wage employment programs in the rural areas,[110] supplemented by Food-for-Work Programs (FFWPs); and the Integrated Rural Development Program (IRDP).[111] I formalize these programs as a subsidy to rural labor rather than a subsidy to rural employers. I do this through the introduction of a shift parameter β and by rewriting the labor market equilibrium condition (7.3) as $\beta w_r = \lambda \bar{w}_r + (1 - \lambda) w_i$. It is clear that β affects only the LL curve, and in such a way[112] that, for a given value of w_r, λ increases with an increase in β. This is illustrated by $L'L'$ in figures 7.5 and 7.6. If factor intensities conflict, w_r falls and leads to a deterioration in welfare. The same is true if intensities coincide provided that I assume local asymptotic stability of equilibrium in terms of my process $\mathcal{Q}$. I can therefore present the following proposition.

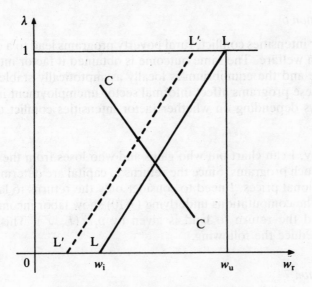

Figure 7.5 Intensity rankings conflict.

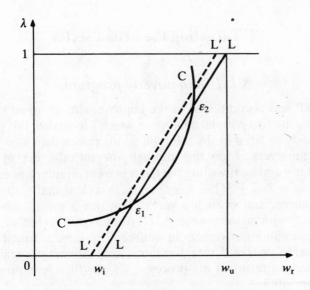

Figure 7.6 Intensity rankings coincide.

Proposition 6

If factor intensities conflict, rural poverty programs lead to a deterioration in welfare. The same outcome is obtained if factor intensities coincide and the equilibrium is locally asymptotically stable. However, these programs affect informal sector unemployment in opposite ways depending on whether factor intensities conflict or coincide.

Finally, I can chart out who gains and who loses from the institution of such programs. Since the returns to capital are determined by international prices, I need to consider only the returns to land and labor. The computations underlying (7.10) show labor income to be $w_r \mathcal{L}$ and the return to land is given by $p_r F_r^T(L_r, \mathcal{T})$. This allows me to deduce the following.

Proposition 7

Rural poverty programs have no effect on the income of capital but they lower the income to labor and raise that accruing to land.

8 Targeting the urban sector

8.1 Urban poverty programs

The MNP was also directed at the improvement of urban slums.[113] This leads me to a parallel analysis in which I formalize this program as a subsidy to labor in the informal sector rather than as subsidy to urban employers. I do this through the introduction of a shift parameter γ and by rewriting the labor market equilibrium condition (7.3) as $w_r = \lambda \bar{w}_u + \gamma(1 - \lambda)w_i$. Again, it is clear that γ affects only the LL curve, and in such a way[114] that, for a given value of w_r, λ decreases with an increase in γ. If factor intensities conflict, w_r rises and leads to an improvement in welfare. The same is true if intensities coincide provided that I assume local asymptotic stability of equilibrium in terms of my process $\mathcal{Q}$. I can therefore present the next proposition.

Proposition 8

If factor intensities conflict, urban poverty programs lead to an improvement in welfare. The same outcome is obtained if factor intensities coincide and the equilibrium is locally asymptotically stable. However, these programs affect informal sector unemployment in opposite ways depending on whether factor intensities conflict or coincide.

Finally, I can chart out who gains and who loses from the institution of such programs. Since the analysis is analogous to the one presented above, I shall simply state proposition 9.

Proposition 9

Urban poverty programs have no effect on the income of capital but they raise the income to labor and lower that accruing to land.

8.2 *Import substitution*

It is also argued . . . that if the Indian development strategy, instead of emphasizing import substitution, had given greater attention to exploiting the opportunities provided by the external economic environment, the growth performance would have been much better.[115] Clearly, whether a country should pursue an outward-looking or an inward-looking policy is not an issue that can be decided on the basis of first principles only. One has to reckon with the size and composition of a country's resources, but also with the nature of the world economic "conjecture".[116]

My model is not suited to handling questions of growth but I can use it to formalize how a country's resources impinge on improvements in the terms of trade. It can also be used to consider the desirability of tariff reform by viewing the exogenously given international prices as tariff inclusive and by perturbing the tariff. I concentrate on the question of an improvement in the terms of trade represented by an increase in (say) p_{u1}, and indicate how the analysis can proceed for a decrease in the tariff.

The first step is to note that a change in any of the international prices for the urban commodities changes factor prices and hence the choice of techniques. Routine differentiation of the price-equals-cost equations, with θ_{jk} denoting the share of the kth factor in the value of the jth formal output, yields

$$\begin{bmatrix} \theta_{1L} & \theta_{1i} & \theta_{1K} \\ \theta_{2L} & \theta_{2i} & \theta_{2K} \end{bmatrix} \begin{bmatrix} \hat{w}_u \\ \hat{a} + \hat{w}_i \\ \hat{R} \end{bmatrix} = \begin{bmatrix} \hat{p}_{u1} \\ \hat{p}_{u2} \end{bmatrix} \qquad (7.14)$$

Since I am not interested in changes in a, $\bar{w}_u$, or p_{u2}, I am reduced to the conclusion that the LL curve shifts outward or inward depending on the movement of w_i, which in turn is completely characterized by the sign of Λ, where

$$\Lambda = \theta_{1i}\theta_{2K} - \theta_{2i}\theta_{1K}$$

and thus

$$\text{sign}(\Lambda) = \text{sign}\left(\frac{X_{1i}}{K_{u1}} - \frac{X_{2i}}{K_{u2}} \right) \qquad (7.15)$$

Next, I turn to the curve CC. for this, I assume a fixed value of w_r and by rewriting (7.6) in a way that emphasizes changes in the choice of technique rather than those in endowments, and by substituting $\hat{R}$ and $\hat{w}_i$ from (7.14), and finally for changes in L_{u1} and L_{u2}, I obtain[117]

$$\frac{\hat{\lambda}}{\hat{p}_{u1}} = \frac{1}{(L_{u1} + L_{u2})D\Lambda}$$
$$\times [a\theta_{2i}(K_1\sigma_{KL}^1 + K_2\sigma_{KL}^2)\Delta + \theta_{2K}(X_{1i}\sigma_{iL}^1 + X_{2i}\sigma_{iL}^2)D_\rho] \quad (7.16)$$

where σ_{rs}^j is the elasticity of substitution of factor r for factor s in sector j.

The difficulty with this compartive statics exercise is now explicit. In a nutshell, a change in p_{u1} shifts both the LL and the CC curves. Nevertheless, I can cull some propositions out of this algebraic morass. I identify two sets of sufficient conditions.

Proposition 10

If factor intensities conflict, and if D_ρ and Λ are both negative, an increase in the price of the first formal urban commodity leads to a fall in welfare. If factor intensities coincide and the equilibrium is locally asymptotically stable, and if D_ρ and Λ are both positive, an increase in the price of the first formal urban commodity leads to a rise in welfare.

This proposition keeps within the guidelines provided by definition 4 on the conflict or the coincidence of the factor intensities represented by D and Δ. If I abandon these, I can obtain proposition 11.

Proposition 11

Let the signs of Δ, D, D_ρ, Λ all coincide, and the equilibrium be locally asymptotically stable. If this sign is positive (negative), an increase in the price of the first formal urban commodity leads to a rise (fall) in welfare.

When I turn to the analysis of a reduction in the tariff walls, I have to take into account the disbursement of tariff revenue. The methodology for this is clear and well understood.[118] I leave a detailed analysis of this question for another occasion.[119] What is clear is that even for the static allocation case clear results cannot be had. All of this is of course to be expected from an elaboration of the theory of distortions.[120] In summary, the results of this section bring out the perspicacity of the remark that results on this issue cannot be obtained on *a priori* principles, even if we abstain ourselves from the complexities of dynamics and growth.

9 Concluding remarks

I conclude this chapter with three observations. The first relates to the omission of dynamics from my model, the second concerns the "plan versus market" dichotomy, and the third the intimate connection between economic development and cultural change.

I have already emphasized that my model falls squarely within the Marshallian partial equilibrium tradition – the exogenously given international prices place the analysis within the rubric of production theory with fixed factors. With a little more generosity, one can follow writers influenced by Harry Johnson[121] and think of the model as static general equilibrium theory – a miniature Walrasian system

but with distortions. In either case, this is a tradition in which
Sukhamoy Chakravarty never worked and, given that his primary
interests were growth and dynamics, my work draws attention to his
more by omission than by emulation.

Of course, to the extent that understanding the allocation of
resources at a particular point in time is a prerequisite to understanding it over time, very much in the same spirit as the understanding
of continuum or nonstandard economies is a prerequisite for understanding large but finite economies, my model simply represents a
first step, to be followed by one in which capital $\mathscr{K}$ is made
endogenous and the law of population growth is made explicit. What
I am not clear about is whether Chakravarty saw this as *the* methodological route on which to proceed, or whether he leaned towards an
alternative position which starts with the dynamics by itself, on its
own, and as a substitute for, rather than as a complement of, static
general equilibrium theory. Such a view is best exemplified in a
recent statement of an economist that Chakravarty admired.

> The method consists in asking what would a rational man (now
> fashionably called an "agent") do when confronted by the manifold
> problems of an economic nature. Under the banner of General
> Equilibrium Theory, this has been developed into an imposing analy-
> tical web of how a system of a large number of such agents would
> interact in a unified market mechanism. This programme, in an
> increasingly mathematical form, has produced impressive results,
> which may be considered "mainstream" economics. Some tentative
> efforts at a kind of experimental economics have raised serious doubts
> about this "rational" behavior. [The] analysis appeared to work well
> for a single moment in time, but there always remained the awkward
> fact that both agents and goods have a future. Since the future had to
> be regarded as unknown and hence uncertain, it all needed to be
> reformulated as a gambling game. John von Neumann's formulation
> of game theory proved too weak a tool to resolve such a gigantic
> problem. It is at this point that economic dynamics becomes
> relevant.[122]

To reiterate, it remains for me an open question whether or not it
was sympathy with such a methodological position that led Chakravarty to show increasing restlessness with the dominant paradigm,[123]
and to welcome, as well as to some extent anticipate,[124] recent
applications of chaos theory.[125]

Discussion of paradigmatic shifts leads me to the "market versus plan" dichotomy and to the necessity of the deconstruction of the terms[126] *market* and *plan*. He began this program in his Suzy Paine Lecture and devoted full attention to it in his Asian Development Bank article.[127] He was well aware of the "chameleon" nature of the two words and had conceded that

> earlier discussion of the market *versus* the Plan was much too crude.[128] I believe that the term "plan" should distinguish between planning as a form of instrumental inference and . . . as an alternative to the market system based on "command and fulfilment". Similarly, the word "market" also permits different interpretations. It may be first viewed as a coordinating system, or in the language of cybernetics as a "servomechanism" and secondly as an expression of an industrial system based on "consumers' sovereignty" judged as an ultimate value in itself. The first interpretation is not necessarily inconsistent with planning as a mode of "instrumental inference".[129] A deeper understanding of the interface between market and planning may prove to be of strategic significance in ensuring a humane existence for vast masses of people, whether they are living in the so called "third world" or in what used to be called the "second world".[130]

However, the fact that the planners themselves have their own interests and are beholden to other interests is never explicitly brought to the fore. Even if in Chakravarty's conception planners may not have what Putnam[131] calls a "God's-eye view," or better still a "view from nowhere," they are clearly in the driver's seat. In this sense, the fact that the Gibbard–Satterthwaite theorem[132] is one of the messages arising from Hurwicz's insight is not as lucidly seen and effectively incorporated in his thinking as some would have liked it to be. He drew a basically optimistic message from this work.[133]

Of course, once one gets into interpretation and deconstruction, the importance of culture and cultural change is not far behind. Referring to Lewis's list of new models invented by development economists, he wryly observed, "This may soothe the consciences of those who judge the importance of a subdiscipline by its ability to develop models."[134] Elsewhere he had already contrasted "the use of mechanistic modes of thought [with the] perverse pleasure taken by the policy-makers in ignoring the dictates of efficiency."[135] It would have been interesting to see his response to Henry Wan's comment on his Suzy Paine Lecture.[136] In any case, he was clear about the importance of changing one's mind. Paying tribute to Suzy Paine, he wrote,

These days, when doing economics is often treated just as an intellectual game, her attitude towards her subject was very strikingly different. She was a deeply serious economist, willing to re-examine from time to time her favorite set of preconceptions, and honest and bold enough to reject views which she might have held at an earlier stage, if she felt that they were turning out to be fetters on further movements in understanding.[137]

These words are a fitting conclusion to this chapter.

Notes

This is a revised version of Johns Hopkins Working Paper 277; the revision has benefited from the thoughtful comments of an anonymous referee and from the firm editorial hand of Tapan Mitra. The technical portions of this work were completed when the author was visiting Bilkent University in June 1991. I am grateful to Saleha Jilani for drawing Ikemoto's work to my attention, and to her, Vandana Chandra, Ralph El-Chami, Ken Kletzer, and Naeem Siddiqui for encouragement and helpful discussion. I also thank Carl Christ, Tatsuo Hatta, and Louis Maccini for sharing with me their memories of Chakravarty's stay at Hopkins during the academic year 1968–9. I retain sole responsibility for errors, be they of analysis or of interpretation.

1 See Berlin (1953, p.1). I have rearranged parts of the text.
2 For the last two, see, in particular, his R. C. Dutt Lecture published as Chakravarty (1982).
3 His first book, dated 1959, on the logic of investment planning was written in Rotterdam. For his obituary, Tinbergen was to write, "Professor Sukhamoy Chakravarty came to me as my student and left me as my teacher"; quoted in Panchamukhi (1990).
4 His second book, dated 1969, on capital and development planning was written in Cambridge and finished in Baltimore.
5 See Chakravarty (1975). The occasion was an address delivered by Chakravarty on being awarded the first Mahalanobis Gold Medal by the Indian Econometric Society.
6 The questions in both of these paragraphs were all posed in his Suzy Paine Memorial Lecture; see Chakravarty (1987a).
7 The distinctions are Hayek's; see his 1975 essay on two types of mind.
8 See Chakravarty (1984, p. 354) for drawing the relevance of Clifford Geertz's 1968 study of Central Java to the Eastern Gangetic delta.
9 See Chakravarty (1984). In Chakravarty (1987a, p. 19), he wrote "Wealth can be viewed as 'power', and not merely as an aid to

further gratification, and that under capitalism, the dynamics of power are largely exercised through the extraction of labour out of labour power – [all this is] strongly highlighted by East Asian experience."

10 See Chakravarty (1991, p. 20). In his comment on Chakravarty's Suzy Paine Lecture, Byres (1987) writes: "I would like to see him develop what he has to say . . . about the idea of 'morphogenesis' which [according to him] pervades Marxist analysis."

11 See Chakravarty (1991, p. 17; 1987d, p. 135).

12 See Chakravarty (1991, p. 15; 1987a, p. 18; 1987d, p. 136). Also Wan (1988, 1990).

13 See Chakravarty (1991, p. 15) where he refers to a sympathetic review of Goldschmidt's work by Stephen Jay Gould.

14 See Chakravarty (1982, p. 12, fn. 9, and section V).

15 Chakravarty (1989, p. 78) mentions that this "point [was] explicitly noted by Chapernowne in his commentary [on the von Neumann model]."

16 Chakravarty (1989, pp. 73, 78) writes: "The fact that certain equilibrium systems permit double descriptions as 'causal' or 'teleological' have been long well known to students of classical mechanics. Furthermore, canonical conjugacy between pairs of quantities such as prices and activity levels which is by now well understood in economics has long been understood by students of physics when they refer to positions and momenta." The fact that both Samuelson and Tinbergen have deep interests in physics also deserves mention in this context.

17 See his Radhakrishnan Lectures in Chakravarty (1987b); also Chakravarty (1990).

18 The phrase *conjuncture specific* keeps recurring in his later writings; see Chakravarty (1987a, p. 7, paragraph 4; 1987b, p. 84, paragraph 2; 1991, p. 19, paragraph 3). However, unlike Marx, and *pace* Panchamukhi (1990), there is no violent contrast between the early Chakravarty and the late Chakravarty.

19 See the conclusion to his Suzy Paine Lecture; Chakravarty (1987a).

20 The distinction is Amartya Sen's; see Klammer's (1989) interview with Sen. As an example of this virtuosity, I am partial to his 1962 *Econometrica* piece which clearly poses the question that Bewley (1972) and Brown and Lewis (1981) were later to solve; see in particular footnote 9 in Chakravarty (1962b). Professor Brown tells me that his first reading on optimal growth theory was Chakravarty (1962a,b); an assignment of Tjalling Koopmans.

21 The distinction is Robert Merton's; see Merton (1972).

22 The distinction is Pencavel's; see Pencavel (1991).

23 In his survey on the contributions of Indian economists his title is given

as Professor of Mathematical Economics; see Chakravarty (1969c).

24 In India, he taught at Presidency College and at the Delhi School of Economics, and abroad he taught at Massachusetts Institute of Technology (1959–61 and 1963–4), at Johns Hopkins University (1968–9), at the University of Erasmus (1976–7), and at Cambridge University (1984–5). He was repeatedly offered, and rejected, positions at Johns Hopkins University (and, for all I know, elsewhere). However, he did send one of his promising undergraduate students to complete his graduate work at Johns Hopkins – I refer, of course, to Rajiv Vohra, now at Brown University.

25 He was Chairman both of the Economic Advisory Council to the Prime Minister since 1983 and the Indian Council of Social Science Research since 1987. Harcourt and Singh (1991) write: "Unlike Mahalanobis, Chakravarty was involved not only in the technical and theoretical work of economic planning, but also directly in the implementation of the 5-Year Plans during the last two decades."

26 See Samuelson (1969),

27 See the tribute to Chakravarty by Harcourt and Singh (1991).

28 Such details are available in Portes et al. (1989, Part I, ch. 1) and are further highlighted in Chandra (1991, chs 2 and 3).

29 A good survey of the voluminous empirical and descriptive literature is available in Portes et al. (1989, part IV, chs 9–12).

30 See Portes et al (1989, p. 41).

31 Extensive empirical evidence on the magnitude of substitution between formal and informal labor motivated by the cost-minimizing behavior of producers is available in Portes et al. (1989).

32 Since there is no money in my model, I am assuming constancy of real, as opposed to nominal, wages in the urban formal sector.

33 See Dasgupta (1985, p. 143). Chakravarty, too, was comfortable with this assumption even in the context of a long-run planning exercise; see Lefeber and Chakravarty (1966). Their work was to see an extension in the form of Dixit's MIT PhD dissertation; see Dixit (1968) and also the references to Marglin's work therein.

34 See Gorman (1976) and, for my context, Khan and Naqvi (1983).

35 There are eight derivatives of the three unit-cost functions; given linear homogeneity of each of the three functions, I am left with five independent equations.

36 See, for example, the relevant chapter in Caves and Jones (1985) and Jones (1965).

37 By this, I simply mean that not all the factor prices and the production techniques are determined solely by international prices independently of factor endowments; or, as in the Harris–Todaro variant of the HOS model, by international prices in conjunction with the exogenously given urban wage. For the latter, see Corden and Find-

lay (1975) and Khan (1987) and his references, as well as the discussion below. The observation is not relevant to the version of the Harris–Todaro model exposited in Basu (1984).

38 See, for example, the relevant chapter in Caves and Jones (1985) as well as Ikemoto (1969), Jones (1971, 1975), and Samuelson (1971).

39 See Gruen and Corden (1970) and Marjit (1990a). In Marjit (1990b), this model is also interpreted as a north–south model.

40 This difference between the two versions is by now well appreciated and well understood; see Khan (1982), Basu (1984, ch. 6), and Khan (1987) and his references.

41 A notable exception is Fields (1975). Harberger (1972, ch. 7) is clear and explicit about the importance of this *unprotected* sector, but he does not present a fully articulated model in which such a sector is incorporated.

42 See Chandra (1991); also Chandra and Khan (1991).

43 For Chakravarty's views on whether the Indian economy was constrained by land, see, for example, Chakravarty (1990, p. 136, paragraph 1; 1987b, p. 5, paragraph 3; also pp. 25–6).

44 In addition to Grinols (1991), also see Chandra and Khan (1991).

45 I would also like to mention in this connection recent work of Fields (1989) and Gupta (1991) who allow for unemployment in addition to informal employment. Fields's primary focus is on job-search models, while a discussion of Gupta's interesting conception will require more space than I have.

46 See Cahkravarty (1987d, p. 129).

47 See Bhagwati and Chakravarty in Chakravarty (1969c, pp. 6–7). I should also reproduce, however, the following footnote to this sentence: "Whether, however, the Mahalanobis-assumed non-shiftability from consumer goods to investment goods capital equipment is greater than that within the former group, and how important it is anyway, are matters on which *evidence* is scant and, as we shall soon argue, was in any case not sought by the Indian planners before adopting Mahalanobis's ideas."

48 See Chakravarty (1969b, p. 2).

49 See Chakravarty (1982, p. 8).

50 See Chakravarty (1987a, Preface).

51 See Chakravarty (1969b, p. 2).

52 See Chakravarty (1987b, p. 89). It is of interest that the subject is again receiving sustained attention; see Pindyck (1991).

53 See the precise references in note 38.

54 See Chakravarty (1987a, p. 12).

55 See Chakravarty (1969b, p. 2).

56 See Chakravarty (1987d, p. 138).

57 See his entry on optimal savings in *The New Palgrave*.

58 I have in mind the work of Bose, Bardhan, Kurs, Srinivasan, Ryder, Weitzman, among others. Dasgupta and Johansen were outside the Cambridge, New Haven circle. Even the Arrow and Kurz (1970) extension of the one-sector Ramsey problem to a setting with irreversibilities, or the Dixit (1968) extension to a setting with surplus labor, do not make it in the references to his entry. The Arrow and Kurz book, however, is referenced.

59 Whitaker (1987, section VI) states: "Period analysis is Marhsall's most explicit and self-conscious application of the comparative-static, partial equilibrium method with which his name will always be associated. [In the words of Marshall himself], 'the most important among the many uses of this method is to classify forces with reference to the time they require for their work; and to impound in *Caeteris Paribus* those forces which are of minor importance relatively to the particular time we have in view.' Short-period-normal equilibrium analysis permitted output to be varied, but not the stock of productive 'appliances' available to produce that output. 'Appliances' must be taken here to cover skilled labour and business organization as well as fixed capital assets."

60 See Chakravarty (1987d, p. 135).

61 See Chakravarty (1982, p. 9), where he refers to Solow (1956) and writes, "[Marshall], therefore, clearly anticipated the so-called neoclassical growth model of Solow and other contemporary authors."

62 I return to this point in the concluding section of this essay.

63 Of course, it is easy to find examples in his earlier work in which he was so involved; see Lefeber and Chakravarty, referenced as Chakravarty (1966).

64 See Chakravarty (1975).

65 See Chakravarty (1989, pp. 72, 74).

66 See Samuelson's (1987) treatment.

67 See Newman (1962).

68 See equations (1)–(3) in Samuelson (1987).

69 See Solow (1962), Stiglitz (1970), Cass (1973), Findlay (1978), and their followers.

70 See the very first quotation to the introduction to this chapter.

71 See the discussion of all of these models, excepting that of Weitzman (1971), in the Bhagwati and Chakravarty survey quoted as Chakravarty (1969).

72 See Srinivasan (1965, pp. 256–7).

73 I do not consider the second stage in which these optimized values go towards the determination of the flows of prices and stocks. Putting this sequential twist to the argument has methodological significance – I return to it in the concluding section of this chapter.

74 See Chakravarty (1969c, p. 8).
75 Throughout the sequel, I shall denote partial derivatives by super-scripts.
76 Again, as a consequence of (7.4).
77 All of this can be seen most simply with reference to the input–output table given above. Focus on the rows pertaining to $\mathscr{L}$, $\mathscr{K}$, and X_i. Material balance for labor, capital, and informal input furnishes me with three equations in the three unknowns X_{u1}, X_{u2}, and X_i. Since the input–output coefficients are already determined, I can calculate the labor requirements.
78 I ignore the case where D is zero.
79 Again, I ignore the case where D_ρ is zero.
80 This can be seen most simply in my modification of the Jones diagram presented as figures 7.3 and 7.4.
81 For details, see the author's Johns Hopkins Working Paper 277.
82 I again ignore the case where the sign of Δ is zero.
83 The exact shape of the downward-sloping curve CC will depend upon the second derivatives. For my purposes, it suffices to point to the possibility of multiple equilibria.
84 See Chipman (1972) and his references.
85 See Chakravarty (1962a, b) and also note 22 above.
86 On these issues, see Debreu (1976) and the references therein.
87 See theorem 1 in Dierker (1972).
88 See theorem 2 in Dierker (1972).
89 For details, see Jaffé's Note 5 to Lesson 7 in Walras (1874); also see Marshall (1879).
90 For the details of a formal proof relying on results in Hirsch and Smale (1974, pp. 181, 187), see the author's Johns Hopkins Working Paper 277.
91 The *physical* and *value* intensities for the first model, and *unemployment-adjusted* and *elasticities-adjusted* intensities for the second; see Neary (1978) and Khan (1980) respectively. The latter collapse to a positive number in the case of an exogenously given sector-specific urban wage, as for example in Neary (1981).
92 See the entry entitled "cost–benefit analysis" in *The New Palgrave*.
93 See Harberger (1972, ch. 7); also Srinivasan and Bhagwati (1978) and Stiglitz (1977, 1982).
94 See Chakravarty (1975).
95 This is precisely the gross national product function of Samuelson (1953) and the production function for foreign exchange of Chipman (1972).
96 Simply note that $w_i L_i + \bar{w}_u (L_{u1} + L_{u2}) = (\mathscr{L} - L_r)[\lambda \bar{w}_u + (1 - \lambda) w_i]$.
97 Note that the derivation relies on the fact that

$$T \frac{\partial \tau}{\partial \alpha} + L_r \frac{\partial w_r}{\partial \alpha} = 0 \qquad \alpha = \mathcal{T}, \mathcal{K}, \mathcal{L}$$

and on the constant returns to scale property of the function $F_r(.,.)$ implying $TF_r^{LT} + L_r F_r^{LL} = 0$ and $TF_r^{TT} + L_r F_r^{LT} = 0$.

98   Harberger's (1972, pp. 180–2) words present a useful contrast to those of Chakravarty at the beginning of section 6.

99   See, for example, the introduction to Stiglitz (1977); also Stiglitz (1982). This issue also has obvious epistemological implications – see section 3 in Khan (1991).

100   See Stiglitz (1982).

101   See Gupta (1991) for a model with an informal sector and open unemployment.

102   See Bhagwati (1971) and the references therein.

103   See Srinivasan and Bhagwati (1978) and, in the context of the Harris–Todaro model, also Khan (1982), Khan and Naqvi (1983), and Chao and Yu (1992).

104   See, for example, proposition 4.2 in Khan (1982).

105   See Chakravarty (1990, p. 142).

106   Harcourt and Singh (1991, last two paragraphs) add "Although Chakravarty sketched out the essential argument of the 'agriculture first' strategy, he unfortunately did not get a chance to analyze its implications fully before his untimely death."

107   See Chakravarty (1987b, p. 25). Also Chakravarty (1990, p. 137).

108   See Chakravarty (1987, p. 26).

109   This is essentially investment in human resources including "elementary education, adult education, rural health, rural roads, rural water supply, rural housing, rural electrification and nutrition"; see Chakravarty (1990, p. 146). In the Seventh Plan (1985–90), the MNP was integrated with other rural development and anti-poverty programs.

110   Two types of wage employment programs have been in operation in India during the 1980s. One is the National Rural Employment Program (NREP) – see table 3 in Chakravarty (1990) for the performance of the NREP in India during the period 1980–8 – and the other is the Rural Landless Employment Guarantee Programme.

111   Under this program assets provided to the target group households are financed through a mix of government subsidies and institutional credit on an average subsidy to credit ratio of 1:2. See table 3 in Chakravarty (1990) for the performance of the IRDP in India during the period 1980–8.

112   In order to see the direction of the shift, differentiate the reformulated labor market equilibrium condition with respect to β to obtain $\partial \lambda / \partial \beta = w_r / (\bar{w}_u - w_i)$.

113   See Chakravarty (1990, p. 146).

114 In order to see the direction of the shift, differentiate the reformulated labor market equilibrium condition with respect to γ to obtain $\partial\lambda/\partial\gamma = -(1 - \lambda)w_r/(\bar{w}_u - \gamma w_i)$.

115 See Chakravarty (1990, p. 139).

116 See Chakravarty (1987b, p. 84).

117 For the details as to the derivation, see the author's Johns Hopkins Working Paper 277.

118 See Hatta (1977a, b), and for the distorted context at hand, Chandra and Khan (1991) and their references.

119 For a parallel analysis, see Chandra and Khan (1991).

120 See Bhagwati (1971) and the references therein.

121 See, in particular, his Yrjö Jahnsson Lectures. The 1974 Krauss and Johnson textbook is titled simply *General Equilibrium Analysis*.

122 Preface to Goodwin (1990).

123 Chakravarty (1989, last paragraph) states: "I believe that while von Neumann was concerned with equilibrium thermodynamics, . . . recent work by Prigogine (1980) and others dealing with 'non equilibrium thermodynamics' may allow us to extend the scope of von Neumann's work by allowing for the emergence of order through fluctuations. The paradigm shift urged by Prigogine in his epistemologically oriented writings fits in well with the extended von Neumann type models, whereas the neoclassical equilibrium model rested on explicit and implicit analogies with the Newtonian model."

124 Hayles' (1991, p. 8) recent statement furnishes an interesting parallel to that of Chakravarty's in note 123 above. "Whereas the Newtonians focused on the clock as an appropriate image for the world, chaos theorists are apt to choose the waterfall. The clock is ordered, predictable, regular, and mechanically precise; the waterfall is turbulent, unpredictable, irregular, and infinitely varying in form. The change is not in how the world actually is – neither clocks nor waterfalls are anything new – but in how it is seen."

125 For descriptive theory, see, in particular, the work of Goodwin and his school – as in Goodwin (1990) and Ricci and Velupillai (1988) – and in the context of optimal growth theory, the work of Benhabib, Majumdar, Mitra, Nishimura, and others; see Majumdar and Mitra (1992), Nishimura and Yano (1992), and their references.

126 For a preliminary attempt at charting the multi-faceted nature of the concept of *market*, see Khan (1991).

127 See Chakravarty (1987a) and Chakravarty (1990) respectively.

128 See Chakravarty (1987d, p 137).

129 See Chakravarty (1987b, p. 4). Also Chakravarty (1987d; 1991, p. 16).

130 See Chakravarty (1991, p. 19).

131 See especially chapter 1 in Putnam (1991).

132   See the entry on strategy-proof allocation mechanisms in *The New Palgrave*.

133   In particular, Chakravarty (1991, p. 15, fn. 1) writes: "Efforts made by Hurwicz and others have been aimed at overcoming the Hayekian objections to any form of central planning through developing alternative designs of decision making which are incentive compatible and, to that extent, avoid some of the problems that attach to Lange's classical scheme defining a 'competitive socialist' system."

134   See Chakravarty (1987d, p. 133).

135   See Chakravarty (1987d, p. 136).

136   See Wan (1990). Professor Wan tells me that Chakravarty was in the process of working on a response to his comment but his illness and untimely death prevented him from completing it.

137   See Chakravarty (1987b, p. 3).

References

Selected work of S. Chakravarty

1959: *The Logic of Investment Planning*. Amsterdam: North-Holland. Also translated into Spanish in 1966.

1962a: Optimal savings with finite planning horizon. *International Economic Review*, 3, 338–55.

1962b: The existence of an optimum savings program. *Econometrica*, 30, 178–87.

1965: An optimizing planning model (co-author, L. Lefeber). *Economic Weekly*, 17, 237–52.

1966: Wages, employment and growth (co-author, L. Lefeber). *Kyklos*, 19, 602–19.

1967: Optimal programmes of capital accumulation in a two-sector model with non-shiftable capital. Working Paper 17A, Delhi School of Economics.

1968: Optimal growth when the instantaneous utility function depends upon the rate of change in consumption (co-author, A. S. Manne). *American Economic Review*, 58, 1351–4.

1969a: *Capital and Development Planning*. Cambridge, MA: MIT Press.

1969b: Some aspects of an optimal investment policy in an underdeveloped economy. In H. C. Bos (ed.), *Towards Balanced International Growth*, Amsterdam: North-Holland.

1969c: Contributions to Indian economic analysis: a survey (co-author, J. Bhagwati). *American Economic Review*, 59, Part 2, 1–73.

1973: Theory of development planning: an appraisal. In H. C. Bos, H.

Linnemann, and P. de Wolff (eds), *Economic Structure and Development: Essays in Honour of Jan Tinbergen*, Amsterdam: North-Holland.

1975: Mahalanobis and contemporary issues in development planning. *Sankhya, Series C*, 37, 1–11.

1982: *Alternative Approaches to a Theory of Economic Growth: Marx, Marshall and Schumpeter*. Calcutta: Orient Longman.

1984: Power structure and agricultural productivity. In Meghnad Desai, S. H. Rudolph and A. Rudra (eds), *Agrarian Power and Agricultural Productivity in South Asia*, New Delhi: Oxford University Press.

1987a: Marxist economics and contemporary developing economies. *Cambridge Journal of Economics*, 11, 3–22.

1987b: *Development Planning: The Indian Experience*. Oxford: Oxford University Press.

1987c: Entries on "Cost–benefit analysis," "P. C. Mahalanobis," "Optimal savings," and "Jan Tinbergen." In J. Eatwell, P. Newman and M. Milgate (eds), *The New Palgrave*, New York: Macmillan.

1987d: The state of development economics. *Manchester School of Economics and Social Studies*, 55, 125–43.

1989: John von Neumann's model of an expanding economy: an essay in interpretation. In M. Dore, S. Chakravarty and R. Goodwin (eds), *John von Neumann and Modern Economics*, Oxford: Oxford University Press.

1990: Development strategies for growth with equity: the South Asian experience. *Asian Development Review*, 8, 133–59.

1991: Development planning: a reappraisal. *Cambridge Journal of Economics*, 15, 5–20.

Other work

Arrow, K. J. 1968: Optimal capital policy with irreversible investment. In J. N. Wolfe (ed.), *Value, Capital and Growth*, Edinburgh: Edinburgh University Press.

—— and Kurtz, M. 1970: Optimal growth with irreversible investment in a Ramsey model. *Econometrica*, 38, 331–44.

Bardhan, P. K. 1970: *Economic Growth, Development and Foreign Trade*. New York: Wiley Interscience.

—— 1971: Optimum growth and allocation of foreign exchange. *Econometrica*, 39, 955–71.

Basu, K. 1984: *The Less Developed Economy: A Critique of Contemporary Theory*. Oxford: Blackwell.

Berlin, I. 1953: *The Hedgehog and the Fox*. New York: Simon & Schuster.

Bewley, T. F. 1972: Existence of equilibria in economies with infinitely many commodities. *Journal of Economic Theory*, 4, 514–40.

Bhagwati, J. N. 1971: The general theory of distortions and welfare. In J. N.

Bhagwati, R. W. Jones, R. Mundell and J. Vanek (eds), *Trade, Balance of Payments and Growth*, Amsterdam: North-Holland.

Bose, S. 1968: Optimal growth and investment allocation. *Review of Economic Studies*, 35, 465–80.

—— 1970: Optimal growth in a nonshiftable capital growth model. *Econometrica*, 38, 128–52.

Brown, D. J. and Lewis, L. M. 1981: Myopic economic agents. *Econometrica*, 49, 359–68.

Byres, T. J. 1987: Sukhamoy Chakravarty on Marxist economics and contemporary developing economies: some comments. *Cambridge Journal of Economics*, 11, 173–8.

Cass, D. 1973: On the Wicksellian point-input, point-output model of capital accumulation: a modern view (or neoclassicism slightly vindicated). *Journal of Political Economy*, 81, 71–97.

Caves, R. E. and Jones, R. W. 1985: *World Trade and Payments*. Boston, MA: Little, Brown.

Chandra, V. 1991: The informal sector in developing countries: a theoretical analysis. Unpublished PhD dissertation, Johns Hopkins University, Baltimore, MD.

—— and Ali Khan, M. 1991: Foreign investment in the presence of an informal sector. Johns Hopkins Working Paper 276; in *Economica*, forthcoming.

Chao, C. and Yu, E. S. H. 1992: Capital markets, urban unemployment and land. *Journal of Development Economics*, 38, 407–13.

Chaudhuri, T. D. 1989: A theoretical analysis of the informal sector. *World Development*, 17, 351–5.

Chipman, J. 1972: The theory of exploitative trade and investment policies: a reformulation and synthesis. In L. E. Di Marco (ed.), *International Economics and Development*, New York: Academic Press.

Corden, W. M. and Findlay, R. 1975: Urban unemployment, intersectoral capital mobility and development policy. *Economica*, 62, 59–78.

Dasgupta, A. K. 1985: *Epochs of Economic Theory*. Oxford: Blackwell.

Dasgupta, P. 1969: Optimum growth when capital is non-transferable. *Review of Economic Studies*, 36, 77–88.

Debreu, G. 1976: Regular differentiable economies. *American Economic Review*, 66, 280–7.

Dierker, E. 1972: Two remarks on the number of equilibria of an economy. *Econometrica*, 40, 951–3.

Dixit, A. 1968: Optimal development in the labour surplus economy. *Review of Economic Studies*, 35, 23–34.

Fel'dman, G. A. 1928: K. teorii tempov narodnogo dokhoda. *Planavoe Khoziaistvo*, 146–70. English translation: On the theory of growth rates of national income, in N. Spulber (ed.), *Foundations of Soviet Strategy for Economic Growth*, Bloomington, IN: Indiana University Press, 1964.

Fields, G. S. 1975: Rural–urban migration, urban unemployment and underemployment, and job-search activity in LDCs. *Journal of Development Economics*, 2, 165–87.

—— 1989: On-the-job search in a labor market model. *Journal of Development Economics*, 30, 159–78.

Findlay, R. 1978: An Austrian model of international trade and interest rate equalization. *Journal of Political Economy*, 86, 989–1007.

Goodwin, R. M. 1990: *Chaotic Economic Dynamics*. Oxford: Oxford University Press.

Gorman, W. M. 1976: Tricks with utility functions. In M. Artis and A. Nobay (eds), *Essays in Economic Analysis*, Cambridge: Cambridge University Press.

Grinols, Earl L. 1991: Unemployment and foreign capital: the relative opportunity costs of domestic labor and welfare. *Economica*, 57, 107–22.

Gruen, F. H. and Corden, W. M. 1970: A tariff that worsens the terms of trade. In I. A. McDougall and R. H. Snape (eds), *Studies in International Economics*, Amsterdam: North-Holland.

Gupta, M. R. 1991: Rural urban migration, informal sector and development policies: a theoretical analysis. *Journal of Development Economics*, forthcoming.

Harberger, A. C. 1972: *Project Evaluation: Collected Papers*. Chicago, IL: Markham Publishing.

Harcourt, G. and Singh, A. 1991: Sukhamoy Chakravarty, 26 July 1934–22 August 1990. *Cambridge Journal of Economics*, 15, 1–3.

Harris, J. R. and Todaro, M. 1970: Migration, unemployment and development: a two sector analysis. *American Economic Review*, 60, 126–42.

Hatta, T. 1977a: A recommendation for a better tariff structure. *Econometrica*, 45, 1859–65.

—— 1977b: A theory of piecemeal policy recommendations. *Review of Economic Studies*, 44, 1–21.

Hayek, F. A. 1975: *New Studies in Philosophy, Politics, Economics and the History of Ideas*, Chicago, IL: University of Chicago Press.

Hayles, N. K. 1991: *Chaos and Order: Complex Dynamics in Literature and Science*. Chicago, IL: University of Chicago Press.

Hirsch, M. W. and Smale, S. 1974: *Differential Equations, Dynamical Systems and Linear Algebra*. New York: Academic Press.

Ikemoto, K. 1969: Specific factors of production and the comparative costs theory. *Kobe University Economic Review*, 15, 23–32.

Johansen, L. 1967: Some theoretical properties of a two-sector model of optimal growth. *Review of Economic Studies*, 34, 125–41.

Johnson, H. G. 1971: *The Two-Sector Model of General Equilibrium*, Yrjö Jahnsson Lectures. Chicago, IL: Aldine-Atherton.

Jones, R. W. 1965: The structure of simple general equilibrium models. *Journal of Political Economy*, 73, 557–72.

—— 1971: A three factor model in theory, trade and history. In J. Bhagwati, R. W. Jones, R. Mundell and J. Vanek (eds), *Trade, Balance of Payments and Growth*, Amsterdam: North-Holland.

—— 1975: Income distribution and effective protection in a multi-commodity trade model. *Journal of Economic Theory*, 11, 1–15.

Khan, M. Ali 1980: Dynamic stability, wage subsidies and the generalized Harris–Todaro model. *Pakistan Development Review*, 19, 1–24.

—— 1982: Social opportunity costs and immiserizing growth: some observations on the long run versus the short. *Quarterly Journal of Economics*, 97, 353–62.

—— 1987: Harris–Todaro model. In J. Eatwell, P. Newman and M. Milgate (eds), *The New Palgrave*, New York: Macmillan.

—— 1991: On the languages of markets, Paper presented at the 7th Meeting of the PSDE, *Pakistan Development Review*, 30, 503–49.

—— and Naqvi, S. N. H. 1983: Capital markets and urban unemployment. *Journal of International Economics*, 15, 367–85.

Klammer, A. 1989: A conversation with Amartya Sen. *Journal of Economic Perspectives*, 3, 135–50.

Krauss and Johnson 1974: *General Equilibrium Analysis*, Chicago, IL: Aldine.

Kurz, M. 1965: Optimal paths of capital accumulation under the minimum time objective. *Econometrica*, 33, 42–66.

Mahalanobis, P. C. 1953: Some observations on the process of growth of national income. *Sankhya*, 12, 307–12.

—— 1955: The approach of operational research to planning in India. *Sankhya*, 16, 3–130.

Majumdar, D. 1976: The urban informal sector. *World Development*, 4, 655–79.

Majumdar, M. and Mitra, T. 1992: Periodic and chaotic programs of optimal intertemporal allocation in an aggregative model with wealth effects. *Economic Theory*, forthcoming.

Malinvaud, E. 1953: Capital accumulation and efficient allocation of resources. *Econometrica*, 21, 233–68. Corrigendum in *Econometrica*, 30, 570–3.

Marjit, S. 1990a: A simple production model in trade and its applications. *Economics Letters*, 32, 257–60.

—— 1990b: Terms of trade, capital mobility and welfare. In B. Dutta, S. Gangopadhyay, D. Mookherjee, and D. Ray (eds), *Essays on Economic Theory and Policy*, Oxford: Oxford University Press.

Marshall, A. 1879: *The Pure Theory of Foreign Trade*, privately published.

Merton, R. K. 1972: Insiders and outsiders: a chapter in the sociology of knowledge. *American Journal of Sociology*, 77, 9–47.

Neary, J. P. 1978: Dynamic stability and the theory of factor market distortions. *American Economic Review*, 68, 672–82.

—— 1981: On the Harris–Todaro model with intersectoral capital mobility. *Economica*, 48, 219–34.

Newman, P. K. 1962: Production of commodities by means of commodities. *Schweizerische Zeitschrift für Volkswirtschaft und Statistik*, 98, 58–75.

Nishimura, K. and Yano, M. 1992: Non-linear dynamics and chaos in optimal growth. *Economic Theory*, forthcoming.

Panchamukhi, V. R. 1990: Professor Sukhamoy Chakravarty: a tribute. *IASSI Quarterly*, 9, 196–9.

Pencavel, J. 1991: Prospects for economics. *Economic Journal*, 101, 81–7.

Pindyck, R. S. 1991: Irreversibility, uncertainty and investment. *Journal of Economic Literature*, 29, 1110–48.

Portes, A., Castells, M. and Benton, L. A. 1989: *The Informal Economy: Studies in Advanced and Less Developed Countries*. Baltimore, MD: Johns Hopkins University Press.

Putnam, H. 1991: *Realism with a Human Face*, Cambridge, MA: Harvard University Press.

Raj, K. N. and Sen, A. K. 1961: Alternative patterns of growth under conditions of stagnant export earnings. *Oxford Economic Papers*, 13, 43–52.

Ricci, G. and Velupillai, K. 1988: *Growth Cycles and Multisectoral Economics: the Goodwin Tradition*, Lecture Notes 309. Berlin: Springer.

Ryder, H. 1968: Optimal accumulation in a two-sector neo-classical economy with non-shiftable capital. *Journal of Political Economy*, 76, 655–83.

Samuelson, P. A. 1969: Foreword. In S. Chakravarty, *Capital and Development Planning*, Cambridge, MA: MIT Press.

—— 1953: Prices of factors and goods in general equilibrium. *Review of Economic Studies*, 21, 1–20.

—— 1971: Ohlin was right. *Scandinavian Journal of Economics*, 73, 365–84.

—— 1987: Sraffian economics. In J. Eatwell, P. Newman and and M. Milgate (eds), *The New Palgrave*, New York: Macmillan.

Solow, R. M. 1956: A contribution to the theory of economic growth. *Quarterly Journal of Economics*, 70, 65–94.

—— 1962: Substitution and fixed proportions in the theory of capital. *Review of Economic Studies*, 29, 207–18.

Srinivasan, T. N. 1962: Investment criteria and choice of techniques of production. *Yale Economic Essays* 2, Spring, 59–115.

—— 1965: A critique of the optimizing planning model. *Economic Weekly*, 17, 255–64.

—— and Bhagwati, J. N. 1978: Shadow prices for project selection in the presence of distortions: effective rates of protection and domestic resource costs. *Journal of Political Economy*, 86, 97–116.

Stiglitz, J. E. 1970: The badly behaved economy with the well behaved production function. Cowles Foundation Discussion Paper 303. Published in J. A. Mirrlees and N. H. Stern (eds), *Models of Economic Growth*, New York: Wiley, 1973, chs 6 and 7.

—— 1977: Some further remarks on cost–benefit analysis. In H. Schwartz and R. Berney (eds), *Project Evaluation*, Washington, DC: Inter-American Development Bank.

—— 1982: The structure of labor markets and shadow prices in LDCs. In R. H. Sabot (ed.), *Migration and the Labor Market in Developing Countries*, Boulder, CO: Westview Press.

Walras, L. 1874: *Elements of Pure Economics*, translated by W. Jaffé. London: Allen & Unwin, 1954.

Wan, Jr, H. 1988: Nipponized Confucian ethos or incentive-compatible institutional design. *International Economic Journal*, 2, 101–8.

—— 1990: Comments on Chakravarty's "Marxist economics and contemporary developing economies." *Cambridge Journal of Economics*, 14, 233–9.

Weitzman, M. 1971: Shiftable versus non-shiftable capital: a synthesis. *Econometrica*, 39, 511–29.

Whitaker, J. K. 1987: Marshall, Alfred. In J. Eatwell, P. Newman and M. Milgate (eds), *The New Palgrave*, New York: Macmillan.

8

Efficiency wage theory with monopolistic landlords

Kaushik Basu

1 Introduction

The efficiency wage theory of Leibenstein (1957) has had a large revival of interest since the mid-1970s.[1] The *basic axiom* behind this model is that the productivity of a worker depends positively on the level of consumption of the worker. This is formalized by assuming that output from a landlord's plot of land depends not on labor *hours* that go into it but on the number of *efficiency units* of labor that go in. And the number of efficiency units produced by a laborer depends on the wage rate that he or she receives. This axiom allows us to explain the existence of open unemployment in equilibrium.

Somewhat surprisingly the entire literature that has grown around this theme models labor markets in competitive terms. This is surprising because in most other studies of rural markets in backward economies the monopolistic power of the landlord is a constant theme.[2] The purpose of this chapter is to rectify at least a part of this anomaly by building a model of a labor market characterized by the basic axiom described above but with a single landlord, who is aware that he confronts an upward-sloping supply curve. My aim is not just to characterize the equilibrium of such a model but to explore the possibility of explaining "surplus labor." A labor market with no open unemployment is described as having *surplus labor* if the withdrawal of some of the laborers does not cause a fall in output. It can be shown (see Basu, 1984) that in the traditional

Leibenstein-type model of efficiency wage surplus labor cannot occur. It will be shown here that once we allow landlords to have monopoly (or, to use more traditional terminology, monopsony) power in the labor market, the existence of surplus labor can no longer be ruled out.

The monopoly model discussed in this chapter is of interest not only because it plugs a gap in the existing literature but also in the light of some recent developments in the literature. Let me explain.

When one first becomes familiar with the Leibenstein-type models, one feels some *empirical* discomfort with the basic axiom. It seems unrealistic to suppose that employers consciously pay higher wages to workers just so that they will be more fit to work. This skepticism, however, is difficult to reconcile with the view that the basic axiom must be true for sufficiently poor countries because, after all, if the wage is *sufficiently* low, a worker's productivity will be zero because he or she will be unable to do any work. But as one reflects on the matter it becomes clear that the problem is not with the basic axiom but with the fact that in the existing literature the basic axiom has almost invariably been used in implicit conjunction with what I described in Basu (1992) as the "perception axiom."

The *perception axiom* says that the basic axiom, i.e. the positive relation between wage and worker productivity, is perceived by each individual landlord (cum employer). There are good reasons to suppose that in many a competitive market even though the basic axiom may be true at the level of the aggregate labor market the perception axiom is false. This is so in the same sense that in models of perfectly competitive industry we assume that the aggregate demand curve is downward sloping but single firms do not perceive this and they behave like price-takers.

There are many reasons why this may be so in the Leibenstein-type framework. Recent studies have shown (for a survey see Osmani, 1991) that although consumption does influence productivity there may be quite a substantial time lag involved in this relation. Hence if there is some turnover in the labor market a landlord may not be able to fully capture from his workers the effect of the wage *he* pays. In the most extreme case of a casual labor market which is by no means negligible in reality (for a discussion of some evidence, see Drèze and Mukherjee, 1989), the productivity of workers will depend on the average wage prevailing in the market and not on a single landlord's wage because workers keep moving from employer to employer.

Table 8.1 A taxonomy of efficiency wage models

		Basic axiom	
		True	False
Perception axiom	True	Leibenstein-type models	/////////
	False		Traditional labor market models

Once we grant that the perception axiom may or may not be valid we get a scheme of possible models as illustrated in table 8.1. In traditional labor market models, there is no relation between wage and productivity and nor is any such relation perceived by individual employers. So the traditional models belong to the bottom right-hand slot. The possibility that there is no relation between wage and productivity but employers believe that there is such a relation is quite unrealistic, and so that square is shaded and disregarded. Virtually the entire literature that uses the Leibensteinian basic axiom also assumes that the perception axiom is true. Hence, works like those of Leibenstein (1957), Mirrlees (1975) and Stiglitz (1976) belong to the top left-hand corner. Note that these models are also of competitive labor markets. The category that is most natural for competitive labor markets but seems to have been ignored is the bottom left-hand corner. I tried to examine this systematically in Basu (1992). Guha's (1989) paper also belongs to this category. It is now known that it is in this slot that surplus labor can arise.

If we move away from the competitive assumption and instead consider a single landlord, clearly the validity of the perception axiom is natural. So in this chapter I want to investigate the top left-hand box but under monopolistic conditions. This turns out to be a very interesting set-up because in it one can find parametric conditions for explaining open unemployment and also for explaining surplus labor.

Section 2 sketches the model, characterizes the equilibrium and demonstrates the possibility of open unemployment in equilibrium. Section 3 shows how within a large parametric class of models surplus labor cannot exist, but also that there are conditions under which it does exist. Section 4 consists of brief concluding observations.

2 The model

Let w be the hourly wage rate and h the number of efficiency units produced in one hour by one laborer. It will be assumed that h depends on w:

$$h = h(w) \tag{8.1}$$

In addition, for all $w \le a$, $h(w) = 0$; for all $w > a$, $h'(w) > 0$, $h''(w) < 0$; and $h(w)$ is bounded from above. Figure 8.1 illustrates equation (8.1). The wage which minimizes $w/h(w)$ is called the *efficiency wage*. Note that $w/h(w)$ is the cost of each efficiency unit when the wage is set at w. Therefore the efficiency wage is that wage which minimizes the cost of efficiency units. If such a wage is feasible, an employer would like to hire labor at that wage. This would be so even if at that wage there was an excess supply of labor and, hence, open unemployment. Figure 8.1 illustrates the efficiency wage w^*. Note that w^* is defined implicitly by

$$\frac{h(w^*)}{w^*} = h'(w^*) \tag{8.2}$$

We are considering here a rural economy with a monopsonist landlord. That is, he is the sole employer of labor. His production function is

$$X = f[nh(w)] \tag{8.3}$$

where n is the number of labor hours employed by him and w is the wage paid. We assume $f(0) = 0$, $f' > 0$, $f'' < 0$.

The rural economy has t laborers. Each laborer supplies s hours of labor, depending on the wage being offered:

$$s = s(w) \tag{8.4}$$

We assume $s' > 0$.

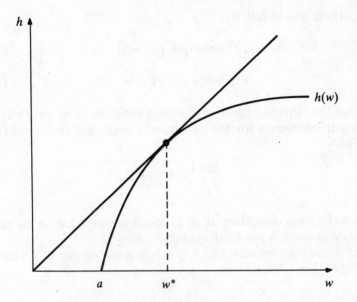

Figure 8.1 The wage–efficiency relation.

Assuming the product price to be fixed and, without loss of generality, equal to 1, the landlord's profit is given by

$$R(n, w) \equiv f[nh(w)] - nw$$

The landlord's problem is as follows:

$$\begin{aligned} &\max\ R(n, w) \\ &\text{subject to } n \leq ts(w) \end{aligned} \tag{8.5}$$

Let the solution of this problem be $(\bar{n}, \bar{w})$. Note that the solution is a function of t. So the effect of changing the size of the labor force on wages and employment can also be analyzed. When we do such an analysis, I shall write $(\bar{n}(t), \bar{w}(t))$, instead of $(\bar{n}, \bar{w})$, to make it clear that these values do depend on t.

In solving the landlord's maximization problem first ignore the constraint and work out the first-order conditions for the maximization. These are as follows:

$$f'[nh(w)]nh'(w) = n \qquad (8.6)$$

$$f'[nh(w)]h(w) = w \qquad (8.7)$$

Since the objective function is strictly concave, (8.6) and (8.7) are sufficient conditions for the optimum. Check that (8.6) and (8.7) imply

$$\frac{h(w)}{w} = h'(w)$$

This is the same condition as (8.2) and it implies that, if the labor supply condition is not binding, then $\bar{w} = w^*$.

Let n^* be the solution of (8.7) when wage equals w^*. That is, $f'[n^*h(w^*)] = w^*/h(w^*)$, or

$$n^* = f'^{-1}\left[\frac{w^*}{h(w^*)}\right]\frac{1}{h(w^*)} \qquad (8.8)$$

Hence what we have established is that, if $n^* \leq ts(w^*)$, then $\bar{w} = w^*$ and $\bar{n} = n^*$. In this case we have open unemployment equal to $ts(w^*) - n^*$ in equilibrium. This equilibrium is similar to what happens in the competitive case. The interesting case in analyzing a monopsonist landlord's equilibrium arises when $n^* > ts(w^*)$, i.e. when the demand for labor at the efficiency wage exceeds the supply at that wage.

Before analyzing this case it is useful to form a geometric charactization of what happens in the competitive case. I follow the analysis in Basu (1984). Suppose the employer is a wage-taker, i.e. he cannot pay wages below a given wage $\underline{w}$. Then his problem is as follows:

$$\max R(n, w)$$
$$\text{subject to } w \geq \underline{w}$$

Let the solution to this be $n(\underline{w})$, $w(\underline{w})$. Figure 8.2 shows $n(\underline{w})$.

It is easy to check from the first-order condition that, if $\underline{w}$ is above w^*, then as $\underline{w}$ rises $n(\underline{w})$ falls. If $\underline{w} < w^*$, then $n(\underline{w}) = n(w^*)$. Note also that $n(w^*) = n^*$, and if $\underline{w} > w^*$ then $n(\underline{w}) = \underline{w}$.

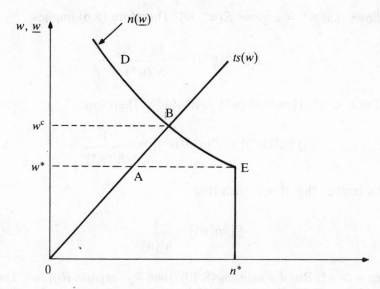

Figure 8.2 The competitive equilibrium.

Superimpose on this graph the supply curve of labor, $ts(w)$, with w, $\underline{w}$ on the vertical axis. We are now considering the case where $n^* > ts(w^*)$ and this is exactly what happens in the case illustrated in figure 8.2. It will be seen that in the monopolistic case being discussed in this chapter the equilibrium wage–employment pair, i.e. $(\bar{w}, \bar{n})$, will lie somewhere between A and B. In other words the equilibrium wage will be somewhere between the competitive wage w^c and the efficiency wage w^*.

To see this, note that the graph of $(w, \text{argmax}_n R(n, w))$ coincides with DBE in figure 8.2 and then continues as a downward-sloping line after point E. Since R is strictly concave in n, it follows that the solution of (8.5) must lie somewhere on 0BD. It is also easy to see that profit rises as we move along the "demand" curve from D towards B. Next, let us check the following:

$$[n < n^*] \rightarrow [\underset{w}{\text{argmax}}\ R(n, w) > w^*] \qquad (8.9)$$

To prove (8.9), observe that, since $(n^*, w^*) = \text{argmax}\ R(n, w)$, it follows that $w^* = \text{argmax } R(n^*, w)$. Therefore (8.6) implies

$$f'[n^*h(w^*)] = \frac{1}{h'(w^*)}$$

Let $n < n^*$. Hence $nh(w^*) < n^*h(w^*)$. Therefore

$$f'[nh(w^*)] > f'[n^*h(w^*)] = \frac{1}{h'(w^*)}$$

This implies that if w is such that

$$f'[nh(w)] = \frac{1}{h'(w)} \tag{8.10}$$

then $w > w^*$. But if $\bar{w}$ satisfies (8.10), then $\bar{w} = \text{argmax } R(n, w)$. This establishes (8.9). Equation (8.9) implies that the solution to (8.5) cannot be on 0A, because for every point on 0A there exists a point

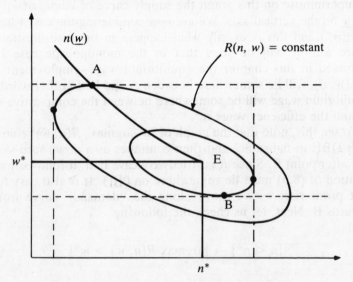

Figure 8.3 The monopolist's iso-profit curve.

vertically above it (and also above the line w^*A) which is better than the point on 0A from the landlord's point of view. This establishes that the wage–employment equilibrium in the case illustrated in figure 8.2 (i.e. where E is to the right of A) is always on the supply curve, somewhere above the efficiency wage w^* and below the competitive wage w^c.

To aid intuition it is useful to draw the monopolist's iso-profit curves in the wage–employment space. This is illustrated in figure 8.3. The iso-profit curves are elliptical lines. The highest profit "curve" is the point E. For any $w > w^*$ the best n (i.e. the point of tangency) is to the left of E, as shown by point A. If $w < w^*$ the best n is to the right of E, as shown by B. If n is fixed below n^*, the best w is above E. If $n > n^*$, the best w is below E.

3 Surplus labor

As mentioned above, an important area of investigation in classical development economics which has seen some recent revival of interest is surplus labor. An economy is said to be characterized by *surplus labor* if an outmigration of a part of the labor force results in no drop in output. As mentioned in the introduction, the traditional Leibenstein model cannot explain surplus labor but, if we do away with the perception axiom while retaining other features of the Leibenstein framework, surplus labor becomes a possibility. What I wish to investigate here is the existence of surplus labor in a monopoly-landlord model such as discussed here. It is first shown that within a fairly large class of reasonable parametric specifications surplus labor cannot exist. Nevertheless, there exist cases outside this class where surplus labor can occur. Let us first consider the class of supply curves given by

$$s = s(w) = Aw^\alpha \qquad \alpha > 0 \qquad (8.11)$$

Note that (8.11) admits a very large class of supply functions which include the linear case ($\alpha = 1$) and also allows for both convex ($\alpha > 1$) and concave ($\alpha < 1$) functions. It will be shown that within this class surplus labor cannot occur.

To check for surplus labor we have to focus on the case where there is no open unemployment. Hence we are considering a case where the labor supply constraint is binding on the landlord. Therefore the landlord's problem (8.5) reduces to

$$\max f[ts(w)h(w)] - ts(w)w$$

The first-order condition yields

$$f'[ts(w)h(w)] = \frac{ws'(w) + s(w)}{h(w)s'(w) + h'(w)s(w)} \qquad (8.12)$$

By using (8.11) this reduces to

$$f'[ts(w)h(w)] = \frac{\alpha + 1}{\alpha h(w)/w + h'(w)} \qquad (8.13)$$

Now, if t falls, then f' rises, since $f'' < 0$. To restore the equality in (8.13) w will have to be raised because, as w rises, $s(w)$ and $h(w)$ rise, $h'(w)$ falls and $h(w)/w$ falls, since in the absence of open unemployment w exceeds w^* as seen in the previous section.

Hence, after t falls, the equality (8.13) is restored at a higher level of f'. But a rise in f' implies a fall in its argument which, in turn, implies a fall in f. Thus output necessarily falls. So in this case there is no surplus labor: an outmigration of labor (i.e. a fall in t) always results in a fall in production.

What is interesting to note, however, is that there are cases outside (8.11) where a withdrawal of the labor force can raise output. To see this, let me describe the right-hand expression of (8.12) as $g(w)$. Note that

$$g(w) \equiv \frac{w + s(w)/s'(w)}{h(w) + h'(w)s(w)/s'(w)}$$

Suppose $s(w)$ is such that there exists $w' < w''$ such that $s(w'')/s'(w'') = 0$ and, as w goes from w'' towards w', $s(w)/s'(w) \to \infty$. Hence, as w goes from w'' to w', $g(w)$ goes from $w/h(w)$ towards $1/h'(w)$. If we are operating on a domain above w^* (as we must be since open unemployment is assumed to be zero in this section), i.e. $w^* < w'$, then note that $w/h(w) < 1/h'(w)$. Hence as w goes from w'' to w', $g(w)$ rises. Hence $g(w)$ can indeed be a downward-sloping curve. Clearly, we can choose different specifications of $s(w)$ to make the gradient of $g(w)$ of any order over a small region. It is therefore possible that, as f falls and f' rises, the equality in (8.12) can be restored by raising w so much that f' is lower than in the original equilibrium. But a lower f' means a higher f and this establishes the existence of surplus labor.

4 Conclusion

Although the literature on rural markets is replete with references to the "power" of the landlord and the relative lack of options for the poor laborers, it has been common in the efficiency wage literature following Leibenstein to assume that landlords in the labor market are perfectly competitive. The purpose of this chapter was to remove this anomaly and to model a labor market in which a laborer's efficiency depends on wages, but allowing for monopsony powers on the part of the landlord. In other words we model a case where a single landlord operates taking into account the fact that the supply curve of labor is (generally) upward sloping.

The equilibrium in such a model was characterized. It was shown that open unemployment can occur in equilibrium. The case where there is no open unemployment was then examined in some detail. It was shown that, despite there being no open unemployment, the labor market can in special cases have surplus labor. In this monopoly-landlord model, the question of rejecting the perception axiom discussed in section 1 does not really arise. Hence the result demonstrates that surplus labor can be explained even without having to reject the perception axiom as long as we recognize the market power of employers in backward rural economies.

Notes

A few references from a large literature are as follows: Mirrlees (1975), Stiglitz (1976), Bliss and Stern (1978), Agarwala (1979), Dasgupta and Ray (1986), Guha (1989), Basu (1992).
For a survey of such studies, see Basu (1990).

References

Agarwala, N. 1979: On Leibenstein's theory of disguised unemployment. *Indian Economic Review*, 14, 29–40.

Basu, K. 1984: *The Less Developed Economy: A Critique of Contemporary Theory*. Oxford: Blackwell.

—— 1990: *Agrarian Structure and Economic Underdevelopment*. Chichester: Harwood Academic.

—— 1992: The broth and the cooks: a theory of surplus labour. *World Development*, 20, 109–18.

Bliss, C. and Stern, N. 1978: Productivity, wages and nutrition. *Journal of Development Economics*, 5, 363–98.

Dasgupta, P. and Ray, D. 1986: Inequality as a determinant of malnutrition and unemployment. *Economic Journal*, 96, 1011–34.

Drèze, J. P. and Mukherjee, A. 1989: Labour contracts in rural India: theory and evidence. In S. Chakravarty (ed.), *The Balance between Industry and Agriculture in Economic Development*, London: Macmillan.

Guha, A. 1989: Consumption, efficiency and surplus labour. *Journal of Development Economics*, 31, 1–12.

Leibenstein, H. 1957: Underemployment in backward economies. *Journal of Political Economy*, 65, 91–103.

Mirrlees, J. 1975: Pure theory of underdeveloped economies. In L. G. Reynolds (ed.), *Agriculture in Development Theory*, New Haven, CT: Yale University Press.

Osmani, S. R. 1991: Nutrition and economics of food. In J. P. Drèze and A. Sen (eds), *The Political Economy of Hunger*, vol. I, Oxford: Clarendon Press.

Stiglitz, J. 1976: The efficiency wage hypothesis, surplus labour and the distribution of labour in LDCs. *Oxford Economic Papers*, 28, 185–207.

PART III

Markets, capitalism, and socialism

9

Optimal redistribution

Jan Tinbergen

Sukhamoy Chakravarty was one of my best students, if not the best. His scientific work done after he obtained his PhD degree and his career have shown this. His death was a sad shock to his many friends, of whom I was one. I am happy that this book is meant to honor Sukhamoy.

I am sure that the subject I choose to deal with would have interested him. By "optimal redistribution" I mean the degree of income redistribution – by taxes, social security systems and government expenditures – that maximizes national welfare. Sukhamoy's intensive work on planning certainly also showed his interest for this feature of future society (Chakravarty, 1987, p. 88).

Whether he would have agreed with my treatment we shall never know. He would certainly have liked an attempt to express my treatment in simple language so as to make it understandable to as many people as possible.

The program may be considered for single countries as well as for the world at large. The model to be used will be as simple as possible. Redistribution requires the presence of at least two groups of people. Within a nation these two groups typically are capital owners and workers, where capital includes land as well as human capital. Land will be the most important component in a feudal nation, and physical or human capital in more developed countries. For the world at large the two groups are the developed and less developed countries.

In the present phase of world history and politics the problem is of crucial importance. The important part of the world that in 1980 had a communist regime around 1985 revolted against that regime, after having at least forty years of experience. The regime was the extremely left version of socialism, of which also more rightist versions existed, in particular democratic socialism in Western Europe, Australia and Canada. Together with the United States of America these countries were called *social market economies* or *mixed economies*, since they combine "capitalist" or market features with "socialist" or interventionist features.

The revolt was introduced by Mikhail Gorbachev in 1985 who, as the Secretary-General of the Communist Party of the Soviety Union, admitted what the American economist Abram Bergson had stated in 1971 and further elaborated in subsequent years: productivity of labor, after correction for differences in capital per worker, was 25 to 34 percent lower than in the United States (Bergson, 1987).

In a way Gorbachev's statement seemed to constitute the victory of capitalism over socialism; or of a system of free markets (*laissez-faire*) over planning. But here a more careful analysis is needed. Precise definitions are required. Capitalism is the system prevailing in England around 1850, the time when Karl Marx lived and wrote. present-day England or any developed Western country (including Japan) is not capitalist but a mixture between capitalism (free markets) and socialism (intervention of public authorities). The concept of free markets also needs a more precise definition. Markets must be subdivided into *stable* and *unstable* markets. Unstable markets are not tending to an equilibrium and therefore need regulation. There are two types of unstable markets: raw material (in particular agrarian) markets and markets of industrial products of which the production requires high fixed costs. Unstable markets of raw materials tend to price and quantity cycles (pigs, coffee). High fixed costs imply that marginal costs are lower than average costs. Free competition leads to prices equal to marginal costs and will therefore lead to permanent losses. The latter will force producers to create a monopoly by a cartel or a trust.

Both types of unstable markets should not be left free but *require regulation*, either by a commodity agreement or by antitrust legislation. In addition to these consequences of free markets the stable free markets lead to a highly unequal income distribution. This too leads to government intervention in the income distribution by social security systems. All Western countries established, after 1850, legal protection against the worst aspects of income inequality. Prohibition of child labor, protection against dangerous work, unemployment, illness, accidents were some of these social security systems.

The previously communist-ruled countries are now advised to introduce market economies. The market economies to be created should not be pure capitalism or *laissez-faire*, however, but the mixed form of market economies that grew out of capitalism between 1850 and 1950 (as an average). The main problem they have to solve before or during that transformation is *the degree of redistribution* to introduce. That indeed is the subject of discussion that remained in the mixed economies. Additional subjects of discussion are the new challenges that society was confronted with after the discussions Marx had introduced. Two important new problems are those of the environment and those of sustainability. Mankind must take care that the environment is not polluted and that present generations are not using resources that must be left to later generations.

These new problems, although very important, will not be dealt with in this chapter. The reader should refer to other publications for help in solving them (Tinbergen, 1990a, b; Tinbergen and Hueting, 1991).

The problem here is to find the *rate of redistribution* that maximizes the total welfare of the two groups of people considered. Their numbers, their incomes per capita and the transfers from one group to the other are the phenomena ("variables" in mathematical language) that enter into the model. Two relationships are also used, namely the production function and the welfare function. The former indicates how much product is obtained from the employment of the two groups of people. In the optimal situation all are employed. The incomes earned are equal to the marginal product obtained. The other relationship indicates how welfare depends on income and employment. Income can be used for consumption and investment and both contribute to – mainly – satisfaction of consumption. Employment also, negatively or positively, contributes to welfare. Both relationships have been the object of economic research and provide us with useful information.

A standard method is used to find the "equations" (mathematical language for relations) between the variables that must exist in order to maximize total welfare. The method is known as the Lagrange method. There are as many equations as there are variables (among which are the Lagrange "multipliers"). The values of all variables can be determined. Some of the equations are very complicated. Fortunately, as a consequence of our being interested only in the degree of redistribution, we need not solve the whole system, but only a relatively simple group of equations. The complicated part is needed only to find an uninteresting coefficient appearing in the production function.

Two production functions have been used in order to obtain a variety of alternatives: the Cobb–Douglas function and the constant elasticity of substitution function, both for a number of values of the coefficients. The results are shown in table 9.1.

The intervals found for the two production functions partly overlap. From table 9.1 we conclude that the optimal rate of redistribution is situated between 0.08 and 0.15. The value 0 found for $\rho = -1$ applies to a case where the incomes need no redistribution since they are equal. An additional piece of research shows that the probability that the incomes are equal is lower the larger the number of groups of people considered, and tends towards zero if that number grows without limit. This justifies our elimination of the value zero for optimal redistribution.

Figures about the *actual rate of redistribution* in a large number of countries have been published by the International Labour Office (Geneva) (ILO) in the World Labor Report (1984, pp. 210–13). These figures are not exactly identical to our concept of redistribution. They constitute the benefits of public social security schemes as a percentage of the gross domestic product (i.e. gross national income). This means that private charity and advantages from public subsidies are not included. Table 9.2 shows some of the maximum and minimum figures of each continent as well as the figures for large countries in 1977 or the last year available to the ILO.

Some interesting conclusions may be derived from the two tables. Neglecting the differences between the redistribution rates as defined in the tables we find that all *developed* countries show redistribution rates in the optimal range from 8 to 15 percent or beyond it. Several Western European countries, even Italy, are beyond the optimal rate; and Hungary as well. My interpretation of this fact is that, in addition to an *optimality* target, these countries give some weight to an *equity* target. My definition of equity is equality of welfare, which does not necessarily mean equality of incomes. Part of welfare is derived from the (positive or negative) satisfaction from

Table 9.1 Absolute values of optimal redistribution rates

Production function	Cobb–Douglas		
Values of coefficients	$v = 0.75$	0.71	0.60
Redistribution rates	0.15	0.15	0.09

Production function	Constant elasticity of substitution							
Values of coefficients	$\varsigma = -2$	-1	0	$+1$	$+2$	$+3$	$+4$	8
Redistribution rates	0.08	0	0.08	0.09756	0.09973	0.09997	0.09999	0.10

Table 9.2 Redistribution rates of selected countries around 1977

Continental extremes		Large countries	
		Underdeveloped	Developed
Africa minimum, Rwanda	0.2		
Africa maximum, Mauritius	5.9	Brazil 5.3	United States 12.4
Latin America minimum, Haiti	0.7	Kenya 1.6	Australia 13.6
Latin America maximum, Chile	9.4	India 2.4	France 24.7
Asia minimum, Bangladesh	0.3		Italy 20.5
Asia maximum, Japan	10.3	*Ex-Communist*	United Kingdom 17.1
Europe minimum, Turkey	3.3	Minimum, USSR 13.4	Germany, FR 23.0
Europe maximum, Sweden	29.9	Maximum, Hungary 16.4	

employment. In this choice Sweden is the champion (followed by the other Scandinavian countries and the Netherlands).

Although within the optimality range, the United States show clearly less interest in equality as I define it; and so do Australia and the Soviet Union.

The *developing* countries – with the remarkable exception of Chile! – are all below the optimal range and some even considerably. A useful *condition* to impose on development assistance evidently consists of a higher rate of redistribution. The argument in favor of such a low rate of redistribution is that the relatively rich people in developing nations could use part of their income for the financing of investments and so *intensify development*. A tax on luxury goods may induce the relatively rich to behave that way and save enough. Alternatively, income saved may be tax exempt.

References

Bergson, A. 1987: Comparative productivity: the USSR, Eastern Europe, and the West. *American Economic Review*, 77, 342–57.

Chakravarty, S. 1987: *Development Planning. The Indian Experience.* Oxford: Clarendon Press.

Tinbergen, J. 1990a: Zuinig aan met energie (Save energy). *NRC/Handelsblad*, June 22, p. 8.

—— 1990b: Energieverbruik en nageslacht (Energy consumption and later generations). *NRC/Handelsblad*, August 17, p. 7.

—— and Hueting, R. 1991: Wrong signals for sustainable economic success that mask environment destruction. Forthcoming.

10

Economics of market socialism and the issue of public enterprise reform in India

Pranab Bardhan

The set of presuppositions which equated a "market system" with "capitalism" and "socialism" with "central planning" needs critical reexamination. As I see it, there is obvious scope for combining markets with socialism, if only to reduce the command element which a bureaucracy has so far treated as the principal regulative feature of a socialist system.

Chakravarty (1991)

I

Historically state socialism has had dramatic initial success in creating a basic capital goods base in early stages of industrialization and in its spectacular feats of mass literacy and public health campaigns made possible by mass-based organizations and forces of human mobilization unleashed by socialist revolutions in poor countries like China, Vietnam or Cuba. But from the post-mortem reports of the collapse of the command economy in different parts of the world it is now clear that centralized state socialism is largely incapable of coping with the technological demands of the increasing sophistication in product quality and diversity and the needs of quick flexibility in decision-making and risk-taking in a whole range of economic activities spanning the technological spectrum from agriculture to semiconductors. There is no doubt that a more decentralized market-mediated allocation of resources and greater competition can correct much of the wastage and dynamic inefficiency of the bureaucratic command system and introduce more agility and flexibility in economic decisions. But the big question is how effective the stimulus of competition and markets can be without large-scale private ownership.

In the 1930s debate on market socialism, when Oskar Lange proposed a way of combining the market mechanism with public ownership, the question raised by Hayek and the other Austrians about how to ensure motivation and incentive in decision-making without private ownership were not fully answered. Socialist planning may be able to mimic market prices, but the question remains, as Kornai (1986b) posed it: "can ownership be simulated by an artificially created body, which is commissioned to represent society as the owner?" The idea has gained ground, reinforced by the failure of attempts at partial reform in some East European countries, that the answer to this question is unambiguously negative. Private ownership is regarded as indispensable for resolving the incentive and agency problems underlying Kornai's query. Privatization is thus supposed to be the key to unlock the door of economic efficiency in the reforming socialist countries as well as in developing countries like India which has a large public sector. In this chapter we address the key incentive and agency problems in the management of a public firm and claim that privatization is not the only or even the better way of handling those problems. We then draw some lessons from this for the burning issue of public enterprise reform in India. In particular we propose a scheme for denationalization without privatization.

II

Some of the horror stories we hear about inefficient public firms may have more to do with their being public monopolies than with the fact of their public ownership *per se*. Examples of efficient public firms in a competitive environment are many around the world. Contrary to popular impression, empirical evidence of significant efficiency differentials between public and private firms *after adjusting for* market structure (and regulatory policy) is quite scanty. As Vickers and Yarrow (1991) note in their survey of the evidence on ownership and efficiency, in competitive industries, even in cases where private ownership seems to have the edge, competition rather than ownership *per se* is the key to efficiency.

But the Lange–Lerner model of market socialism, in its preoccupation with the feasibility of price calculations ("getting the prices right"), has largely ignored the fundamental question that competition among public firms may not be enough to motivate their managers to maximize profits. Under private ownership the entrepreneur has a stake in the firm; he or she gains or loses money depending on the performance of the firm. The salaried manager of a public firm has usually much less at stake, and therefore may not have the full drive or incentive to pursue the Lange–Lerner rules of the game. In particular, the latter operates under the built-in expectation of what Kornai calls "the soft budget constraint." Various political considerations interfere with the harsh exit mechanism of the market and the state remains as the ultimate bailer-out of losing concerns. Political accountability prevails over financial accountability. Kornai (1986a) spells out the mechanisms of softening the budget constraint in terms of (a) soft subsidies, open-ended and negotiable, (b) soft taxation, i.e. easily arranged tax reliefs, (c) soft credit – easy renegotiation of debt, often forced upon suppliers and other creditor firms – and (d) soft administered prices, often involving cost-plus pricing.

There are at least two conceptually separable elements in the essential soft budget constraint problem: one is an information or agency problem, and the other is a political problem (largely involving the problem of credible pre-commitment on the part of the state). Let us take the agency problem first. The state, as the principal, even when it has the "political will" to demand efficiency of management, may not have the full information to sort out whether the agent-manager's bad performance is due to factors beyond the latter's control or not. This agency problem is clearly absent in owner-managed firms under private ownership. But if one goes beyond nineteenth-century owner-entrepreneurial capitalism and looks to sectors outside the small-scale sector of trade, crafts, services and agriculture, large-scale enterprises under corporate capitalism also face qualitatively similar agency problems in management. With the separation between ownership and management in such a capitalist firm, the manager may not maximize the share value of the firm and may instead feather his or her own nest or simply take wasteful or foolhardy decisions, and the large body of shareholders, the principal in this case, may have a difficult monitoring problem at hand: the individual investor has neither the ability nor the full incentive to monitor. Just as a socialist firm, as it is owned by everybody, is really owned by nobody, in the sense that nobody takes responsibility, similarly, when shares of a capitalist firm are owned by thousands or even millions of investors, one may have difficulty in ensuring the proper line of responsibility. Only a small part of the agency costs under corporate capitalism can be gauged from the astronomical salary rises that the chief executive officers in American and British companies regularly give themselves – this is clearly a case of the soft budget syndrome, in respect of the shareholders' money rather than the taxpayers'.

Finance theorists concerned with the agency problem in corporate capitalism – for example, Alchian and Demsetz (1972), Jensen and Meckling (1976), Fama (1980) – claim that the primary disciplining of managers comes through (a) the capital market and (b) the managerial labor market (both within and outside the firm). In principle it is possible to reproduce (b) under market socialism if managerial reputation and future wages crucially depend on the performance of the currently managed firm (although it requires time and considerable depoliticized institution-building, but not necessarily a capitalist property system, to nurture a corporate culture of competitive bidding in the market for professional managers). But reproducing (a) without private ownership is much more difficult. Socialism essentially lacks an institution like the stock market which is supposed to provide a mechanism of continuous assessment of managerial performance. The threat of corporate takeover is supposed to keep the managers honest and the firm efficient, and thus to resolve the conflict of interest between those who bear risk and those who manage risk.

But the financial discipline of corporate takeover is usually a delayed and wasteful process. Jensen (1989) notes that in the United States the fact that takeover and leveraged buyout premiums average 50 percent above market price illustrates how much value corporate managers can destroy before they face a serious threat of disturbance. Even in the takeover process there is a basic asymmetry of information: managers are more informed about the real reasons for a firm not performing well than outside buyers are. As Stiglitz (1985) suggests, takeovers are like buying "used firms" and Akerlof's "lemons principle" applies here as well.

We also should not forget that the threat of corporate raids, a peculiarly Anglo-American game, has not been necessary for strong performance in some countries in continental Europe (like France or Germany), and particularly in Japan. The predominent practice in postwar Japan (at least until the middle 1970s) of mutual stock-holding of private companies within the *keiretsu*, a corporate financial grouping, often with a "main bank" as the nucleus, provides an important alternative model of monitoring by involved parties. We have drawn upon some of the features of the Japanese system in our proposed alternative financial system of monitoring under market socialism in the next section.[1] Even in the United States, as Jensen (1989) points out, in recent years new organizational forms (the leveraged buyout association is a major example) are evolving in which the key organizational principle is the active involvement by investors who hold large equity or debt positions in the long-term strategic direction of the companies they invest in. In other words, in the trade-off between risk diversification (facilitated by the diffuse stock ownership system) and control (which is diluted by that system), the balance is shifting in favor of more control by large investors.

III

In our proposed scheme, the state will not directly own a public firm. It will be a joint stock company with some of its shares owned by its workers, but also a major part of its shares owned by other public firms (including their workers) in the same financial group together with the main investment bank and its subsidiaries. The share-owning workers in one firm will have the motivation and some leverage in prodding other firms in the group to maximize profits. Some shares will be owned by companies outside the group, other financial institutions, pensions funds, local governments, etc. The firm will also borrow from the main bank (which may sometimes organize a loan consortium for the firm) and those loans are convertible into equities under some pre-specified conditions.[2] As Horiuchi (1989) suggests for the Japanese system, the primary role of the main bank may be that of what Diamond (1984) has called "delegated monitoring": through its commitment to the affiliate firm the main bank communicates to other investors and lenders about the firm's credibility.

The shares of a firm can be sold to the main bank. At the first signs of significant attempts by other firms at unloading the shares of a particular firm, and usually much earlier, the main bank will take measures to prod and discipline the management, renegotiate the debt contract if necessary, orchestrate financial rescue strategies, help the firm with interest moratorium and emergency loans, and arrange for technological assistance from affiliated firms and for temporary selling of the firm's stocks in the latter to make up for its operating losses. With the bank's substantial shareholdings it will even have the power to take over the management of the ailing firm temporarily if necessary. (In cases where bankruptcy cannot be prevented, the assets of the firm will be disposed of by the bank among a number of other enterprises.) Aoki (1988) gives the example in Japan of Sumitomo Bank taking over the management of the distressed Toyo Kogyo Company, the maker of Mazda cars, in the mid-1970s, until it was salvaged and nursed back to health. The main bank is motivated to arrange the rescue operation (a disproportionate share of the cost of which is borne by the main bank) since it wants to retain its reputation or credibility as a delegated monitor (in a system of reciprocal delegated monitoring with a small number of other main banks who do it for their affiliate firms) and since otherwise it may lose the intangible asset it has accumulated specific to its relationship with the affiliate firm. In the Japanese case long-term workers also have an incentive to work harder in order to avoid liquidation of the firm (which involves a significant loss of firm-specific benefits and seniority). As Berglof (1989) has found in his comparative study of alternative financial systems, creditor reorganization of problem firms is relatively common in bank-oriented financial systems. Such reorganization is more informal and less costly than involvement by outsiders (like courts or corporate raiders) and is also in line with the incomplete contracting approach to capital structure in the literature (see, for example, Aghion and Bolton, 1988) where the parties agree *ex ante* to let the banks act as reorganization specialists. Even in the United States venture capital often plays a similar role, in getting involved in active management of a company in times of trouble.

The maximum size of a corporate group should not be very large and would depend on the monitoring ability and technical and financial expertise of the main bank. On the other hand, it should not be too small, at least for the sake of risk diversification. It will be desirable for members of a corporate group to be technologically somewhat interrelated, either at the vertical upstream–downstream level or at the horizontal contracting level. This is for three reasons: (a) technological interrelatedness makes it easier to be somewhat knowledgeable about one another's production and market conditions, so that sharing of information, closer monitoring and early detection of trouble become feasible; (b) there may be spill-overs in the results of research and development, so that the usual externalities in the generation and diffusion of technology can be internalized within the mutual stock-holding corporate group; and (c) it becomes easier for the main bank to specialize in some realtively narrow and well-defined technological area for the purpose of monitoring and scrutinizing its loans and equity involvements in the associated companies. On the other hand, if the technologically interrelated firms are prone to have covariate risks, the main bank needs to have a sufficiently diversified portfolio of loans and equities in firms outside the corporate group to reduce the danger of bank failure.

The proposed bank-centric financial system thus solves in a major way the planner–manager principal–agent problem and does it in a potentially better way than the stock-market-centric system. The main bank and the group partners have a large stake in and more "inside" information about a company than the ordinary shareholders in a stock-market-centric system, are likely to be capable of detecting and acting on early signs of trouble (at least the collective action problem is somewhat less acute in what is basically a mode of internal conflict resolution), and are prone to take a longer view in the matter of risk-taking and innovations (i.e. they will be more tolerant of temporary low returns). Under the stock market system even fully rational investors, in a situation of highly imperfect information about the activities of the firm, may be too much concerned about short-run profitability. This is partly confirmed by Berglof (1989) who notes that a feature that distinguishes the bank-oriented systems from their stock-market-oriented counterparts is the longer-term shareholdings in the former.

IV

But the major problem of depending on the main bank as the primary monitor of the public firms in a corporate group is the inevitable question: who monitors the monitor? If the main bank depends substantially on the state for finance, the political aspect of the soft budget constraint again looms large, and the politics of soft budget expose, so to speak, the soft underbelly of socialist economics.

Whenever the beneficiaries from a state policy of leniency in underwriting losses, in refinancing or in providing relief or subsidies are concentrated and highly visible while the costs of such a policy are diffuse, there is inevitable political pressure on the state to follow such a policy, whether in a capitalist or in a socialist country. But such pressure is clearly more irresistible in the latter than in the former. In capitalist countries, while large bail-outs by the state are not uncommon, the prevailing hegemonic ideology makes lay-offs and bankruptcies politically more tolerable. All systems make costly mistakes from time to time; under socialist monitoring (including under our proposed system) what are called type 2 errors (i.e. bad projects are allowed to continue too long) are likely to be more common than type 1 errors (i.e. projects are abandoned too soon) that seem to characterize the harsh, if occasionally myopic, exit mechanisms of capitalist market economies. Different societies have different degrees of tolerance for these two types of error. Societies that value stability and security more than mobility and change seem to have a larger degree of tolerance for type 2 errors.

While it is difficult to get away completely from the politics of the soft budget constraint, there are some reasons to believe that they may be less virulent under our proposed insider monitoring system with proper safeguards. Let us spell out these reasons.

1 In our system between the state treasury and the public firm which is an independent joint stock company, there is a hard layer formed by equity-holding technologically interdependent affiliate firms and the main bank which orchestrates the reciprocal monitoring. This layer provides some financial discipline on public firms and acts as a buffer against directly political accountability. This is not enough, of course, to prevent the whole affiliate group from acting as a lobby with the government for a troubled member.

2 The reputational concerns of the main bank managers may act as an antidote to easy susceptibility to political pressures. In Japan, even though the banks have been closely regulated by the Ministry of Finance, there is some keenness on the part of the bank managers to preserve their reputation as good monitors, and there is competition among banks in seeking the position of main bank for well-run firms. In our proposed system it may not be difficult to keep track of the reputational record of bank managers, since the number of main banks will be relatively small. The managerial labor market may not "forget" if a bank manager "forgives" bad loans or nonperforming firms on his or her watch too often.

3 It is obviously important to introduce incentive features in the payment structures of main bank managers linked to their monitoring performance of the firms. While the social loss from a bad project may be many times the resulting loss to the bank manager's linked income, it may be a significant enough fraction of his or her income to make negligence rather costly.

4 It is very important to keep the doors of international competition open, as a check on the institutional monitors' laxity. The use of international market signals can also provide valuable guidelines and comparative reference points in the main banks' monitoring process and raise cost and quality consciousness all around. There are obviously some genuine cases for infant-industry protection, but to prevent the much too common degeneration of infant industries into inefficient geriatric protection lobbies, there should be a clearly specified fixed duration announced for such protection, after which the firm has to sink or swim in international competition. To make such pre-commitments credible some binding international trade agreements may be tried.

5 It is often claimed that under the soft budget constraint the state remains as the risk-absorber of last resort, and so there is little incentive on the part of managers to avoid very risky projects. Yet in actual cases of public sector management one often finds too few, rather than too many, risks taken by the managers. This is largely because of too much accountability to the politicians: the managers are constantly wary of taking bold decisions that might be seen by their nosy political bosses as rocking the boat of the pre-existing patronage distribution system. Even in our proposed system it may be difficult for the state credibly to pre-commit not to intervene too often with the main bank managers' decisions. So

some difficult-to-change constitutional guarantees on the infrequency of state intervention in the short- to medium-run operations of the bank managers may be necessary.

6 Although in our system the state is to own a majority of the shares of a bank directly, some significant fraction of the shares is to be owned by pension funds, insurance companies, and other banks, to allow for some diversification of interest and professional control in the main bank's operations.

One major problem in our proposed bank-centric corporate groups is the possibility of collusion and industrial concentration facilitated by interlocking shareholding and exchange of inside information. It is therefore very important to preserve the discipline of product market competition (along with some antitrust regulations) in this system. In the formation of these corporate groups it is necessary to keep major competitors in separate groups around different main banks. In our proposed system we are not ruling out cases of a firm leaving one corporate group and joining another (although in the Japanese case the relationship between a main bank and its customers is usually quite stable), but new entry applications to a group should be subject to strict scrutiny against collusion possibilities by an independent antitrust authority.

There are some situations, particularly when the market size is small, where economies of scale considerations may make it difficult to have many competing firms in the same industry. In these situations a corporate group with mutual stock-holding among companies linked in input–output interdependence might be helpful in providing some mutual accountability. For example, a steel firm having a stake in a coal company belonging to the same group may, through its own levers of control and those of the main bank, pull up the latter if it indulges in monopoly-induced sloth and high costs. Of course, partial vertical integration through mutual stock-holding may increase market power and make new entry difficult. It is here that international competition can provide a crucial safeguard. There are lessons to learn here from the cases of South Korea and Taiwan where the state has often energetically used the carrot of easy loans and other benefits and the stick of international competition to prod the firms (many of them in the public sector) onto the technological frontier.

V

Let us now take up the issue of public enterprise reform in India and consider the implications for this of the foregoing analysis of market socialism. Over the last four decades the public enterprise sector in India has acquired mammoth proportions. The total investment in public enterprises (even at historical cost) had exceeded 3 trillion rupees by the end of the 1980s. But the overall financial performance of these enterprises has been rather poor. The after-tax profits of the central government commercial enterprises as a ratio of capital employed was only about 4.5 percent in the last two years of the 1980s. The average performance is actually much worse if one takes out the petroleum sector enterprises. As for the public sector enterprises under state governments (including Union Territories) the performance is much more dismal. These enterprises ran a net loss of about 19 billion rupees a year at the end of the 1980s. Unless a drastic reorganization of the public enterprise sector is carried out soon it will remain a massive albatross on the Indian nonagricultural economy, far from being the leading sector that the founding fathers of Indian planning wanted it to be.[3]

First, a minimum necessary condition of this reorganization is to introduce competition. More than two-thirds of output produced by public sector enterprises is currently under monopoly conditions. Mere privatization, converting a public monopoly into a private monopoly, will shelter the same kind of inefficiency, and be worse in terms of concentration of economic (and political) power. Easing entry barriers both in capacity licensing and in foreign trade will undoubtedly bring more market pressure on public firms and raise their cost-consciousness. In the core industries, like the steel–power–fuel–transport complex, economies of scale considerations may sometimes limit the number of viable firms in an industry. But, as we have noted at the end of the preceding section, in our proposed system of mutual stock-holding in a given financial group there is some mutual check, as a public steel firm will have a significant stake and control in the operating efficiency of an affiliate public coal firm.

We have also seen before that competition is not enough to ensure responsibility in investment and management decisions. We have discussed some of the agency and political problems involved and ways of safeguarding against them. The principal–agent problems are, of course, much more serious in the Indian public sector (as also in many of the actual cases of state socialism), because (a) the public firm often faces multiple goals and a manager (or his or her political patron) can sometimes explain away the nonperformance in making profits by referring to other goals of the firm (like employment creation or job protection, self-reliance or indigenization of materials supply, industrialization of backward areas, etc.) and (b) there are multiple organs of the government (too many "principals") exerting control over the firm management (the relevant production ministry, the Bureau of Public Enterprises, the program implementation ministry, influential members of Parliament, the various auditing and investigating agencies, and so on), which, on the one hand, dilutes the manager's responsibility and, on the other, makes him or her too vulnerable.

Financial profitability has to be unambiguously announced as the primary goal of the public firm (this is particularly salient in the context of the acute importance of generating public sector surplus in facing the deep fiscal crisis and macroeconomic imbalance that the Indian economy is currently undergoing). All other goals, however worthy, are to be openly serviced not through commands on public enterprises but by direct and goal-specific subsidies from the government, the cost of which should be separately budgeted and made transparent for the purpose of public discussion. (For example, the goal of employment creation calls for a direct payroll subsidy; the goal of encouraging indigenous production of materials and components calls for a direct production subsidy to their producers.) For keeping public firm profitability at the centre stage it is necessary, on the one hand, to discontinue most distribution and price controls on the output of public firms and, on the other, to remove all special input and credit subsidies. Privileged access of public firms to subsidized credit, for example, leads to costly distortions in managerial decisions: as Kelkar (1989) has pointed out, at every stage of a public sector project capital is substituted for good management (in the form of overdesigning at the project stage, low capacity utilization, poor maintenance of plant and equipment, over-large inventories, etc.)

In our proposed financial system the public firm management is accountable only to the major shareholders, particularly the other affiliate public firms in the financial group and the "main bank," not to the various organs of the government. In India the state-owned financial institutions are heavily involved in industrial finance, but they usually play a relatively passive role on the issue of efficient management of the firms they control. We are envisaging here a major restructuring of these financial institutions and activization of their monitoring functions on the lines delineated in sections III and IV or, preferably, creation of new financial institutions for this purpose. One should also note that our financial monitoring system is quite different from the idea, floated in India from time to time, about reorganizing groups of public sector enterprises in the form of holding companies.

Of course, as long as the umbilical cord between the financial institutions and the state remains, the problem of soft budget constraint will persist – hence the necessity of the safeguards discussed in section IV, particularly those relating to substantial incentive payments in the salary and promotion of the managers of financial institutions linked to their monitoring performance of the public firms and the financial discipline of international competition (tradeable product prices linked to import prices regulated only by moderate tariffs). A constitutional amendment forbidding central and state governments from providing revenue support to losing public firms and enforcing budgetary discipline will be necessary to make the state's commitment of nonintervention more credible. Similarly, there should be, as Sah and Weitzman (1991) have suggested, well-publicized liquidation pre-commitments for public sector projects *before* they are launched, if their cumulative performance at pre-specified dates in the future is not above a certain threshold level. The rescue strategies by the main financial institution of a corporate group that we have indicated in section III will be subject, by prior legislative enactment, to this kind of liquidation pre-commitment.

Of course, the major constituency opposed to liquidation or scaling down of unprofitable enterprises is the workforce. As Jalan (1991) has observed, in Indian public enterprises today, while the chief executives have unsecure tenure, the rest of the employees enjoy total job security. Not merely are their jobs protected even in the most hopelessly losing public sector enterprise, but when a private sector concern falls "sick" the political pressure is on the state to take it over to protect the jobs. In this way the public sector has become a charitable dispensary of chronically sick firms. This is, of course, politically the most difficult nut to crack. In public enterprises where year after year the revenues do not cover even the nonwage costs, it is cheaper to shut down the enterprise and keep on paying the workforce on some kind of a welfare payment system. All kinds of "golden handshake" schemes and adjustment and training and transfer programs can be thought of. Sah and Weitzman (1991) have pointed out the advantages of profit-sharing payment schemes in this context. If pre-commitment to profit-sharing is part of a public sector project right from the beginning and if workers must sign on to this provision when they take a job, then in chronically unprofitable concerns the attraction of clinging onto the job is obviously much less and to that extent the resistance of the workforce may be weaker.

With regard to managerial personnel policy, both at the level of the monitoring financial institutions and that of the public firms, new systems making for increased professionalization and depoliticization in appointments, promotions and dismissal have to be devised. This is particularly important in view of the widespread practice of using public sector management jobs or membership on the boards of directors of nationalized banks as political sinecures and of automatic promotions for the administrative personnel without much reference to performance or technical qualifications for the specific job. In this context we approve of Jalan's suggestion of the creation of a new autonomous body for recruitment of managerial personnel with somewhat similar terms of reference as the Union Public Service Commission. This should be dovetailed with a vigorous managerial labor market competing with the private sector.

We do not have any illusion about the formidable problems, political and adminstrative, that such suggestions for drastic reforms will face in implementation. The vested interests (particularly in the bureaucracy, politicians, and the unions) for preserving the status quo (often converting new organizational ideas into hollow rituals) are enormously strong. Yet one hopes that new ways of thinking about this vital part of the Indian economy will some day generate enough pressure to bring about desperately needed changes. One can only point out that the institutional problems in reform implementation in India are probably somewhat less severe than what socialist economies in Eastern Europe are currently facing: India has a vigorous mixed-economy base, a framework of market competition already in place, although not in the public sector, and a viable pre-existing legal, contractual, and financial system which one can mold for the purpose of reform – in Eastern Europe much of this needs to be built from ground up.

Notes

1   As M. Aoki has pointed out to us, in Japan there are two, overlapping but conceptually distinguishable, types of *keiretsu*: one is a financial corporate grouping across industries, bound by mutual stock-holding and a main bank as the nucleus; the other is a hierarchical grouping of firms connected by inter-industrial input–output relations, with a major manufacturing firm at its apex. Although in our proposed system we emphasize the former, there are one or two institutional features that we have borrowed also from the latter system.
2   When lenders are also important equity-holders, credit-rationing and other onerous terms of lending may be largely avoided and more risk-taking encouraged.
3   Nagaraj (1991), however, has noted that the declining contribution of the public sector to gross domestic saving is more on account of the deteriorating saving record of administrative departments; the contribution of nondepartmental enterprises has actually improved in the 1980s, possibly because of the large rise in adminstered prices in recent years.

References

Aghion, P. and Bolton, P. 1988: An "incomplete contract" approach to bankruptcy and the financial structure of the firm. MIT Department of Economics Working Paper, March.

Alchian, A. and Demsetz, H. 1972: Production, information costs, and economic organization. *American Economic Review*, 62, 777–95.

Aoki, M. 1988: *Information, Incentives, and Bargaining in the Japanese Economy*. New York: Cambridge University Press.

Berglof, E. 1989: Capital structure as a mechanism of control: a comparison of financial systems. In M. Aoki, B. Gustafsson and O. E. Williamson (eds), *The Firm as a Nexus of Treaties*, London: Sage.

Chakravarty, S. 1991: Development planning: a reappraisal. *Cambridge Journal of Economics*, 15, 5–20.

Diamond, D. 1984: Financial intermediation and delegated monitoring. *Review of Economic Studies*, 51, 393–414.

Fama, E. 1980: Agency problems and the theory of the firm. *Journal of Political Economy*, 88, 288–307.

Horiuchi, A. 1989: Informational properties of the Japanese financial system. *Japan and the World Economy*, 1, 255–78.

Jalan, B. 1991: *India's Economic Crisis*. New Delhi: Oxford University

Jensen, M. 1989: Eclipse of the public corporation. *Harvard Business Review*, 89, 61–74.

—— and Meckling, W. 1976: Theory of the firm: managerial behavior, agency costs and ownership structure. *Journal of Financial Economics*, 3, 305–60.

Kelkar, V. 1989: On efficiency of the public sector. Merchant Memorial Lecture at Indian Institute of Technology, Bombay.

Kornai, J. 1986a: The soft budget constraint. *Kyklos*, 39, 3–30.

—— 1986b: The Hungarian reform process: visions, hopes, and reality. *Journal of Economic Literature*, 24, 1687–734.

Nagaraj, R. 1991: Public sector performance in the eighties: some tentative findings. *Economic and Political Weekly*, December 14.

Sah, R. and Weitzman, M. 1991: A proposal for using incentive pre-commitments in public enterprise funding. *World Development*, 19, 595–605.

Stiglitz, J. 1985: Credit markets and the control of capital. *Journal of Money, Credit, and Banking*, 17, 133–52.

Vickers, J. and Yarrow, G. 1991: Economic perspectives on privatization. *Journal of Economic Perspectives*, 5, 111–32.

11

Sustainable full employment and real wage flexibility

Amit Bhaduri

1 Intellectual background to the problem

In this chapter we seek an economic answer to a political question. The question concerns the sustainability of full employment, in particular whether full employment tends to become self-destructive over time owing to the increasing economic power of the organized workers in a capitalist economy. Major theorists of industrial capitalism from Marx to Keynes have provided two somewhat different analytical perspectives on this question. While Marx viewed "periodic crisis" as essentially a phenomenon triggered off in the *labor market*,[1] Keynes as well as later "Keynesians," with their emphasis on the centrality of effective demand, focused attention on the *product market*.

In the Marxian perspective, a high level of economic activity and employment during a sustained economic boom raises the bargaining power of the working class, leading to higher *real* wages. As a result, both profit and saving (assuming a classical savings function) are squeezed. In the pre-Keynesian framework where saving decisions are not treated as independent of investment decisions, lower saving results in lower investment to destroy the full employment boom (Marx, 1967; Mandel, 1978; also Norton, 1988). Set in the longer term context of accumulation with rising labor productivity, this view was formalized elegantly in a model of cyclical growth by Goodwin (1967) with extensions and generalizations by several writers later (e.g. Desai, 1973; van der Ploeg, 1983; Goodwin *et al.*, 1984; Skott, 1989).

Viewing the same problem from a different angle, the Keynesian tradition, with its emphasis on an autonomous investment function independent of savings decisions, needed to explain how an investment boom collapses. Keynesians addressed this question by shifting their attention from wage bargaining in the labor market to mutual feedback mechanisms between investment decisions and the size of the product market, captured by the interaction between the multiplier and the accelerator mechanism in their different specifications (e.g. Kalecki, 1935; Keynes, 1936, ch. 22; Samuelson, 1939; Kaldor, 1940; Hicks, 1950; Goodwin, 1951).

The difficulty inherent in integrating the labor market with the product market through a plausible theory of collective wage bargaining continued to surface in different ways in the Marxian as well as in the Keynesian perspective. For instance, it resulted in the somewhat contradictory reasoning in Marxian economics on the relation between real wage and profit. From its under-consumptionist perspective, a "high" real wage is considered helpful in alleviating the problem of demand for the "realization" of surplus (value) into monetary profit. However, from its perspective of distributive class conflict, a high real wage is considered detrimental to the generation of surplus (value), leading to a "profit squeeze" as an important ingredient of periodic crisis.[2] In contrast, Keynes's own attempt in the *General Theory* (1936) was to resolve this problem of integration of the labor market with the product market by assuming a passive labor market, where persistent "money illusion" on the part of the workers result in endogenous contracyclical movement in the real wage rate. The relevant dynamic process is sketched only in its barest outline in the *General Theory* (pp. 301–3): a higher autonomous investment increases demand which drives prices up faster in the product market than money wages in the labor market. The consequent reduction in the real wage induces profit-maximizing firms to expand production and employment until the lower real wage rate equals the lower marginal product of labor at a higher level of output.[3]

Note that Keynes's own reconciliation between demand-determined output and the Marshallian (neoclassical) postulate of profit-maximizing equilibrium left no room for the distinction drawn by later authors (e.g. Malinvaud, 1977; Benassy, 1986) between

"Keynesian" and "Classical" unemployment. But the reconciliation was possible only at the cost of at least three questionable assumptions. First, the level of aggregate demand was treated as exogenous, i.e. independent of income distribution through endogenous variations in the real wage rate.[4] Second, firms were supposed to face rising marginal cost through diminishing returns to labor as a factor of production, in order to reconcile the assumption of *precise* profit maximization with the price-taking behavior of competitive firms. Finally, the passivity of the labor market which allowed real wages to fall even in the face of expansion of demand in the product market and led to the prediction of contracyclical real wage movement ruled out satisfactory treatment of the power of workers' unions to resist a fall in real wages. Thus it left little room for introducing workers' organized power into the analysis in the form of an independent wage bargaining equation. Therefore the reconciliation attempted in the *General Theory* between the labor market and the product market turned out to be vulnerable theoretically as well as empirically. The empirical support for contracyclical movement of the real wage rate was dubious;[5] nor did the assumption of rising marginal cost with precise profit maximization by price-taking firms find much support in empirical investigations.[6]

Departing from these Marshallian tradition-bound aspects of Keynes's theory, Kalecki (1939, 1971) had suggested independently an alterative formulation based on "cost-determined" prices. Instead of viewing firms as passive price-takers, he viewed them as makers of prices, who used "mark-up" on more or less constant unit prime cost (which equals marginal cost) and set prices in the manufacturing sector. Thus, the inverse relation between real wage and output or employment implied necessarily in traditional theory could be replaced by this alternative postulate of cost-determined prices which allows real wages to increase, decrease or remain constant at higher levels of output depending on the behavior of the mark-up or profit margin with respect to the level of economic activity. But it left unexplained how the level of the mark-up is either determined or changed through the interaction between the labor market and the commodity market.

The problem with the "neoclassical synthesis," attempted first by Keynes in the *General Theory*, between the labor market and the commodity market through the profit-maximizing inverse relation between the level of employment and the real wage rate, surfaced again recently in the Keynesian–monetarist controversy over the effectiveness of fiscal policies in combating unemployment. Neoclassically oriented Keynesians failed to take the clue from Kalecki's cost-determined prices; instead, they retained the postulate of precise profit maximization under rising marginal cost. Consequently, they were forced to concede to the monetarists' claim that the effectiveness of expansionary fiscal policy depended ultimately on its ability to reduce the real wage rate through inflation. This, in turn, had to be reflected in the relevant coefficient of the augmented Phillips curve (Friedman, 1968; 1975; Tobin, 1972).[7] Ironically, this revised Keynesian argument became essentially a supply-side argument which accepts that any expansion in employment is possible only through a reduction in labor cost (real wage). This should be recognized as a false trail in so far as it loses sight of the main Keynesian feature of the centrality of effective demand in determining output and employment.

In this chapter we wish to follow a line of enquiry for integrating the labor market with the product market which, according to our view, incorporates the valuable features of the different analytical schemes outlined above without carrying their excess intellectual baggage. Thus, in conformity with the Keynes–Kalecki scheme and in contrast with both the Marxian and the neoclassical theory, the *real* wage rate is treated as an *endogenous* variable. It is an endogenous outcome of the price-setting behavior by the firms in the product market and the money-wage-setting behavior by the workers in the labor market.

As a result, at a higher level of economic activity, the real wage may rise (as assumed by Marx) or fall (as assumed by Keynes of the *General Theory* and the neoclassics) or may even stay roughly constant (as suggested by Kalecki, and also by Keynes in his later (1939) writings). A general model of the interaction between the labor market and the product market must accommodate these diverse possibilities as particular cases.

At the same time, in contrast with the analysis of the *General Theory*, variations in the real wage rate are also expected to influence different components of aggregate demand, i.e. consumption, investment, and trade balance. Broadly speaking, higher real wages and a more favorable distribution of income in favor the working class would tend to increase the consumption demand C in the economy as suggested by the under-consumptionist trait in the

Marxist analysis. However, the under-consumptionist argument is one-sided: because a higher real wage worsens the "climate" for investment by reducing the profit margin, it decreases investment demand *I*. In a more general framework depending on the relative strength of the two opposing tendencies, aggregate demand in a *closed* economy (*C* + *I*) may go either up or down as a result of an *exogenous* increase in the real wage rate. Moreover, if a higher real wage rate erodes the international price competitiveness of the economy, it may depress its exports *E* and increase its imports *M*. The resulting decrease in trade surplus (*E* − *M*) would further counteract the higher consumption demand associated with that higher real wage.

The ambiguity of the effect of real wage variations on aggregate demand through its contradictory effects on the different components of aggregate demand gives rise to two analytically distinct regimes. In one regime, aggregate demand and the size of the market increase with the real wage rate, conforming to the under-consumptionist logic, because the increase in consumption demand at a higher real wage outweighs quantitatively its possible negative effects on investment and trade surplus. However, in the other regime aggregate demand *decreases* as real wages increase, contradicting the under-consumptionist logic for exactly the opposite reason (Bhaduri and Marglin, 1990).

2 A formal analysis with two special cases

In the light of the preceding discussion, an analytical taxonomy of the integration between the product market and the labor market needs to capture the interaction between two basic relations. First, both (money) wage bargaining by the workers and nominal price-setting behavior by the firms would be influenced by the "state of demand," which may be related in the simplest case to the previous period's capacity utilization through the assumption of static expectations. However, since the *real* wage is an endogenous outcome of money wage bargaining and the price policy of the firms, it is impossible to postulate the precise behavior of real wages in relation to the "state of demand" proxied by last period's output without specifying the exact form of the wage bargaining equation (e.g. Phillips/augmented Phillips curve) and the price-setting equation (e.g. profit maximization under incomplete information, mark-up pricing, etc. (see Bhaduri, 1986, ch. 3; Bhaduri and Falkinger, 1990). Nevertheless, for the present purpose of an analytical taxonomy, we may use a "black-box specification" and simply assume that the level of the real wage rate is related to the previous period's capacity utilization in a general way. Thus, the endogenous real wage outcome equation is given by

$$w_{t+1} = m + nz_t \qquad (11.1)$$

where m and n are constants of unknown sign, w is the real wage rate and z is the degree of capacity utilization.[8] Viewed in this way, equation (11.1) *cannot* be interpreted simply as a wage bargaining equation. It is as much a wage bargaining equation as a profit bargaining equation because it is the outcome of both wage bargaining by the workers and the price policy of the firms, and captures in our view the "endogeneity" of the real wage rate, stressed by Kalecki (1971) and Keynes (1936, 1939).

Along with the endogenous real wage outcome of equation (11.1) we must specify the effective demand formation equation as the second basic relation of the model. Assuming a closed economy with a minimal role for the government, where a constant fraction s ($1 \geq s > 0$) of profit R and no wage W is saved, the savings behavior is given by

$$S = sR = s\frac{R}{Y}\frac{Y}{Y^*} Y^* = shz \qquad Y^* = 1 \qquad (11.2)$$

where the full capacity (potential) output $Y^* = 1$ by normalization, h is the profit share, $1 \geq h \geq 0$, and z is the degree of capacity utilization, $1 \geq z \geq 0$.

By definition,

$$w = x(1 - h) \qquad (11.3)$$

where w is the real wage rate and x is labor productivity. Therefore, profit share is inversely related to the real wage rate if labor productivity x is roughly constant. At the same time, profit share h is an increasing function of the proportional profit margin v on unit variable (labor) cost of the form

$$h = \frac{v}{1 + v}$$

Investment I is assumed to respond positively to both profit share h (and to profit margin v) and the degree of capacity utilization z (through some form of the "acceleration relation"), as the two main constituents of the rate of profit in the short period.[9] In the simplest linear form this yields

$$I = a + bh + cz \qquad b > 0, c > 0 \qquad (11.4)$$

The IS curve or the product market clearing degree of capacity utilization is obtained by equating (11.2) and (11.4). By inserting (11.3) in the equation of the IS curve, the market clearing level of capacity utilization is obtained as a function of the real wage rate at time period t:

$$z_t = \frac{(a + b)x - bw_t}{(s - c)x - sw_t} \qquad (11.5)$$

As mentioned earlier, equation (11.5) is capable of generating two alternative paths of demand expansion for raising the degree of capacity utilization. Depending on whether $dz/dw \gtrless 0$ according as $as + bc \gtrless 0$, capacity utilization increases or decreases at higher real wage rates. When the slope is positive, i.e. $dz/dw > 0$, the positive effect of a higher real wage on consumption dominates quantitatively its negative effect on investment through lower profitability. As a result, *wage-led economic expansion* becomes feasible in this case in conformity with the under-consumptionist logic. In the opposite case, $dz/dw < 0$ because the negative investment effect of a higher real wage rate dominates the positive consumption effect, and the possibility of *profit-led economic expansion* emerges, contradicting the under-consumptionist logic (see Bhaduri and Marglin, 1990).

In order to examine more closely the possibility of the two alternative paths of economic expansion, note that, by the usual "stability condition" of the Keynesian income adjustment process, dSdz > dI/dz, which, in view of (11.2), (11.3), and (11.4), implies

$$(s - c)x - sw > 0 \tag{11.6}$$

i.e. the denominator of (11.5) is positive. Thus, profit-led economic expansion is feasible when investment responds more strongly than saving to profit share/margin, i.e. dI/dh > dS/dh, which in view of (11.2)–(11.6), yields $as + bc < 0$, implying dz/dw < 0.[10]

The interactive process between endogenous real wage outcome and the formation of effective demand is evident from equations (11.1) and (11.5). At any initial real wage, the level of aggregate demand and the corresponding market clearing level of capacity utilization are determined by equation (11.5) within the same period. But current capacity utilization, as a proxy for the "state of demand" through static expectations, influences both money wage bargaining by the workers and the price-setting policies of the firms. These lead to a different real wage outcome for the next period in accordance with (11.1) which in turn again affects demand and capacity utilization through (11.5) and so on. More formally, the recursive dynamics are described by using (11.5) in (11.1) to yield the basic difference equation for capacity adjustment as

$$z_{t+1} = \frac{[(a + b)x - bm] - bnz_t}{[(s - c)x - sm] - snz_t} \tag{11.7}$$

This difference equation of the Riccati type can be solved analytically by means of suitable substitutions (see Brand, 1966, pp. 392–3.) to yield

$$z_t = (sn)^{-1}[(s - c)x - sm] - (sn)^{-1}\left(\frac{Mk_1^{t+1} + Nk_2^{t+1}}{Mk_1^t + Nk_2^t}\right) \tag{11.8}$$

where M and N are arbitrary constants and k_1 and k_2 are the (distinct) roots of the equation

$$k_{t+2} + (bn + sm + cx - sx)k_{t+1} + x(as + bc)k_t = 0 \tag{11.9}$$

Despite the artificial assumption of strict linearity introduced for simplification in equations (11.1), (11.3), and (11.4), the analytical solution (11.8) to equation (11.7) shows a rich variety of possibilities with regard to the time path of z. Assuming that meaningful economic solutions (i.e. $1 \geqslant z \geqslant 0$) exist, the time path of capacity utilization z may converge steadily to an equilibrium value ($sc - cx - sm - 1$)/sn when the roots of (11.8) are real, distinct, and of the same sign.[11] Otherwise the time path may show oscillatory convergence or divergence (in the case of real roots of opposite signs) or continuous oscillations (in the case of conjugate complex roots). Given the variety of possibilities, a better economic understanding may be gained by concentrating on heuristic graphical solutions in two important prototypes or special cases – the Marxian case and the Keynesian case. (Linearity is assumed in the diagrams as a local property around an equilibrium, assumed to be existing at high capacity utilization and employment levels.)

In the Marxian case workers bargain successfully in terms of higher *real* wages as employment and capacity utilization increases.[12] Thus the parameter n in equation (11.1) is positive. Since the Marxian model also assumes a profit squeeze despite the validity of the under-consumptionist view, this implies a special version of wage-led expansion. This means that a large (percentage) increase in the real wage rate brings about only a relatively small (percentage) increase in aggregate demand and capacity utilization. Because the volume of increased sales fails to compensate for the decline in profit margin per unit of sale at a higher real wage, a profit squeeze must result when aggregate demand (AD) and capacity utilization are positively sloped but inelastic or "flat" with respect to real wage variation (Bhaduri and Marglin, 1990). Accordingly, in the Marxian case of figure 11.1, we have a rising real wage outcome line RW (equation (11.1)) cutting a relatively flat aggregate demand line AD (equation (11.5), linearly approximated) from below in the w, z space. Note that, despite class conflict over distribution entailed by the profit squeeze resulting from the low elasticity of the line AD, "workers' militancy" in terms of successful real wage bargaining represented by a positively sloped line RW may lead to a stable equilibrium even at high employment levels, as long as the real wage outcome line has a steeper slope than the aggregate demand line AD. Further, the greater the inflexibility of the real wage rate, the steeper is the slope of RW, and the greater the profit squeeze, the flatter is the AD curve. Consequently, greater real wage inflexibility in a situation of high distributive conflict entailed by a sharp profit squeeze may contribute to stabilizing the (high) level of economic activity and employment. This casts some doubt on the Marxian argument of "periodic crisis" through profit squeeze.

Contrast the above Marxian prototype model with the Keynesian case. A lack of workers' militancy reflected in imperfect wage indexation or money illusion denies workers the possibility of a higher *real* wage at a higher level of activity. Thus, in equation (11.1) $n < 0$ and the real wage outcome line RW is negatively sloped (figure 11.2).[13] However, economic cooperation among the classes along the "social democratic" line is a typical Keynesian presumption which would hold if a relatively small (percentage) increase in the

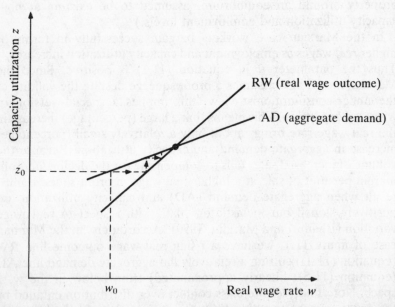

Figure 11.1 The Marxian prototype: distributive conflict with moderately favorable real wage outcome for the workers. Class conflict over distribution results from the profit squeeze which is shown by the relatively "flat" or inelastic aggregate demand (AD) with respect to variations in the real wage rate w. The real wage outcome is favorable to the workers in so far as real wages increase with capacity utilization (and employment), shown by the positive slope of RW. But RW has to be relatively steep (compared with AD), which means that real wages must be sufficiently inflexible in order to ensure stability.

real wage leads to a relatively large (percentage) increase in aggregate demand (Bhaduri and Marglin, 1990). In this case the volume of sales increases sufficiently to allow *total* profit to rise despite a lower profit margin per unit of sales at a higher real wage rate. As a result, aggregate demand AD and capacity utilization z are elastic with respect to real wage variation, shown by a rather steeply rising AD curve in figure 11.2 in contrast with the flat AD curve of figure 11.1. It is easy to see that the time path of capacity utilization in this prototype Keynesian case is oscillatory; it converges to equilibrium provided that (in absolute value) the slope of the real wage outcome

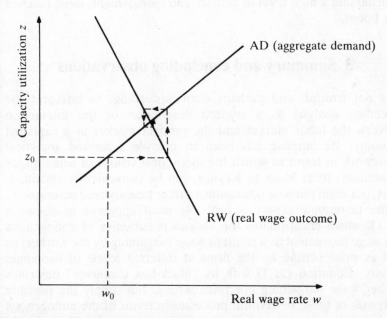

Figure 11.2 The Keynesian prototype: distributive cooperation with moderately unfavorable real wage outcome for the workers. Class cooperation over distribution results from a relatively large increase in aggregate demand (AD) and capacity utilization (z), shown by the relatively steep or elastic AD curve with respect to variations in the real wage rate w. The real wage outcome is unfavorable to the workers in so far as real wages decrease as capacity utilization (and unemployment) increases, shown by the negative slope of RW. But RW has to be relatively steep (compared with AD) which means that real wages have to be sufficiently inflexible in order to ensure stability.

line RW exceeds that of the aggregate demand line AD. However, since cooperative capitalism along Keynesian lines entails a rather steeply sloped aggregate demand AD, an even steeper sloped real wage line RW is required to ensure stability. This implies that the *real* wage rate has to be sufficiently inflexible, i.e. *insensitive* to variation in capacity utilization. Therefore, a sufficiently inflexible real wage is seen again to exert a stabilizing influence on the level of economic activity and employment. In other words, within the common framework of wage-led expansion, with or without the class conflict over distribution of income suggested by Marx and Keynes respectively, "sufficient" *inflexibility* of the real wage rate may help in sustaining a high level of activity and employment, once reached in a boom.

3 Summary and concluding observations

It is not fruitful, and perhaps even misleading, to interpret the preceding analysis as a stylized description of the interaction between the labor market and the product market in a capitalist economy. Its purpose has been to provide a unified analytical framework in terms of which the theoretical visions of some major economists, from Marx to Keynes, can be conveniently classified. Thus, our main purpose is taxonomy rather than stylized description.

The taxonomic aspect is probably most apparent in equation (11.1), which encapsulates the various possibilities of endogenous real wage movement as a result of wage bargaining by the workers as well as price setting by the firms at different levels of economic activity. Equation (11.1) with its "black-box character" describes neither wage bargaining nor price setting, but simply the possible outcomes of these behavioral processes in terms of the endogenous level of the real wage rate. Descriptively equation (11.1) is of little value but it is useful for our classificatory scheme.

The novel aspect of the chapter may be its attempts to integrate these various possibilities of endogenous real wage outcomes with the theory of formation of effective demand. In turn, this provides a convenient classification of the two-way interaction between the level of economic activity (assumed to be demand determined) and the class distribution of income (assumed to be reflected in the real wage rate at constant labor productivity). Our analysis shows that the possibilities are many. Once we liberate the analysis from the artificial assumptions of precise profit maximization and diminishing returns to labor as a factor (i.e. rising marginal cost), the necessity of an inverse relation between output level and the real wage disappears (equation (11.1)). At the same time, a higher real wage is seen either to increase or to decrease aggregate demand in the wage-led regime and in the profit-led regime respectively (equations (11.2)–(11.6)).[14]

Once we recognize explicitly the effect of real wage variation on the level of effective demand, it becomes plausible to argue that a sufficiently inflexible real wage rate exerts a stabilizing influence on the level of economic activity in many situations, and a high level of employment reached in a boom may become more sustainable through a less flexible real wage. If this sounds paradoxical, it is only because conventional neoclassical arguments, by emphasizing mostly the supply side or the cost of production aspect, fail to incorporate the demand effect of real wage variations.

Our analytical framework illustrated this point about the stabilizing influence of a relatively inflexible real wage in two important prototype cases – the Marxian case and the Keynesian case. Because of the importance both these authors placed on demand – Marx in his identification of the realization problem and Keynes in his formulation of effective demand – they were acutely aware of the positive demand-generating impact of a higher real wage. Nevertheless, Marx emphasized the distributive class conflict and the tendency towards periodic crisis through profit squeeze at higher real wages caused by workers' militancy in a boom. Keynes and particularly Keynesians of "social democratic" persuasion emphasized class cooperation through sufficient expansion of demand and output at higher real wages. Our analysis suggests that in both these cases – with or without distributive conflict – relative inflexibility of the real wage rate may exert a stabilizing influence on the level of employment and output.

Nevertheless, a crucial question remains unanswered in our analysis through its neglect of the nominal variables. For instance, a highly inflexible real wage may entail a large but more or less equal proportional increase in nominal prices and money wages. Therefore the stabilizing influence of a relatively inflexible *real* wage rate on economic activity may be gained at the cost of its destabilizing effects on the *nominal* economic variables. The economic advantages of "counterveiling power" in terms of output and employment stability may be intertwined inextricably with the dangers of nominal price–wage instability or inflation in advanced capitalist economies.

Notes

This chapter is dedicated to the memory of Professor Sukhamoy Chakravarty with whom I had an interesting discussion in the early 1980s on the role of real wages in Marx's "crisis theory." The chapter is stimulated partly by that discussion. I am also grateful to an anonymous referee of this volume for very helpful comments.

1 The distinction is an oversimplification. Marx, in particular, had many causes of crisis – the crisis of generation of surplus value, the crisis of profit realization and the crisis of proportionality. Nevertheless, the main thread of his argument seems to run in terms of real wage bargaining in the labor market, as indicated in the text.

2 Thus, the crisis of generation of surplus value through higher real wages could alleviate at the same time the crisis of realization of surplus value due to the expansion of demand caused by higher real wages; see Marglin and Bhaduri (1990).

3 See Bhaduri (1988). Note that this line of reasoning involves two different assumptions: (a) rising marginal cost and (b) precise profit maximization by price-taking firms. When confronted with uncomfortable empirical evidence, Keynes (1939) tried to justify the former assumption but paid little attention to the latter.

4 The Cambridge distribution theory, e.g. by Kaldor (1955–6) and by Pasinetti (1962), tried to generalize the analysis in this direction. But they also required the real wage rate to decline at full employment through the mechanism of forced saving, for generating a higher level of savings to match a higher (exogenously) given level of investment.

5 See Schor (1985) which provides recent empirical evidences as well as a survey of the issues involved.

6 Bhaduri and Falkinger (1990) refer to the relevant empirical and theoretical literature on this issue.

7 Cf. Lucas (1983): "*any* average inflation rate was consistent theoretically with *any* level of unemployment. This conclusion, arrived at via impeccable neoclassical reasoning conflicted with the prediction of a real output–inflation trade-off, which was at the centre of all models based on the neoclassical synthesis" (p. 283; emphasis in original). The neoclassical "synthesis" required the coefficient of money wage adjustment to price change to be less than unity via the augmented

Phillips curve, while pure neoclassicism with strict *real* wage bargaining (without money illusion) would make it unity.

8 As explained in connection with the later equation (11.2), all relevant variables including the real wage rate w are expressed as proportions of full capacity output Y^* by our procedure of normalization.

9 By definition, the rate of profit $r = R/K = (R/Y)(Y/Y^*)(Y^*/K) = hza$ where K is the given book value of invested capital in the short period (by accounting convention) and $a = Y^*/K$ is the technological output–capital ratio, a constant without technological progress in the short period. The rationale for an investment function like (11.4) is discussed in appendix A of Bhaduri and Marglin (1990).

10 Since s, b, and c are positive, a must be negative. This negativity of a is needed (in the simplified linear form of equation (11.4)) only to make investment more responsive than savings to profit share or margin. Thus it can be interpreted as a (local) linear property of the investment function.

11 With repeated roots $k_1 = k_2$ the time path of z converges to $(sx - cx - sm - k)/sn$.

12 It is assumed that high capacity utilization also means high employment, an assumption which is not always easy to justify empirically.

13 Note that RW is not the profit-maximizing equilibrium locus which Keynes accepted in the *General Theory*. The assumption of constant labor productivity x makes marginal cost constant (since labor is the only input) and without the assumption of imperfect competition the postulate of profit maximization has nothing to bite on. Nevertheless, a negatively sloped RW line in figure 11.2 resembles analytically the profit maximization postulate.

14 For elaboration, see Bhaduri and Marglin (1990). Note that both the Marxian and the Keynesian prototype cases discussed earlier belong to the wage-led regime and are consistent with the postulate of an exogenous level of investment. However, an investment function like equation (11.4) is needed for a more complete classification which not only includes the profit-led regime but distinguishes the conflictive case (figure 11.1) from the cooperative case (figure 11.2) within the wage-led regime.

References

Benassy, J. P. 1986: Theories of unemployment. In his *Macroeconomics: An Introduction to the Non-Walrasian Approach*, London:Academic Press, ch. 3.

Bhaduri, A. 1986: *Macroeconomics: The Dynamics of Commodity Production*. London: Macmillan.

—— 1988: Microfoundations of macroeconomic theory – a post-Keynesian view. *Ökonomie und Gesellschaft*, Jahrbuch 6: *Die Aktualitatt Keynesianischer Analysen*, Frankfurt: Campus.

—— and Falkinger, J. 1990: Optimal price adjustment under incomplete information. *European Economic Review*, 34 (5), 941–52.

—— and Marglin, S. 1990: Unemployment and the real wage: the economic basis for contesting political ideologies. *Cambridge Journal of Economics*, 14, 375–93.

Brand, L. 1966: *Differential and Difference Equations*. New York: Wiley.

Desai, M. 1973: Growth cycles and inflation in a model of the class struggle. *Journal of Economic Theory*, 6, 527–45.

Friedman, M. 1968: The role of monetary policy. *American Economic Review*, 53 (1), 1–17.

—— 1975: *Underemployment versus Inflation*. London: Institute of Economic Affairs.

Goodwin, R. M. 1951: Non-linear accelerator and the persistence of the business cycle. *Econometrica*, 19, 11–17.

—— 1967: A growth cycle. In C. H. Feinstein (ed.), *Socialism, Capitalism and Growth*, Cambridge: Cambridge University Press.

——, Kruger, M. and Vercelli, A. (eds) 1984: *Non-linear Models of Fluctuating Growth*. Berlin: Springer.

Hicks, J. R. 1950: *A Contribution to the Theory of the Trade Cycle*. Oxford: Oxford University Press.

Kaldor, N. 1940: A model of the trade cycle. *Economic Journal*, 50, 78–92.

—— 1955–6: Alternative theories of distribution. *Review of Economic Studies*, 23, 212–26.

Kalecki, M. 1935: A macrodynamic theory of business cycles. *Econometrica*, 3, 327–44.

—— 1971: *Selected Essays on the Dynamics of the Capitalist Economy*. Cambridge: Cambridge University Press.

Keynes, J. M. 1936: *The General Theory of Employment, Interest and Money*. London: Macmillan, ch. 22.

—— 1939: Relative movements of real wages and output. *Economic Journal*, 49, 34–51.

Lucas, Jr, R. E. 1983: Methods and problems in business cycle theory. In his *Studies in Business-Cycle Theory*, Cambidge, MA: MIT Press.

Malinvaud, E. 1977: *The Theory of Unemployment Reconsidered*. New York: Wiley.

Mandel, E. 1978: *Late Capitalism*. London: Verso.

Marglin, S. A. and Bhaduri, A. 1990: Profit squeeze and Keynesian theory. In S. Marglin and J. Schor (eds), *The Golden Age of Capitalism: Reinterpreting the postwar experience*, Oxford: Clarendon Press.

Marx, K. 1967: *Capital*, vol. 2. New York: International Publishers.

Norton, B. 1988: Epochs and essences: a review of Marxist long-wave and stagnation theories. *Cambridge Journal of Economics*, 12, 203–24.

Pasinetti, L. L. 1962: Rate of profit and income distribution in relation to the rate of economic growth. *Review of Economic Studies*, 29, 267–79.

van der Ploeg, F. 1983: Economic growth and conflict over the distribution of income. *Journal of Economic Dynamics and Control*, 6, 253–79.

Samuelson, P. A. 1939: Interaction between the multiplier analysis and the principle of acceleration. *Review of Economic Statistics*, 21, 75–8.

Schor, J. B. 1985: Changes in the cyclical pattern of real wages: evidence from nine countries, 1955–80. *Economic Journal*, 95, 452–68.

Skott, P. 1989: Effective demand, class struggle and cyclical growth. *International Economic Review*, 30, 231–47.

Tobin, J. 1972: Inflation and unemployment. *American Economic Review*, 62, 1–18.

12

Homage to Chakravarty: thoughts on his lumping Schumpeter with Marx to define a paradigm alternative to mainstream growth theories

Paul A. Samuelson

Sukhamoy Chakravarty was a great economist. I did not write "a great *Indian* economist," but of course he was one of the giants of his Indian generation. Alas, considerable as were his published contributions to economic science, we must feel that fate deprived us of the full potential that his friends and colleagues believed him capable of.

Here are a few reasons for our regrets. First, bad health limited both his life span and the fullness of his activities. This was not all loss: when John Maynard Keynes's health would turn bad in the 1930s, he would be forced to spent more of his time at Cambridge University and his scientific output thereby benfited; similarly Chakravarty's temptations to depart from contemplative scholarship may have lessened in consequence of chronic hypertension. Still, on a net basis, bad health must have deprived us of Chakravarty's potential contribution much as was the case with the brilliant Lloyd Metzler after his tragic brain tumor in 1951.

Second, Chakravarty as an Indian patriot was drafted into government service at the highest level as a member of planning commissions and as personal advisor to Prime Ministers Indira Gandhi and

Rajiv Gandhi. One of the purposes of effective economic science is to provide counsel for society. But, as testified by the descent of Swedish economics from the transcendental heights of Wicksell, Cassel, Heckscher, Ohlin, Myrdal, Lindahl, Svennilson, and Lundberg to its latter day excellence, the creative advance of political economy as a discipline is hampered by concentration over extended periods of time on public and commercial activities. That involves living off capital. It is worse than that. A high advisor must be a team player, arguing against a mixed bag of policies behind shut doors but closing ranks and being circumspect in public utterances and in scientific publications. The economic policies in India, all agree as they look back upon the history, have not been so sophisticated and sage as to require no misgivings. Warren Hastings said in self-defense when accused of nonoptimal governing in India: "When I consider my opportunities, I marvel at my moderation." A brain truster for Indian governments of recent decades sometimes must have recourse to lame arguments that political feasibility had been such that policies actually promulgated were the best the political traffic could then bear. And always there is the insidious danger that one's paradigms may get bent toward fashions that turn out to be losers in the Darwinian jungle of economic science. Did Chakravarty bet on the wrong trends in political economy of the last half of the twentieth century?

A third handicap possibly limiting Chakravarty's realization of his full potential stems from his being confined in most of the last three decades largely to India itself, some thousands of miles away from the strong European and North American centers of lively economic advance. As with Trevor Swan in Australia and Hirofumi Uzawa in Japan, Chakravarty had plenty of the solitude that makes for originality. But too much of that good thing, experience shows in economics and in other disciplines, can lead to a lack of direct participation in frontier debate and critical interchange.

A Ramanujan blessed with good health and accommodated to Saville Row tweeds – can we doubt? – would have produced more mathematics of genius at Oxbridge in the 1913–19 years than the actual scholar of history was able to. The great astrophysicist, S. Chandrasekhar, never returned permanently to India after leaving it at age 20 in 1930. He had good offers; but, comparing conditions for serene research, he decided to stay at the University of Chicago. The revealed preferences of Bhagwati, Sen, Srinivasan, and others of

Chakravarty's generation to accept permanent appointments in the West have similarly helped world science at India's expense. And it has at the same time contributed to their own research accomplishment. Chakravarty chose to forgo such opportunity. Perhaps this partially explains why some of his writings of the 1980s bear resemblance to topics and treatments of earlier days.

Here I shall concentrate on Chakravarty's R. C. Dutt Lectures on Political Economy, which are too little known in the West (see Chakravarty, 1982). They bear the provocative title *Alternative Approaches to a Theory of Economic Growth: Marx, Marshall and Schumpeter*. Peculiarly in the India of colonial days and of early independence, a Laski-like popularity of chic Fabianism prevailed. This is not a trend for me to deplore. The world does not particularly need local Friedrich Hayeks and Milton Friedmans on every subcontinent. Since Sukhamoy Chakravarty was so deep and sage a mind, we can benefit by appraising critically his notions for alternatives to mainstream economics. Here is a selective paraphrase of characteristic interpretations in Chakravarty (1982) and other writings late in life.

1 He contrasts two main systems of growth and development. First there is the mainstream viewpoint associated with J. S. Mill and Alfred Marshall. Second there is the alternative analysis stemming from Marx and Schumpeter. Both of these have as common ancestors the classical models of Adam Smith and David Ricardo. This classical trunk is described as bifurcated into the branches of Mill and of Marx.

2 Chakravarty, while respecting useful elements in the mainstream branch, pretty clearly wishes to defend the alternative branch in these current years when planning has become a dirty word and when the ideology of *laissez faire* has been making a strong comeback.

3 He is distinctive in picking Mill as the first of the mainstream writers, removing him from the usual classical trio of Smith–Ricardo–Mill and using Mill rather than the neoclassical triad of Jevons–Menger–Walras as the Abraham of the modern mainstream genealogy. Also Chakravarty is distinctive in selecting Marshall as the prototype of neoclassical growth theorists rather than naming a committee of Knut Wicksell, Eugen von Böhm-Bawerk, J. B. Clark,

and Vilfredo Pareto to represent the neoclassical school. Chakravarty realizes that he is being idiosyncratic in giving Joseph Schumpeter pride of place beside Karl Marx, and knows he must argue his contention before his Marxian contemporaries. And, I would add, before the mainstream crowd.

4 At this point it is worth enumerating some of the features Chakravarty approves of in the Marxian paradigm.

(a) Marx, both in Hegelian and non-Hegelian terms, has a theory in which change from *laissez faire* capitalism is a natural expectation. Although Chakravarty points out explicitly that Marx has no clear-cut unambiguous paradigm of the collapse of capitalism, Marx does specify important aspects purporting to explain the laws of motion of the mid-nineteenth-century economy.

(b) Chakravarty cites with approval Marx's basic notion of a "surplus" as characterizing the mode of production in the bourgeois society. Exploitation of non-capital-owning labor by the capitalist owners of capital is regarded as a central feature of capitalism's evolution. *Capital*'s 1867 paradigm of *surplus value* (*mehrwert*), which an analyst like me dismisses as a gratuitous detour into unrealism and a swamp of *non sequiturs*, seems to be regarded more favorably by Chakravarty. (In many of his writings defensive of the general philosophy of planning that pervaded the Indian programs of his time, Chakravarty deplores the pressures holding down real wages in the market guided take-offs espoused for Korea, Taiwan, Singapore, Hong Kong, or Chile by economists like Peter Bauer, Ann Krueger, Hia Myint, and even Ian Little. By contrast, despite their imperfections, the prescriptions for a democracy like India by P. C. Mahalanobis, Charles Bettelheim, Nicholas Kaldor, and other deviates from the mainstream are well tolerated by Chakravarty.

(c) Although Keynes himself receives little explicit attention in the Dutt Lectures, Chakravarty values in Marx an appreciation of the "realization problem" that capitalism must sometimes face. Keynes, Malthus, Sismondi, Rodbertus, Rosa Luxemburg, Hobson, and other under-consumptionists are by no means in perfect agreement with Marx's views on the subject. But neither is Marx in perfect agreement with J. B. Say, James Mill, [Robert Lucas,] and neoclassical believers in a version of Say's law that insists upon the impossibility of a problem of general overproduction and of unmaintainable full employment. As will be seen, although Chakravarty attempts to link up Schumpeter and Marx in various dynamic respects, he admits that Schumpeter is more a devotee of full employment economics than Marx is – and Chakravarty clearly lauds Marx for his difference in this regard.

Why "Mill–Marshall"?

Generally, wherever Chakravarty refers to a Mill–Marshall conventional approach, I find myself substituting for it a "mainstream" approach. This is not a matter of importance but it deserves some discussion.

John Stuart Mill used to be underrated as merely an eclectic expositor of the doctrines original with Smith and Ricardo. Marx naturally denounced Mill as a vulgar bourgeois economist. Mill and Marx were contemporaries and Marx was hard on all contemporaries – Mill, Proudhon, Rodbertus, Lasalle. . . . Had mastoid infection spared David to live three extra decades after 1823, one suspects Ricardo would have cut a less favorable figure in Karl's writings. Jevons also had his phobia against Mill. Even Marshall, who mathematized Mill, disliked Mill's feminist sympathies. And Schumpeter, characteristically, patronized Mill for his competence – much as he patronized Smith and Marshall.

Today we know better: Mill and Smith rise in the esteem of connoisseurs as Ricardo's over-blown shares fall on the bourse of antiquarians' rankings. Whatever excellence Mill is guilty of, he cannot be convicted of being neoclassical in the fashion of Gossen, Jevons, Menger, Walras, Wicksteed, Fisher, and Wicksell. Chakravarty may be right that Mill does not give increasing returns the emphasis that Smith did or that Bertil Ohlin and Allyn Young were to do. But in this respect Mill shows no retreat from Ricardo. Moreover, the passages in Marx that hint of monopoly formation as capitalism ripens and decays, they are quite distinct from Marx's theoretical analyses bearing on *mehrwert* equalization versus profit-rate equalization, on the transformation problem, on the tableaux of reproduction, on the laws of decline in the rate of profit, or on the immiseration of wage earners.

My own reading of the classicals – Smith, Malthus, Ricardo, Mill, Marx[1] – found in them essentially one and the same canonical model of growth (see Samuelson, 1978). Where Mill is not identical with Ricardo, he is not inferior. And the same can be said in comparing Mill with Marx.

During the nineteenth century that saw world population double and European population quadruple while life expectancies and real wage rates rose, the time was overripe for a *post*-Mill[2] bifurcation that would jettison the near-empty and out-moded classical paradigm of *"subsistence* real wages." I suppose agreement with this would require Chakravarty to replace his dichotomy of Mill–Marshall and Marx–Schumpeter with the dichotomy of mainstream economists versus Marx–NeoKeynes–Sraffa economics.

I am only half done with my carping. A teacher in India of Chakravarty's earliest teachers would naturally think of Alred Marshall as the quintessential mainstream economist. (So, in lesser degree, would the teachers of my American teachers.) But for thirty-five years now Marshall has been old hat. Nor was he ever much on growth theory as such. An Englishman like John Hicks was much more influenced by Wicksell than by Marshall and it is laughable to explain this away by Hicks's LSE residence. The juvenilia of Marshall in J. K. Whitaker (1975) were not remarkable, compared with writings by other contemporaries, in their treating population and technology trends as largely exogenous and in their emphasis on the need to divert resources from current consumption to capital formation tangible and human.

Where does Schumpeter belong?

If I had to give two names to *mainstream* growth theory, I suppose that I might select instead of Mill–Marshall names like Wicksell–Schumpeter or Kuznets–Solow. This leaves Sukhamoy and Paul jousting over which side of the grand-bifurcation line Schumpeter is to be found.

My principal task in the present chapter will be to conduct with the shade of Chakravarty a respectful debate concerning where Schumpeter does fit into the picture. As one of the diminishing tribe of surviving Schumpeter pupils, I owe it to the memories both of Chakravarty and of Schumpeter to record my judgments on the proposed linking of Schumpeter with Marx.

And now is the time to provide this fresh evaluation of Schumpeter's schema when Robert Loring Allen (1991) and Richard Swedberg (1991a,b) have provided us with fresh biographical material from Schumpeter's own diaries. My guess that the 52-year-old Schumpeter I first met in 1935, for all his gaiety and bravado, was a sad person is more than confirmed; indeed the diaries reveal him to have been a seriously depressed personality under the surface. And although he made no bones about his conservatism in politics, I don't think that any of us realized quite how conservative he really was at heart – a finding that cuts for me rather than for Chakravarty. Schumpeter went along with the popular belief that the mass of people are led by wishful thinking into expecting to happen what they *want* to happen. But as I have noticed in life, among sophisticated people like Schumpeter, all goes into reverse: what they would hate to have happen, they paranoidly expect to happen. Schumpeter's views about the inevitability of socialism reflected in part a shallow understanding of American politics – as, for example, in his stimulating and provocating *Capitalism, Socialism and Democracy* (1942). Schumpeter's hatred of Franklin Roosevelt – and his fear of Roosevelt – bordered on the pathologic.

Of all the points I shall try to make in this chapter, I believe the most important one is this:

> It is a grave misinterpretation to link Schumpeter together with Marx, either as forming a paradigm that is an alternative to mainstream paradigms of Mill–Marshall and others (Hayek, Solow, Samuelson, Debreu, . . .) or as being *two scholars who truly share basic insights*.

I am of course aware that Schumpeter has in many places articulated words of praise and admiration for Karl Marx. But I and other of his students found this puzzling since in neither his lectures nor his writings could we identify the reasons for this admiration. It would be an evasion for us to write it all off as typical Schumpeterian empty praise – as when he would introduce to Harvard audiences with flowery compliments the Mises he looked down on and the Hayek whom he considered overvalued. Somehow his respect for Marx was more long-lasting and seemed genuinely sincere. Despite repeated investigations I never could find the answer to the puzzle.[3] Indeed in the end the evidential record requires me to conclude that, even if under hypnosis Schumpeter were to insist on the genuineness of his admiration for Marx, careful comparison of how the two writers would interpret dozens of different questions and processes will reveal that Schumpeter's answers are 180° different from Marx's – and the differences are generally precisely those differences that neoclassical pedants have with Marxian writers. Pragmatically what counts is not a scholar's rhetoric but rather his substantive hypotheses and descriptions.

Let me contemplate one such issue. Chakravarty (1982, pp. 14–15, 23–4, 40, n. 10) correctly makes much of Marx's qualms about Say's law and the inevitability of full employment. And he does not fail to notice certain ambiguities if not self-contradictions in Marx concerning this matter: under-consumptionists like Rodbertus are chided by Marx, and Marx's own Tableaux of (Expanded) Reproduction accommodate continued saving by capitalists without disturbance to equilibrium; on the other hand, Marx does speak derisively of the childish babble about Say's law, and worries much about cyclical breakdowns in the "realization" process. Schumpeter, as Chakravarty himself points out, was essentially a full employment economist – an anti-Keynesian even before there was the 1936 *General Theory*. Only compare the contradictory reactions of Marx and Schumpeter to Ricardo's belated sections on machinery and its likely harm to wage earners!

If two prophets differ on each essential doctrine of theology, how can they be lumped together as being of the same religion? Chakravarty concentrates on what he perceives to be their common dynamic vision. But is it the *same* dynamic vision? Newton had his mechanics. Aristotle had his mechanics. I would never speak of an Aristotle–Newton paradigm if Aristotle believed that a cannonball needed new pushes to keep flying while Newton believed that new pushes would only serve to accelerate or decelerate its continued motion. There is only one night sky, but Ptolemy and Copernicus are not one. Marx believed that capitalism's contradictions would somehow entail its demise and cause it ultimately to be succeeded by communism. Schumpeter believed the capitalistic system to be *economically stable*: between bursts of innovation it had a rendezvous with a circular-flow equilibrium (involving a zero interest rate); but quasi-endogenously caused clusters of innovation, amplified by a money-creating banking system, will constantly engineer economic growth and development (generating unavoidable business cycles that, often, unnecessarily overshoot and engender unnecessary waves of unemployment and inflation).

Schumpeter's theory of an inevitable progression from capitalism to socialism *is not based on his economics but rather on his sociology*, according to which the very successes of rational capitalism will undermine the irrational feudal traditions that might forestall its decline.

Schumpeter's essential brief is an apologetics for Walras–Mill economics once it is made to be dynamic – not an indictment.

My final summing up finds Marx essentially lacking in a cogent model that helps explain the inequality of capitalism and the laws of motion of the economic system. But what we may call his innuendo about the future of capitalistic dynamics undoubtedly constitutes in his eyes and those of his followers an indictment of mainstream economics (1840–84, and by extrapolation 1885–1992). By contrast Schumpeter admires and commends what markets accomplish, statically and dynamically.

I ought to add my considered opinion that, although Schumpeter's differs from Marx's unsatisfactory dynamics, his own different dynamics is also fundamentally flawed. This is not the place to document in detail this damning verdict but here are a few suggestive hints.

1 As argued in Samuelson (1981), by the trick of defining capitalism too narrowly and socialism too broadly, Schumpeter achieves the empty accomplishment of an almost tautological deduction that capitalism must die and be succeeded by socialism. Events since his death in 1950 quite disconfirm his prophecies of 1919, 1928, 1942, and 1949. Schumpeter's bland blessing of socialism's viability does not prepare us for the post-1970 swing toward the market, nor for the travails of the Soviet and Chinese systems. Schumpeter fell in love with his own 1911 theory of development, and somehow convinced himself that capitalism by its nature could not be stationary (*or steadily growing* in trend).

2 Schumpeter's non-developmental core of pure economics is itself gratuitously flawed. He never reasoned well about the zeroness of the rate of interest in stationary long-run equilibrium. (If land with permanent income is to be traded between overlapping generations endowed with only finite life spans, it is hard to envisage its being bid to *infinite* value, as a zero Schumpeter interest would require.) Indeed, I believe that in the last twenty years of his life Schumpeter came to suspect his own youthful thesis, but like Bre'r Rabbit he preferred to say nuffin' on that score. Capitalism as a

system relying on competitive markets would, in any case, be perfectly viable whether its equilibrium interest rate were or were not to have a rendezvous with zero; but neither the evidence of economic history nor the best theories of modern economies predispose us to believe in a trend towards euthanasia of the rentier. Recall that Schumpeter was always patronizing toward Cassel's *Theory of Social Economy* (1918), dismissing it as being exactly what continental economists could handle. But actually, Cassel's (Harrod–Domar!) model of a system that grows progressively through capital accumulation and technical change is nearer to a correct *historical* account of growth and development trends than are Schumpeter's 1911 or 1938 scenarios. And Cassel's view of the business cycle and technical change is in no way inferior to Schumpeter's. (I add that Cassel is no hero of mine, but he deserves not to be underrated. See Samuelson (1993) for my views on Cassel and on Schumpeter's valuations of him.)

3 Schumpeter unnecessarily overemphasized the importance of *bank creation of money* in initiating business cycles and financing venture capital. If much of European gross national product went through market pricing before 1790, and even if there had been less M-creation by pre-1790 banks, it would be absurd for Schumpeter to try to date the genesis of capitalism to only the end of the eighteenth century. Schumpeter's toy boat carried a deal of gratuitous ballast (as Schumpeter (1946, pp. 184ff.) admits).

4 I delight in the new boom for Schumpeter shares. His personality, literary style, and bold speculations merit our rereading him. His prophecies, right or wrong, are interesting and *ex ante* they were not absurd but merely mistaken. And this is quite aside from his solid writings as a historian of economic analysis and of intellectual thought. Moreover, especially at a time when Poland, Hungary, Czechoslovakia, and the erstwhile Soviet republics are trying to find a path from bureaucratic command to a market system, Schumpeter's emphasis on capitalism as "creative destruction" (a process for ruthless cutting of losses) is indeed important.

But having said that, one must also note various spurious reasons for a vulgar popularity of Schumpeter. Keynes is dead, long live Schumpeter. (Indeed Keynes is dead and 1933–40 model T Keynesianism served its purpose and deserves its honored place in the museums and in the insides of 1992 Mercedes–Cadillac retooled neo-Keynesian versions. But whatever will end up being valid in Robert Lucas or Edmund Phelps is not to be found in 1911 or 1942 Schumpeter.)

Furthermore, in a technical season when the general run of scholars feel oppressed by the rigors and minutiae of mathematics and econometrics, there will always be a derived demand for soft discussions concerning what differentiates the innovator from the inventor and the provider of capital. If Chakravarty and I want to analyze seriously Smith–Ohlin–Young increasing returns to scale, we cannot look to tomes by Marx and Schumpeter but rather must study J. M. Clark, Chamberlin, Paul Krugman, and Paul David. The Schumpeter who first lectured to me in 1935 did not believe that *Fortune 500* giants could stay creative and viable. By 1940 he had a mind change and was prepared to believe that oligopolies could learn to stay creative in competitive innovating and technical research. No Schumpeter I ever shared a drink with feared Galbraithian monarchs as having enough monopoly power to sap capitalistic vigor!

Chakravarty, polymath and sage

My main task, that of analyzing where Schumpeter belongs along the Marx–Walras continuum, is done. It would require a deeper and wider paper to appraise in a friendly but objective way whether a Chakravarty or a Samuelson can find in the post-Sraffian and Marxian literatures genuinely useful corrections or supplements to the dominant post-neoclassical literature.

I have enumerated before the important sources of wealth-and-income inequality from (a) natural resource holdings (Paul Getty, Sheikh Smith), (b) Schumpeterian innovation (Hewlett and Packard, Edwin Land, Henry Ford), (c) Knightian uncertainty (Warren Buffet, Michael Milken, real estate developers), (d) human capital (university-educated subclasses), and (e) organized crime and political dictators (Capone, King Saud). What will strike the reader of Karl Marx's dozen volumes, and the literature spawned from them, is that we are given no understanding of the data on Gini distributions or on the Forbes lists of the top 400 in global affluence by the Marxian calculus of *mehrwert*, the elucidation of the transformation problem from values to prices, or the laws of declining profit and immiseration of the working classes! It is a loss that, now, I cannot look forward to talking to Sukhamoy on a hundred topics like this.

Arthur Spiethoff has spoken of the miracle that the young Schumpeter, who before he was 30 had written a great work on development and a learned treatise on doctrinal history, was so to speak born omniscient. Before Sukhamoy came to the Massachusetts Institute of Technology from Calcutta and Rotterdam, already he knew everything. At least everything that I might want to know. The Hegel dialectic and Hamiltonian conservation of energy. How Locke related to Erasmus. At any round seminar table, where Chakravarty sat was the head of the table! So, inevitably, his death leaves us impoverished.

But right at this time our loss is especially great. When Einstein distrusted quantum mechanics as not providing the ultimate explanation, Max Born bemoaned to him that his generation had to carry on without their leader. Right now when the Soviet Union has disintegrated and Eastern Europe is bolting toward the market, humane economists with misgivings about *laissez faire* outcomes face a crisis, external and internal. Can social Darwinism (or Spencerian) after all be the wave of the future and the *desideratum maximorum*? We could use from Sukhamoy Chakravarty counsel in traversing the new shoals of passage. Has there really been a high-noon showdown in which *pure* capitalism outperformed *pure* socialism? Or was the triumph a triumph of the mixed economy over bumbling bureaucracies? Were Mises and Hayek right that such bumbling is *generic* not singular? Were Lerner and Lange the romantic dreamers? Ideological preferences by the like of Galbraith or Friedman cannot validly pronounce on these vital questions and the wisdom of a Chakravarty was never more in need than at the present hour.

Now, in his memory, we must work away at providing our own answers.

Notes

1   At many places Marx deals with land scarcity and rent. Nevertheless, he despised Malthus and disliked explanations of poverty attributable to technological and geological necessity or to excessive birthrates; he preferred explanations that emphasized exploited labor and the class struggle. Therefore most of his million-odd words relevent to a coherent theory of growth are at best explicated by a version of the canoni-

cal classical models that omits land scarcity (and would tolerate asymptotic exponential growth of populations held down to near-subsistence real wages).

2 In Samuelson (1970) I tried to explain to myself why Schumpeter admired Marx. In the end I failed. Again, for the present chapter I chased down in *The History of Economic Analysis* (1954) every Schumpeter reference to Marx. My notes show it to be thin stuff: much roll of drums and blare of trumpet; few heard melodies. My finding could only be expressed in the old doggerel, with meaning inverted and Dr Marx substituted for Doctor Fell:

> I really love thee, Doctor Fell.
> The reason why I cannot tell;
> But this alone I know full well,
> I really love thee Doctor Fell.

Chakravarty (1982, p. 24, n. 25) is acute to quote from Schumpeter's 1937 preface for the Japanese translation of *Theory of Economic Development*.

> It was not clear to me at the outset . . . that the idea and aim are exactly the same as . . . underlie the economic teachings of Karl Marx . . . precisely a vision of economic evolution as a distinct process generated by the economic system itself.
>
> (see Schumpeter, 1951, p. 160)

As I put it to myself, "Joseph Alois Napoleon, it turned out, in the end admired Karl for his *chutspah* in aiming at a Napoleonically ambitious (if faulty) schema. But, he believed, it was Joseph and not Karl who was the real Napoleon!"

3 Marx called religion the opiate of the masses, evoking from Raymond Aron the aphorism that Marxism is the opiate of the intellectuals. One modern Marxism fad, according to my post mortem, *dulls* understanding of the laws of motion of capitalism by professing to find distributional profundity in the notion of "surplus" under modern modes of production. I cannot concur with Chakravarty's finding fault with Marshall for dropping this standpoint. When past societies became depopulated, that did not mean that their interest rates had to be zero or negative in their final stages! There is no scientific explanatory power for the quantitative degree of inequality for income and wealth among the 4 billion global inhabitants whose real wages are above physiological subsistence levels from the fact that post-Newtonian science has lifted mean incomes above physiological or meaningful definitions of subsistence. Marshall never dropped what was never in Smith or Ricardo. Put in our language, Ricardo's distribution theory was a supply-and-demand analysis of how changing labor-cum-capital goods, relative

to inelastic natural resources, alter market interest rates, wage rates, and rent rates. The mumbo-jumbo of "surplus" adds no iota of insight into the process. And its relevance for the process in which societies die of starvation is understandable only in the supply-and-demand terms that a Marshall or Wicksell uses.

References

Allen, Robert Loring 1991: *Opening Doors: The Life and Work of Joseph Schumpeter*. New Brunswick, Transaction Publishers.

Cassel, Gustav 1918: *Theoretische Sozialökonomie*. Leipzig: C. F. Winter. Translated into English as *Theory of Social Economy*. New York, Harcourt Brace, 2nd edn, 1932.

Chakravarty, Sukhamoy 1959: *The Logic of Investment Planning*. Amsterdam: North-Holland.

—— 1982: *Alternative Approaches to a Theory of Economic Growth: Marx, Marshall and Schumpeter*, R. C. Dutt Lectures on Political Economy, 1980. Calcutta: Centre for Studies in Social Sciences.

Samuelson, Paul A. 1970: A foreword: Schumpeter and Marx. In Alexander Balinky, *Marx's Economics: Origins and Development*, Lexington, MA: D. C. Heath.

—— 1978: The canonical classical model of political economy. *Journal of Economic Literature*, 16, 1415–34.

—— 1981: Schumpeter's capitalism, socialism and democracy. In A. Heertje (ed.), *Schumpeter's Vision: Capitalism, Socialism and Democracy after 40 Years*, New York: Praeger.

—— 1993: Gustav Cassel's scientific innovations: claims and realities. *History of Political Economy*, forthcoming.

Schumpeter, Joseph A. 1934: *Theory of Economic Development*. Cambridge, MA: Harvard University Press. English translation of the 1911 German classic.

—— 1942: *Capitalism, Socialism and Democracy*. New York: Harper & Row.

—— 1946: Capitalism. In Richard V. Clemence (ed.), *Essays on Entrepreneurs, Innovations, Business Cycles, and the Evolution of Capitalism*, Reading, MA: Addison-Wesley.

—— 1951: *Essays on Economics Topics of J. A. Schumpeter*, edited by Richard V. Clemence. Port Washington, Kennikat Press.

—— 1954: *The History of Economic Analysis*, edited by E. Boody Schumpeter. New York: Oxford University Press; London: George Allen & Unwin.

Swedberg, Richard 1991a: *Joseph A. Schumpeter, His Life and Work*. Cambridge: Polity Press.
—— (ed.) 1991b: *Joseph A. Schumpeter, The Economics and Sociology of Capitalism*. Princeton, NJ: Princeton University Press.
Whitaker, J. K. (ed.) 1975: *The Early Economic Writings of Alfred Marshall 1867–1890*. London: Macmillan.

Selected publications of Sukhamoy Chakravarty

Books

1959: *The Logic of Investment Planning*. Amsterdam: North-Holland. Reprinted 1968. Also translated into Spanish, Madrid, 1966.

1969: *Capital and Development Planning*. Cambridge, MA: MIT Press, with a foreword by Professor Paul A. Samuelson.

1973: *The Relationship Between Food Aid and Non-Food Aid* (with P. N. Rosenstein-Rodan). Rome: F.A.O.

1977: *Reshaping the International Order* (with Professor Jan Tinbergen and others). Submitted to the Club of Rome, E. P. Dulton & Company, New York.

1980: *Alternative Approaches to a Theory of Economic Growth – Marx, Marshall, Schumpeter*, R. C. Dutt Memorial Lectures. Calcutta: Longman.

1987: *Development Planning: The Indian Experience*. Oxford: Oxford University Press. Also translated into Japanese in 1989.

1989: *John von Neumann and Modern Economics* (co-editor with Mohammed Dore and Richard Goodwin). Oxford: Clarendon Press.

1989: *The Balance Between Industry and Agriculture in Economic Development*, vol. 3, *Manpower and Transfers* (ed.). London: Macmillan.

Articles

1962: The existence of an optimum savings program. *Econometrica*, 30, 178–87.

1962: Optimal savings with a finite planning horizon. *International Economic Review*, 3, 338–55. (Reply, *International Economic Review*, 7, 119–23, 1966).

1964: Optimal investment and technical progress. *Review of Economic Studies*, 31, 203–6.

1964: An appraisal of alternative planning models (with R. S. Eckaus). In P. N. Rosenstein-Rodan (ed.), *Capital Formation and Economic Development*, London: Allen & Unwin.

1964: An approach to a multisectoral intertemporal planning model (with R. S. Eckaus). In P. N. Rosenstein-Rodan (ed.), *Capital Formation and Economic Development*, London: Allen & Unwin.

1964: Choice elements in intertemporal planning (with R. S. Eckaus). In P. N. Rosenstein-Rodan (ed.), *Capital Formation and Economic Development*, London: Allen & Unwin.

1965: An optimizing planning model (with L. Lefeber). *Economic Weekly*, 17, 237–52.

1965: Optimal programs of capital accumulation in a multisector economy. *Econometrica*, 33, 557–70.

1967: The theory of optimal investment decisions. *Indian Economic Review*, 3, 47–73.

1967: Alternative preference functions in national investment planning. In E. Malinvaud and M. O. L. Bacharach (eds), *Activity Analysis in the Theory of Growth and Planning*, New York: Macmillan.

1968: Some aspects of optimal investment policy in an underdeveloped economy. In H. C. Bos (ed.), *Towards Balanced Economic Growth: Essays Presented to J. Tinbergen*, Amsterdam: North-Holland.

1968: Optimal growth when the instantaneous utility function depends on the rate of change in consumption (with A. S. Manne). *American Economic Review*, 58, 1351–4.

1969: Contributions to Indian economic analysis (with J. Bhagwati). *American Economic Review*, 59, Part 2, 1–73.

1973: Theory of development planning: an appraisal. In H. C. Bos, H. Linneman, and P. de Wolff (eds), *Economic Structure and Development: Essays in Honour of Jan Tinbergen*, Amsterdam: North-Holland.

1975: Mahalanobis and contemporary issues in development planning. *Sankhya, Series C*, 37, Part 2.

1977: Reflections on the growth process in the Indian economy. In C. D. Wadhwa (ed.), *Some Problems of India's Economic Policy*, Bombay: Tata McGraw-Hill.

1984: Power structure and agriculture productivity. In M. Desai, S. H. Rudolph, and A. Rudra (eds), *Agrarian Power and Agricultural Productivity in South Asia*, New Delhi: Oxford University Press.

1987: Marxist economics and contemporary developing economies. *Cambridge Journal of Economics*, 11, 3–22.

1990: Development strategies for growth with equity. *Asian Development Review*, 8, 133–59.
1991: Development planning: a reappraisal, Marshall Lecture at Cambridge University 1989. *Cambridge Journal of Economics*, 15, 5–20.

Index